How to Hire a
HOME IMPROVEMENT CONTRACTOR
Without Getting Chiseled

D0187481

How to Hire a
HOME
IMPROVEMENT
CONTRACTOR
Without Getting Chiseled

Revised Edition

Tom Philbin

St. Martin's Griffin   New York

Design by Carla Weise/Levavi & Levavi, Inc.

Library of Congress Cataloging-in-Publication Data

Philbin, Tom
    How to hire a home improvement contractor without getting chiseled / Tom Philbin.—Rev. ed.
        p.   cm.
    Includes index.
    ISBN 0-312-14620-5
    1. Dwellings—Maintenance and repair. 2. Dwellings—Remodeling. 3. Construction contracts. 4. Contractors.
5. Consumer education. I. Title.
    TH4815.4.P49   1997   90-29405
    643'.7—dc20   CIP

First St. Martin's Griffin Edition: January 1997

10   9   8   7   6   5   4   3   2   1

For Ralph Nader, who taught us all to look at the world a little differently, and who has saved a lot of people a lot of pain. I hope this book saves some pain, too.

CONTENTS

Acknowledgments   xi
Introduction   xvii

PART 1: How to Hire a Contractor   1

OVERVIEW   A Strategy for Greatly Reducing
Risks   3
CHAPTER 1   Educate Yourself About the Job   22
CHAPTER 2   When You Need a Plan—
or More   29
CHAPTER 3   Where to Get the Money   32
CHAPTER 4   Finding Contractors   39
CHAPTER 5   Bids   86
CHAPTER 6   Check the Contractor Out   95
CHAPTER 7   Payment Schedule   98
CHAPTER 8   A Written Contract   104
CHAPTER 9   Be There If You Can   118

PART 2: Buyer's Guide to Home
Improvements   121

How a House Is Built   132
How a Plumbing System Works   141
How an Electrical System Works   144

MORE SPACE   146
▪ Attic Conversion   146
▪ Finishing a Basement   151
▪ Dormers   154
▪ Room Additions   157
▪ Garages   161

KITCHEN REMODELING   165
▪ New Cabinets   165
▪ New Countertop   170

- Refinishing Wood Cabinets — 172
- Refinishing a Refrigerator — 173

BATH REMODELING — 175
- Tubs — 176
- Lavatories — 180
- Toilets — 182
- Lavatory Faucets — 185
- Tub Faucets — 186
- Showers — 187
- Exhaust Fans — 188

FLOORING — 190
- Resilient — 190
- Hardwood — 193
- Carpeting — 195

DOORS — 198
- Garage Doors — 198
- Patio Doors — 201

STANDARD DOORS — 206
- Wood Doors — 206
- Steel Entry Doors — 211
- Fiberglass Entry Doors — 214

WINDOWS — 215
- Double-Hung Windows — 215
- Casement Windows — 223
- Fixed Windows — 224
- Sliding Windows — 226
- Jalousie Windows — 227
- Awning Windows — 227
- Hopper Windows — 228
- Top-Hinged Windows — 228
- Bay or Bow Windows — 228

ELECTRICAL IMPROVEMENTS — 230
- Replacing a Switch — 230
- Replacing a Standard Switch with a Dimmer — 231
- Installing a Receptacle — 232
- Installing a Grand-Fault Circuit Interrupter — 232
- Installing a Ceiling Light Fixture — 233
- Upgrading Electrical Service to 150 Amps — 234

WALLS — 236
- Sheetrocking Walls or Ceilings — 236

WALLCOVERING   239
- Wallpaper   239
- Paneling   242

PAINTING   244
- Interior Painting   244
- Exterior Painting   246

CERAMIC TILE   249
- Wall/Floor   250

INSULATION   253
- Batts or Blanket Insulation   254
- Rigid Insulation on Basement Wall   256
- Loose-fill Insulation   257
- Blown-in Insulation   257

STAIRS   260
- Prefab Fold-up Stairway   260
- Circular Staircase   261
- Simple Wood Steps   262
- Custom Wood Steps   263

SKYLIGHTS   264
- Fixed or Motorized   264

CEILINGS   268
- Acoustical Ceiling Tile   268
- Suspended Ceiling   270

FIREPLACES   272
- Freestanding Fireplace   272
- Built-in Fireplace   274
- Brick Fireplace   275

ROOFING   277
- Asphalt or Fiberglass Shingle   277
- Roll   283
- Clay Tile   283
- Concrete Tile   286
- Cedar Shingle   287
- Cedar Shakes   288
- Slate   289

SIDING   291
- Vinyl   293
- Aluminum   298
- Steel   299
- Plywood   300

- Board 301
- Cedar Shakes or Shingles 303
- Hardboard 305

GUTTERS 306

DRIVEWAYS 309
- Concrete 309
- Asphalt 310

PATIOS AND WALKWAYS 313
- Brick-on-Sand 313
- Flagstone-on-Sand 315

DECKS 316
- Raised 317
- Ground-Level 319

PORCH 321

TERMITE CONTROL 325

WATERPROOFING 327
- Waterproof Basement 327

APPENDIX A: Sample Contract 331
APPENDIX B: Glossary 345
Index 351

▬ ACKNOWLEDGMENTS ▬

I would like to thank the following governmental agencies and individuals for the information they provided for this book.

Note to the new edition: Though some of the organizations and associations have changed or gone out of existence since this book was first published, and some individuals are no longer in the positions listed, my appreciation remains. Their contributions are still invaluable.

Alabama: Susan C. Rief, Consumer Protection Specialist, Office of the Attorney General

California: Steve Kolb, Department of Consumer Affairs

Connecticut: Susan Nichols, Consumer Protection Department; Mary Beth Greaney, Paralegal Specialist, Office of the Attorney General

Delaware: Frederick A. Warwick, Division of Consumer Affairs; Stuart B. Drowos, Deputy Attorney General

Florida: Doyle Conner, Commissioner, Department of Agricultural and Consumer Services

Georgia: Joyce Flournoy, Office of Consumer Affairs

Hawaii: Wayne Fujikane, Department of Commerce and Consumer Affairs

Idaho: Kriss J. Bivens, Consumer Specialist, Business Regulation Division

Indiana: Dan Foley and Vicki Hermansen, Office of the Attorney General

Illinois: Neil Hartigan, Attorney General; Nancy Antonacci, Consumer Protection Division

Iowa: Stephen Switzer, Investigator, Department of Justice

Kansas: Carole A. Harvey, Consumer Protection Division, Office of the Attorney General

Kentucky: Lori Farris, Consumer Education Specialist

Louisiana: Mary H. Travis, Department of Justice

Maine: James E. Tierney, Attorney General

Maryland: J. Joseph Curran Jr., Attorney General

Massachusetts: Mary Ann Walsh, Commissioner of Consumer Affairs

Michigan: Frank J. Kelley, Attorney General; Frederick J. Hoffecker, Consumer Protection Division, Department of the Attorney General

Minnesota: Hubert H. Humphrey III, Attorney General

Mississippi: Tray Bobinger, Director, Consumer Protection Division

Missouri: William Webster, Attorney General; Peter Lumaghi, Assistant AG; Mary Jenkins

New York, NY: Mark Green, Commissioner, Department of Consumer Affairs

North Dakota: Tom Engelhardt, Consumer Fraud Division

Ohio: Anthony J. Cellebreze, Attorney General

Oregon: Jim Stembridge, Deputy Administrator, Construction Contractors Board

Pennsylvania: Ernie Preate Jr., Attorney General

South Dakota: Jeffrey Hallem, Assistant Attorney General, Division of Consumer Affairs

Suffolk County, N.Y.: Jane Devine, Director, Department of Consumer Affairs; Bill Baessler, Director of Licensing; Bob Klein, Investigator; and Patrick Halpin, Suffolk County Executive

Nassau County, N.Y.: Ina Alcabes; Larry DelleVecchia, Investigator Supervisor

New Mexico: Jeffrey Trout, Director, Consumer Protection and Economic Crimes

Utah: Stephen G. Schwendiman, Assistant Attorney General

Virginia: Betty Blakemore, Director, Consumer Affairs Office

Virgin Islands: Olga McBean, Department of Licensing and Consumer Affairs

Washington: Sheila Gooch, Investigator; Byron Brown, Assistant Attorney General

Wisconsin: John Gray, Division of Consumer Affairs

I would also like to thank the following individuals and organizations:

American Hardboard Association

American Homeowners Foundation

American Institute of Architects

American Society of Home Inspectors

Walter D. Anderson, Resilient Floor Covering Institute

James Benney, National Wood Window and Door Association

Ronald M. Boden, Jarro Building Industries Corp.

Matt Breen, Bank of Ireland

Brick Institute of America

Sandy Bugaj, Owens Corning Fiberglass Corporation

Alan Campbell, Executive Director, National Association of the Remodeling Industry

Caren Cinnamon, Seaman & Eisemann Insurance

Tom Conser, National Wood Flooring Association

Patsy Davenport, Administrative Director, Oak Flooring Institute

Nick DeRosa

Judith Donner, Consumer Specialist, Orkin Pest Control

Bill Dunn, Suffolk Building Supply

Pete Fetterer, Kohler Company

Bill Garthe, Adamson Construction Company

Marsha Goldeberger, Director, BBB, Standards & Practices
Fred Gorman, Founder, Shells Only
Susan Grant, Director, Association of Consumer Agency
Administrators
Christine C. Graves, Managing Partner, Homes Guild
Reynolds Graves, Graves, Gold & Darbee
Bob Hartig
Deb Hagen, Mona, Meyer & McGrath
John Heyn, The John J. Heyn Company, Inc.
Richard Hoover, Executive Vice President, Stark
Ceramics
Charley Hudson, Long Island Building Supply Corp.
Charley Hudson, contractor
John Jackson, *Qualified Remodeler* magazine
George Kinneane
Barbara Lagowski
Marilyn LeMoine, American Plywood Association
Wilhelmina Loomis, Executive Director, Tile Contractors
Association of America
Mark McCabe, *Remodeling* magazine
Marylee MacDonald, Building Research Council, University of Illinois
Matt Mahoney, Mahoney Construction Company
Dan Miller, Director, International Remodeling Contractors Association
Bryan Patchan, Executive Director, National Remodelers
Council
Pam Price, Hometime
Walter F. Pruter, Executive Vice President, National Tile
Roofing Manufacturers Association, Inc.
Barri Friedman Rafferty, Burson Marsteller
Bill Rooney
Peter Rush, Sumner Rider & Associates, Inc.
Paul Sandberg, Freelance Garage Doors
Jim Savery
Harvey Seymour, Insurance Information Institute
David Shirley, Tennessee State Legislator
Ronni Shulman, Ronni Shulman Public Relations
Walt Stoeppelwerth, Home Tech
Jack Sturiano

Joe Tarver, Executive Director, National Tile Contractors Association, Inc.
Tile Council of America, Ken Erikson
Ed Thomas, Western Wood Products Association
Gerald Triplett, Director, Asphalt Institute
Dick Wood

INTRODUCTION

California bonds expert Theron Skiles reflected the feelings of many people in a position to know when he said to me one day late in my research, "Hey, man, this is the real world. People don't care about anything but the price of the home improvement. They take the lowest bid, and that's it. And that's why they get taken. It's all dollars and cents."

In some, perhaps most, instances he is probably right. You can get down on your hands and knees and beg some people to pay attention to what you're saying, and they'll listen—and then take the lowest bid that comes along or otherwise act contrary to advice given.

But I know, too, that there are lots of people out there who will listen.

I have no way of confirming this, but I do believe it, and this book is for these people. Those who will really listen.

Let me make it clear that the ideas in this book do not come from me. I am the medium, as it were, but the message comes from all over the country (as well as out of the country) . . . from consumer affairs people, and attorneys general, and lawyers, and consumers, and associations—and contractors. Indeed I think contractors gave me some of the best ideas, just as the foxes would if they were helping to make the henhouse secure against other foxes.

And yet, having said that, I would be ingenuous not to acknowledge some debt to myself. As my research progressed, it became clear that there was no universally consistent counsel that consumer protection people, collectively, could offer consumers about hiring and dealing with contractors. In fact while some advice was very good, some was meaningless, some bad, some downright dangerous—and some crazy, at least when I came to understand the nature of the home-improvement field and the pedigree of the people who work in it.

Unhappily there was no easy formula to pick up and present. Indeed I found myself using ideas from some people to challenge long-held assumptions of others who should have known better. In essence I had to work from a Chinese menu of ideas to—and let's really mangle this metaphor—work out a formula for success.

For example, there is inconsistent advice on what a contractor should be paid up front. In California they'll tell you no more than 10 percent or $1,000, whichever is less. In Maine the law says one-third, but that it's not inflexible; that is, the customer and contractor can collectively waive the provision and the customer is free to put up—gulp—up to 50 percent down. So, for example, you contract to have an extension done for $50,000 and give the contractor a check for half—$25,000 . . . "And then," said one contractor to me, "feel your whatchamacallit puckering when he doesn't show up the first day."

Based on what I've learned, my advice would be to give nothing up front, except under certain circumstances detailed in the text. And believe me, I am not being gratuitously cruel to contractors. There are reasons.

Following the advice in this book will take work and sweat, perhaps precious hours that one would rather spend elsewhere.

But it's okay to accept a little pain at the beginning so that you don't have to take on a massive amount of it later. And you'll not only avoid the pain, you'll realize the pleasure of seeing your home-improvement dreams—maybe dreams that will never be possible again—come true. I'm counting on it.

Good luck.

—TOM PHILBIN

PART 1

HOW TO HIRE
A CONTRACTOR

A Strategy for Greatly Reducing Risks

When it comes to horror stories, the home-improvement field can sometimes make you think you're reading Stephen King.

A few years ago, in Memphis, Tennessee, a legislator we'll call Jim Arnold contracted to have some home-improvement work done. The work was done, and Arnold paid the general contractor—the person with whom he had made the contract—all the money for the job. But there was a problem. The GC hadn't paid his supplier, who slapped a lien—a legal claim for a debt—on Arnold, who ultimately had to pay an additional $20,000. That's right, even though Arnold had paid the GC in full.

In San Jose, California, as reported in *Changing Times* magazine, a couple contracted to have additions put on both ends of their house. The contractor convinced them to pay his entire fee—$125,000—up front. They did. He opened up both ends of the house, then left—never to return, leaving the house open to weather and wild animals.

In Asharoken, New York, neighbors noticed a roofing contractor on a fellow neighbor's roof. He was working with a torch. Before the day was out, the contractor had burned the house to the ground—and he turned out to be unlicensed and working with forged insurance forms.

In Missouri, Assistant Attorney General Peter Lumaghi tells the story of an elderly woman living in the southeastern part of the state who had no understanding of home improvements and contractors. So when a contractor slapped a lien on her home, despair set in and she eventually set the house on fire—and stayed inside, a suicide.

These are, admittedly, horror stories that are atypical. But it's just a matter of degree. There are many, many smaller horror stories out there, which indicates the many perils people face when hiring carpenters, plumbers, roofers, and other home-improvement contractors.

Susan Grant, former director of the Consumer Protection Division of the State of Massachusetts and president of the National Association of Consumer Agency Administrators, says, "Home improvements is a very serious problem in America."

This is reflected in the number of complaints consumer-

1. A not unfamiliar sight. A consumer affairs investigator, this one in Nassau County, Long Island, investigates an improvement gone sour.

protection agencies across the country receive. Home improvements consistently rank second or third among complaints, and in some areas number one.

And the complaints routinely are about jobs worth thousands of dollars. Grant, for example, says complaints to her averaged around $10,000 each. Bill Baessler, director of Licensing of affluent Suffolk County, Long Island, says complaints to the Suffolk Department of Consumer Affairs usually involve $50,000 or $60,000—and more.

Walt Stoeppelwerth, who has conducted hundreds of seminars for contractors on running their businesses better, says, "If you were to canvass a thousand people who have had home improvements done, you might find 20 percent who were totally satisfied with the job, 30 percent who were semisatisfied, and 50 percent who were completely dissatisfied."

Stoeppelwerth is not alone in his thinking. From innumerable interviews with people who have had improvements done, consumer protection people, contractors themselves, and others, there's no question that the dissatisfaction level is quite high. To accept Stoeppelwerth's figure, then, means that 80 percent of the people who get improvements done are dissatisfied to one degree or another.

That's a stunning percentage, and the questions that spring to mind are how and why and, most importantly, what, if anything, can be done to keep oneself from being part of that negative statistic.

To answer the last question first, people can keep themselves from being victimized by contractors. That's the purpose of this book. But it should also be stated that it can't give you 100 percent protection. On the other hand, if you use the strategies presented here, you will vastly reduce your chances of being hurt because you will hire and deal with a reliable, honest, competent contractor—of which there are many. Indeed I would put your chances of not getting burned at around 99 percent—not bad as life situations go.

First one should understand the ways consumers get hurt. There are implicit lessons.

HOW CONSUMERS GET HURT

There are two general contractor groups who victimize consumers: what might be called pure rip-off artists and the mostly well-meaning contractors who don't know what they're doing in one way or another.

The pure rip-off artist is in the minority—but that percentage is still a shocker. Says Fred Gorman, founder of the Medford, Long Island, remodeling firm Shells Only and who has been in the remodeling business for over fifty years, "I would say that one in ten contractors are highbinders. If you let them, they'll rip you off."

In a number of states most of these contractors come from out of town. As Tom F. Engelhardt, director of the Consumer Fraud and Antitrust Section for North Dakota, says, "Most home-improvement scams involve transient merchants mis-

2. Some contractors are better than others. (California State Contractors Board)

representing the need for home improvements and promising excellent bargains. Consumers complain of overpriced repair, substandard repair, and failure to complete repairs."

The Williamson gang is probably the ultimate example of this kind of contractor. They are known to every consumer protection agency in the country because they travel all over the country, usually showing up in the warm months.

They may be into anything now, but they are famed for one asphalt-driveway scam. Indeed William Webster, formerly attorney general of Missouri, calls them "asphalt gypsies."

They wear clean uniforms and drive around in modern trucks until they spot a driveway with a few hairline cracks or other defects. They point out the problems (they usually arrive midday, when, they hope, only a woman is home), then offer to seal the driveway for what seems like a good price, say a five-gallon can for $60.

If they get the go-ahead, they'll be back a half hour later, finished, and ask for *$600*. Naturally the consumer will point out that the agreed-upon charge was $60.

"That's right," says the scamster. "Sixty dollars for a five-gallon can; we used *ten* cans." He expects the person to argue and is prepared to settle for less—say $400. The consumer offers a check, but the gypsy won't take a check, and when the person says he or she doesn't have that kind of cash in the house, the gypsy says he'll take a check—but will accompany the person to the bank. If the consumer agrees and leaves the house, the gypsy's confederates may rob it while she or he is gone. And the driveway won't be properly sealed either. These swindlers may use low-quality sealer, but they've also been known to swab on used motor oil as well as cheap black enamel paint. Looks good until you drive on it—and take it with you into the street. (Susan Grant calls these gypsies the "crankcase-oil brigade.")

The elderly are particularly vulnerable to the pure ripoff artist. A humanoid named Harold Bartlett, for example, specialized in victimizing elderly black women in East Saint Louis, conning them into signing deeds of trust to their homes and then threatening to foreclose if they didn't pay for improvements.

ABC's *Home Show* showed a case where an alert bank

manager saved an elderly client before she was too badly hurt. The manager had noticed that the woman had transferred large amounts of money from her savings to her checking account and was writing fairly large checks to someone he had never heard of. Suspicious, he contacted the Los Angeles bunko squad. An investigating detective found that the woman was having an old shed (which one investigator described as looking "pregnant and drunk") reroofed, a job later determined to be worth perhaps $700. The woman had already paid the roofer $5,000 of the overall price of *$58,000.*

Another scam: "spiking" the house, that is, starting the job by ripping down siding, say—"because I misunderstood," the contractor will tell the homeowner. "I thought you wanted me to start." Then the homeowner is forced to have the job finished, either by the spiker or by someone else. (Get it finished by someone else and take action against the spiker.)

And there are many other kinds of scams. One of the most damaging is the kind suffered by the couple in San Jose mentioned earlier: contractors who will take down payments on a job and never start. Then there are those who start and never finish. And such amounts are not small—usually they're in the thousands, many times the tens of thousands. Sue Nichols, former head of the Connecticut Consumer Affairs Department, says they had one "contractor" who made a livelihood of this. "That's all he did, go from job to job giving estimates, taking advances, and never coming back. He got around eighty thousand dollars before he [disappeared]."

This of course is felonious behavior. The district attorney will be happy to take your complaint—and to pursue it after he or she has gone after the perpetrators of the other complaints on the desk—the robberies, burglaries, assaults, rapes, and murders.

BAD GOOD GUYS—
A MORE COMMON DANGER

The most common peril to consumers comes not from pure rip-off artists but from contractors who are well intentioned

3. A siding job was started on this Suffolk County, Long Island, home because the contractor said he misunderstood the homeowner's desires. In some cases there's no misunderstanding. Contractors "spike" the job by starting it without permission The contractor here paid $4,000 to the homeowner for the misunderstanding. (Suffolk County Department of Consumer Affairs)

but are poor craftsmen, or poor businessmen, or both. They don't know what they're doing. They are what Bill Garthe, a general contractor who operates Adamson Construction Company in Saint James, New York, calls "people who have a pickup truck and a hammer and think they're contractors."

Susan Grant adds, "And sometimes they don't even have that."

For example, there are many moonlighters—mostly firemen and cops—who are doing home improvements but don't know what they're doing. Jobs get botched.

In other cases it can be a "specialty" contractor—someone who normally does one or two things, such as roofing and siding—biting off more than he can chew. Says one insurance specialist with Seaman & Eisemann Insurance in Hicksville, Long Island, "In the winter, when it gets slow, a roofer may decide to get work by contracting to add a room on someone's house. He can do the roof well, but the rest of the addition gets away from him."

In other cases it may simply be that the contractor is not good at what he does. One of the most stunning examples of this was a job I observed at an elderly couple's house. A ceramic-tile installer had secured new water-resistant drywall to the wall framing in a bath and had then installed the tile on top of that. The problem was that the nails used to secure the drywall were too long: The couple showed me the rather stupefying sight of the bedroom wall contiguous to the bath—and the points of nails that had broken through, making it look as if it had a kind of orderly chicken pox.

Many contractors go from one job to the other, doing shoddy work for years because potential customers never get to speak with previous ones.

But being a poor businessman is even more common than being a poor craftsman. Indeed if there is one "heart of darkness" of home-improvement contracting, it's this.

Bill Rooney, a home-improvement expert who is host of the KXL radio show *Around the House* in Portland, Oregon, believes that "almost all contractors are terrible businessmen."

"They work for wages only," says Walt Stoeppelwerth, "and don't have any or enough markup in their estimates. They don't allow money for insurance, tool maintenance, taxes, gas, and the like—or the things that can go wrong on a job."

WOLVES IN THE WALLS

Washington State architect Ken Kraeger calls these the "wolves in the walls." For example, a contractor might have given a price for a new kitchen, but then opens up a wall and there's a gas pipe he didn't know was there and didn't provide for in his estimate. He has to spend the time to deal with it, time that gobbles up his profit. There is little or no markup, no cushion, to absorb the blow. At some point the contractor may become discouraged and depart.

Some contractors, too, are desperate for money and will give an unrealistically low bid just to get the job, perhaps to stanch a hemorrhage they have going at another job or to make their mortgage payment. Or to eat.

Whatever, the low estimating can lead to a variety of problems that in turn lead to the contractor not finishing the job, or cutting corners—or both.

Any homeowner who is involved becomes, of course, enmeshed in the contractor's problems.

That most contractors don't know what they're doing in one way or another is a truism. Reflecting this is a mind-boggling mortality rate. According to the Remodelors Council of the National Association of House Builders, some 80 to 90 percent of all contractors go out of business after five years.

Stoeppelwerth puts the figure at "95 percent after five years. After only one year of business 50 percent of them go under."

In Maryland contractors must be licensed. In 1988 there were eight thousand licensed contractors. In 1989 over four thousand of them did not renew.

Hopefully the contractor will not go out of business halfway through your job—with perhaps all of your money in his pocket.

Contractors who do poor work, or overpriced work, or who go out of business, or who are rip-off artists are not the only perils a homeowner faces: There is also that vicious lien law. If the contractor has not paid the suppliers or subcontractors who work for him, the homeowner could be liable for the charges.

In Tennessee, legislator David Shirley said that suppliers used to not "even bother to check out a contractor's credit. They give him the materials easily because they know that if the contractor doesn't pay them, they could easily move against the homeowner."

Many contractors and suppliers are well aware of the law's existence. The American Subcontractors Association each year publishes a thick document that details the lien law in all the states, in effect making sure that the "sub," as they say in the trade, does it right. The law varies from state to state, except in its thrust: If the supplier or sub isn't paid by the GC, the homeowner can be made to pay even if he's already paid the GC in full.

The law likely started, like many bad things, with good intentions. Byron Brown, a former assistant attorney general with the state of Washington, said that from reading statutes it appears to have been "generated to protect laborers, ordinary workers, from employers who victimized them. The homeowners weren't involved then."

But the homeowner became the proverbial innocent bystander, and today the law seems to exist in at least a few states because the legislators who could change it also have home-improvement businesses and see it as a good thing for them.

Representative Shirley, himself a contractor, knows this well. For ten years he fought unsuccessfully to have a law written that would merely require that consumers be alerted to the law's existence; he finally won some changes in it. In fact just recently consumers in Tennessee were taken out of what Shirley called the "law's line of succession." If the contractor doesn't pay his subs or suppliers, the consumer is no longer responsible: It's strictly between the general contractor and the sub or supplier. For Shirley, it was a hard-fought triumph.

4. Tennessee legislator David Shirley, who fought for ten years against the state's lien law. He finally won.

A STRATEGY FOR PROTECTING
ONESELF

The FBI will tell you that many people who are murder victims often contribute to their victimization. The same thing would seem to hold true for consumers victimized by home-improvement contractors. They set themselves up for it.

For one thing they don't try to protect themselves.

Mark Green, former consumer affairs commissioner of New York City, says, "It is surprising that the same person who will shop all over town to save twenty-five dollars on a television set will do little or nothing to shop an improvement that will cost thousands of dollars."

Indeed a lot of money is usually at stake. Many people—in some areas (such as Long Island, New York) most of them—contract to have improvements done that cost more than the original house—lots more. For example, a 700-square-foot extension in Long Island could cost you around $100 a square foot—$70,000. A kitchen could easily go for $20,000. Bill Garthe, a contractor mentioned above, says that "In 1956 you could buy a house for ten thousand dollars. Today you could pay ten thousand dollars just for the materials for building a garage."

Most people don't even get involved in shopping for the money for the job. According to a report in *Money* magazine, only one-third of the people who need money shop for it. "Those who don't shop," the magazine said, referring to a report prepared by Purdue University's Credit Research Center, "are generally single female parents, retirees, or consumers who were previously rejected for credit." Those who do shop tend "to be college graduates who have annual incomes in excess of $40,000 or household debt burdens that consume at least 40% of their gross pretax income."

Why people don't get involved is perhaps something for a psychologist to determine. Perhaps it simply puts people into a position of dealing with something—a home improvement—where they have little or no knowledge. It all seems so overwhelming; they get scared and assume, as it were, a fetal, passive position.

I recall watching one woman on TV explaining how she was ripped off by a contractor, and the longer she talked, the more stunned I became. It was outrageous. Not to be snide, but her actions, or inactions, in the face of what was so obviously a con made me wonder not only why she didn't detect the aroma of what was being done to her but how, indeed, she had gotten through life. Who fed her?

One high-ranking consumer affairs department head who has handled thousands of consumer complaints and who prefers to remain anonymous says, "Over 90 percent of the problems my agency handled can be directly traced back to people's stupidity."

Jim Stembridge, former deputy administrator of Oregon's Construction Contractors Board, sees problems stemming from stupidity—and greed.

"We find that many of the consumers who have problems are not entirely innocent," he says. "In fact the biggest problems . . . occur where people believe they can get a better deal than anyone else and go for the 'unbelievably low' bid, when they should know that they are not going to get a satisfactory product for the price they are paying.

"The most typical jam people get into in Oregon happens when they hire someone who is not registered with the Construction Contractors Board. Quite often it's someone who's moonlighting, a friend of a friend, an out-of-work carpenter with a five-dollar ad in the *Nickel Ads* throwaway newspaper, or just someone who's 'working in the neighborhood.' Consumers often get what they deserve with these 'special deals' that turn out to be 'special trouble.' "

GET INVOLVED

Whatever the reasons why people don't get involved, the bedrock of a strategy to protect oneself begins with this. Without involvement nothing else is possible, because involvement fuels commitment, and you need commitment, determination to do what is necessary to protect yourself.

Essentially, protecting yourself—and getting a good job

at a fair price—means controlling the job and this means controlling the money. It means being on your guard. It means going, most of all, through a careful screening process in selecting a contractor who is honest, reliable, and competent—and whom you're not afraid of and can talk to.

Following is a lineup of the steps to take that will add up to a winning strategy and that will be fleshed out in subsequent chapters. Give yourself plenty of time to follow them.

1. Become informed about the job.
2. Have a formal plan, if necessary.
3. Get contractors' names from reliable sources; make preliminary checks on them.
4. Get multiple bids.
5. Thoroughly check the contractor you like.
6. Write a detailed contract which includes not letting the contractor get ahead of you on payments and being able to hold out a final payment.
7. Understand the lien law before the job starts, and protect yourself against it.
8. Whenever possible, be there when the job is being done.

Going through these steps, aside from getting you a good contractor, can have an important psychological benefit. The fear and confusion that one might feel in hiring a contractor will fade. It's hard to feel fear when you know what you're doing and have control of things.

Using the Book

It is not necessary to read the entire book to learn how to hire and deal with a contractor. All you need to do, really, is read Part 1, and then look up and study the information in Part 2 Buyer's Guide to Home Improvements which applies to the specific improvement you plan. For example, if it's roofing just look up the roofing section; if siding, the siding section, and so forth.

WHO'S WHO ... AND WHO DOES WHAT

WHO'S WHO

In any given home-improvement job, one of a number of people may be involved. Following is a précis of who these people are and who does what.

General Contractor. As someone once said, "the description doesn't mean the guy is in the army." Rather it refers to an individual, commonly known in the trade as the GC, who oversees big remodeling jobs such as room additions, dormers (where they raise the roof to provide living space in the attic), and other house remodelings that require structural work. GCs also will supervise kitchen remodelings merely because they are big.

The GC orders most of the materials and products to do the particular job and hires the various craftspeople—plumbers, carpenters, electricians, roofers, and so forth—who will do the work. He may also order products and materials.

GCs have varying backgrounds. Many start out as carpenters and then expand their businesses into general contracting. Others start as roofing-and-siding installers and become GCs.

The newest breed of GCs, which may be first generation, are builder-designers, who may have no experience in the home-improvement field but are "packagers," as Bill Rooney, host of the radio show *Around the House* in Portland, Oregon, says. "They sell the entire job, from plans to cleanup." Of course other GCs can do the same thing, except that they usually have "dirty fingernail" experience in the work.

Depending on the size of the company, GCs may have permanent crews going from job to job, or one or more subcontractors, or subs.

Subcontractor. This is a name given to any craftsperson— plumber, electrician, carpenter—who is hired on a piecemeal basis for the one job. He is paid for his share of the work by the GC. The subcontractor will usually have his own jobs on the side. For example, a roofer may work as a subcontractor for a GC but will also be doing individual roofing jobs for his own customers.

Specialty Contractor. This simply means a tradesperson such as a carpenter or a roofer who practices a specific trade, such as roofing or plumbing, rather than being a general contractor. Both permanent crew members and subs are considered to be specialty contractors; they just have different specialties.

WHO DOES WHAT

There is a surprising number of trades within the home-improvement field. Following is a lineup of the various jobs involved in a major extension, pretty much in their order of occurrence and who would do them.

Excavation. The first step in adding a room usually is excavating the earth and preparing it in order to ensure that it is flat and firm. This job is usually done by a specialist in the work.

Foundation. This is the masonry base on which the addition rests. A mason, who is likely skilled in all kinds of concrete work, does this.

Drainage. A plumber would likely do this; that is, install pipes to ensure that ground water will drain away from the house foundation.

Framing. Framing is the making of the wood skeleton of the room or whatever. Carpenters do this, and usually young carpenters—a framing crew—because it is, as they say, "bull work."

Sheathing. This is the exterior wood base of the house. It's another job for the carpenter, or perhaps a siding installer (see below) will do it.

Electrical. The job of snaking the wires through the walls and ceilings to the points where they emerge from the walls is called the electrical "rough in." This job, as well as connecting switches, outlets, appliances, and so on, is a job for a licensed electrician.

Plumbing. Bringing water and drainpipes through walls is called rough plumbing; connecting fixtures and faucets to them where they emerge from the walls is a job only a licensed plumber can do.

Heating/Air-Conditioning. Also a job for a plumber, or a specialist in heating and air-conditioning.

Insulation. If the framing is open, exposed, just about anyone can do this job, but it's usually done by an insulation installer, or the carpenter.

Doors. The carpenter hangs the doors ("hangs" because that's exactly what he does—hangs it on the hinges).

Garage Doors. Usually done by a specialist, but a carpenter could also do it.

Windows/Skylights. This is usually another job for a carpenter, but there are also people who specialize in putting in skylights as well as windows. Carpenters, though, usually do the framing required.

Siding. Done by siding installers, who may be able to install all kinds of siding but usually focus on just one type. Some installers install only vinyl, some only wood, some only aluminum, and so forth. People who do siding often also install roofing.

Roofing. Like siding installers, roofers tend to focus on one or two materials, particularly since some materials, such as slate and tile, require great experience to install well. Most roofers install asphalt or fiberglass shingles, far and away the most popular. It is physically the hardest job to do, requiring strength, agility, endurance, skill, and a love of sunlight and heat. At thirty a roofer is an old man.

Gutters/Downspouts. If you are getting siding installed, this will often be part of the job, and siding installers can do it. Similarly roofers will also install it. However, many individuals and companies specialize in seamless gutter installation.

Drywall. Drywall, commonly known by the brand name Sheetrock, is the flat, hard plaster panels commonly used for walls and ceilings. Carpenters can do it, but it is normally done by someone who specializes in it—in fact two specialists: One person, known in the trade as a "rocker," nails the Sheetrock to the framing members. When he's finished, the joints are taped, and "mud" (joint compound) is applied by a specialist called a spackler, to seal and hide the joints.

Fireplace. If it's a masonry fireplace, a mason will build it; if a prefabricated fireplace, a carpenter will usually do it.

Paneling/Wallcovering. Installing wallcoverings is usually done by someone who specializes in it or by a painter who both paints and does this. A carpenter normally installs paneling.

Molding. This applies to exterior and interior wood trim and is a job for a very experienced carpenter. In fact some carpenters are known as trim carpenters because they specialize in this. (An old-time carpenter I knew once said, "If you watch a house being built, you'll see the framing being put up by the young bucks, but it's the guys with the gray hair who do the trim.")

Cabinets/Built-ins/Countertops. Work for a carpenter.

Interior and Exterior Painting. A painter.

Flooring. Floors require underlayment, or subflooring—a base for the finish flooring material. A carpenter may do it if it's part of a room addition. But, as with siding and roofing, there are a number of different kinds of flooring—vinyl, ceramic, wood—so there is specialization.

Decks/Landscaping. Decks are ordinarily done by people who specialize in them, or by carpenters.

NOTE: If you hire a large company, you may have a host of these different contractors on the job at one time or another; if a small company, you may only get one or two people—a lead carpenter who will sub such specialties as plumbing and electrical work but will probably do other specialties—flooring, Sheetrocking, and much more—himself.

5. When a home improvement is being done, disruption is par for the course.

DUST, DIRT, DISRUPTION— AND POSSIBLE THIEVERY

Many people are taken aback by the dust, dirt, and disruption caused by a remodeling job, and the bigger the job, the more of this one gets.

When the old stuff is taken out—tubs removed or walls or ceilings taken down—a lot of trash is created, but also a great deal of dust and dirt. To keep dust from floating into other rooms, either you or the contractor can hang plastic dropcloths, but don't expect to solve the problem completely.

"There's no way to keep dust out of other rooms," says one contractor.

What can help one maintain an even disposition is the cleanliness and neatness of a contractor. One big remodeling contractor I know hires one person on every job who has just one job—walking around and picking up and discarding debris. Depending on the job it may also mean that the homeowner will have to get involved in daily cleanup.

A good contractor will leave a job clean, and you can also contract for having him leave the house "maid clean." For an extra hundred dollars or so the contractor will have a professional cleaning service clean the house from top to bottom after the job is done.

Also, *expect* disruption in the house. If a kitchen is being redone, you can be sure of taking some meals in restaurants, and you may be without a toilet for some time, or your front yard may look as if it took a couple of direct mortar hits. Contractor Ron Boden says the whole experience is "traumatic."

Also, during the course of the job workers will be, to one degree or another, traipsing in and out of the house to use the bathroom, get a drink of water, whatever. Our homes are our nests—we don't like people disrupting them. Good contractors realize this and give very specific instructions to the people who work for them on being mannerly and considerate.

Finally don't leave valuables lying around. Such items can be an open invitation to sticky fingers.

CHAPTER 1

Educate Yourself About the Job

Most people don't know much about home improvements, perhaps because they think of them as something akin to brain surgery. The fact is they aren't brain surgery, nor are any of them really that complex. The products and materials used are simple enough, and so are the installation methods, once you know them. Their mysteriousness derives, it seems to me, from simply not knowing. With a bit of effort the average person—even, as a friend of mine once said, "those with more than the usual complement of thumbs"—can learn enough to benefit himself or herself in a variety of ways.

For one thing, know-how leads to knowing what you want in the job rather than something you don't need or cannot afford.

For example, you may want wood flooring for your new living room. "So the contractor or the salesman," said Tom Conser, former president of National Wood Flooring Association, "will suggest you get clear-grade acrylic-impregnated strip oak at ten dollars a square foot and he will tell you that it will last eight hundred years. Fine, except that you can get select-grade strip flooring for four dollars a square foot that is absolutely beautiful. Of course it will only last four hundred years."

Know-how will also prevent you from getting less of a product or material.

For example, you may want new windows installed but have no idea what you want. So the contractor sells you a bunch of vinyl replacement windows, which are of far inferior quality than, say, wood windows, which you could in fact afford.

Job know-how should include knowing just what a product looks like. This can be particularly important if the product or material has an aesthetic function.

A few years ago, for example, a consumer affairs specialist told me of a mistake she once made. She contracted to have white vinyl replacement windows installed in her seventy-year-old house but had not fully visualized how they'd look when installed. The job was done while she was at work, and when she came home, she was aghast: "They *screamed* out at me. I almost died. They looked so out-of-place."

Knowledge will also help you in evaluating contractors, particularly the pure rip-off artist.

One of the most egregious—and funny—examples of contractor baloney I have ever heard occurred to my writer friend Barbara Lagowski. At the time that she was taking roofing-and-siding bids on her New Jersey home, she was pregnant, and one contractor cautioned her on the danger of using backer board beneath the vinyl siding.

"Why is that?" asked Barbara, who had done her homework and knew that backer board was nothing but thin plastic that helped stiffen the siding.

"Backer board," the contractor said, "could give out fumes that could seep into the house and damage your unborn baby."

WARRANTIES AND GUARANTEES

Knowledge can also ensure that you get full benefits of manufacturer warranties and guarantees of products and materials.

For instance, some contractors will install asphalt roofing their own way for speed. But if they don't install it the way the manufacturer details, then the warranty may be voided. If something goes wrong with the roof, you—rather than the manufacturer—are responsible. And this applies to many other products and materials as well.

Essentially, know-how mainly relates to the quality of the job you want, and the fact is that quality differs greatly on perhaps *95 percent* of the products out there. For example, there are important quality differences in wood, roofing, siding, windows, flooring, ceiling material, paint, molding, gutter, and much more, as well as important installation differences among jobs. For example, proper preparation of the soil as well as the thickness of the material used and how it's installed can mean life or death for asphalt and concrete driveway jobs.

There are also quality differences within particular brand names, even quality brand names. For example, American Standard makes a whole assortment of faucets that range from high quality all the way down to "builder's special" (commonly used by builders of tract housing) quality. Benjamin Moore makes one of the better paints, but that's its "Regal" line. There is some stuff down the line of quality— with the Benjamin Moore name on it—that is of much lesser quality. CertainTeed makes excellent vinyl siding—in the higher grades. Its bottom-of-the-line material is known as a commodity material.

And of course there are price differences. You can get an American Standard toilet for $100—and one for $900. Both carry the American Standard brand name.

This know-how will also enable you to transmit what you want much better to contractors, and they will be bidding on apples and apples rather than apples and grapefruit. For example, if five roofing contractors come to your house and you can tell them that you want 20-year warranty asphalt shingles of a certain style and color, you'll have a solid beginning basis for comparing prices.

Most contractors like it when consumers know exactly what they want. It militates against misunderstandings. If you tell a contractor the make, model number, style, and color of a toilet you want, he then doesn't have to worry that when he puts it in, you say, "Oh, I don't like that." Too bad. It was your choice.

Such specific know-how will also enable you to write a much better contract. Most contracts I've seen are deficient because they are vague and noninclusive—incredibly so when one considers the thousands of dollars that can be involved. Most people have no idea what they're buying.

Finally quality differences can mean hundreds, even thousands of dollars of difference in the cost of a job—and its longevity.

WHERE TO GET THE KNOW-HOW

Part 2 of this book, "Buyer's Guide to Home Improvements," is designed to deliver job know-how on a wide variety of jobs. It looks at common and uncommon home-improvement and maintenance jobs in terms of what's available, product/material quality, how the job is done (and should be done), any rip-offs to be wary of, whether or not it's a job for the do-it-yourselfer, and approximate costs.

If you need more information, it's certainly out there.

Neighbors or friends who have had or are having jobs done like the one you want can be a source of information. So can clerks at lumberyards, building-supply outlets, home centers, and hardware stores. So can kitchen, bath, flooring, and other specialty dealers. Such places often have products displayed, and on many products you can spot quality differences fairly quickly. Barbara Lagowski told me how shocked she was at the differences in vinyl siding: "The bottom-of-the-line stuff was really thin."

How-to videos can also be helpful. Though they typically don't provide a great deal of help in product selection—they use good stuff but don't detail many alternatives—they are particularly good when it comes to showing how jobs are done.

This Old House is on TV all the time, and so is *Hometime*. *Hometime* also sells a number of low-cost, excellent videos on such things as decks, framing, kitchens, and drywall. Write to them at 6213 Bury Drive, Eden Prairie, MN 55346.

Today many libraries also have free how-to videos on all kinds of subjects and should be checked out. The library is also a source for books and articles, of course. Just tell the reference librarian what you're interested in and he or she will load you up and tell you how to get magazine articles on the subject you're interested in (at least that's the way they do it at my library).

If you've done your homework and still don't feel like you've got all the details you need on the job—for example, you may not be sure if the existing siding has to come off before the new material can be applied (at significant cost differences)—there are still further sources.

One, happily, is contractors. When they come in to give their bids is the time to ask questions—and compare answers. Between what you are finding out on your own and what contractors can tell you, you can glean all you really need to know.

But there are still other sources of information. One is the American Society of Home Inspectors. While their usual task is inspecting entire homes, they also provide inspections for remodeling work. You could hire them before the contractors come in, but I think it would be better to wait. You'll likely have complete know-how after the contractors are finished bidding. ASHI people charge by the hour; you can expect to pay around $125 per hour, but most job evaluations won't take more than an hour.

If the whole idea of dealing with contractors doesn't appeal to you, ASHI can be hired to help supervise the job. According to a spokesperson for the association, this might range anywhere from $500 to $1,000, or about 2 percent of the typical $50,000 to $75,000 rehab cost. For this they would make three or four visits during the job and review it thoroughly before the contractor finishes. As the spokesperson says, "If a contractor knows that his work is being inspected by an objective professional, he is less likely to try to take advantage."

For jobs strictly involving structural work—additions or modification of the house framework—an architect could also be hired on a piecemeal basis. They charge around $60 an hour.

Also available strictly for advice would be members of the National Kitchen and Bath Association. These are designers but may also be designer dealers, some of whom will give advice at about $65 an hour.

DO YOU NEED A PLAN?

On many jobs you won't need a plan. These would include siding, roofing, windows, flooring, replacing wall material, painting, and the like where essentially cosmetic things are happening to the house.

However, where structural modifications are involved—rooms added, roof raised, dormers added, walls rearranged, and so on—you will need a formal plan. This is necessary not only so that you can show the plan to contractors, but also because you will probably be legally liable to have one and in many instances—it depends on the building code where you live—A plan prepared by a licensed architect as well. Whatever, you should always inquire of the town building-code officials to ensure that you get the necessary paperwork: A plan may not be needed, but approval almost certainly will be. (I say "almost" because there are some towns in America that have *no* building codes.) Building departments are concerned with how safe a particular job is and that it doesn't violate zoning laws. For example, they might frown on someone wanting to build a ten-story apartment building in an area zoned for two-story homes.

While you're talking to inspectors, it might also be a good time to ask a question or two. These people see a lot of home improvements. And while you're there, by all means read the building code relevant to the job you're having done. It can give you some good insight into all the details that are involved.

Incidentally, some contractors like to say their products are "up to code." But that doesn't necessarily mean it's a quality product. A builder's special low-quality toilet may be "up to code," meaning that it's safe for eliminating human waste, but that doesn't mean it's a good product and will work every time so that you don't have to be involved with noisome tasks.

If you need a plan, there are a variety of ways to go, and these are covered in the next chapter.

When You Need a Plan—or More

Professional remodeling contractors do over 80 percent of the work required in the plus-$120-billion remodeling business. It is generally accepted that about half is spent on renovations and repairs, and half on alterations.

That division reflects just how often one must get a formal plan for the job at hand. As mentioned in chapter 2, such jobs as siding, roofing, new windows, new walls and flooring material—anything where the house structure is not involved—will not likely require a plan. Anything that is, will.

There are a few sources for this plan. One is an architect.

ARCHITECTS

Architects will prepare working drawings that are acceptable to the building department and from which the contractor can build. The plan will commonly consist of a floor plan, elevations—side and front views of the house—and

details. It can cost anywhere from $400 to $800, depending
on complexity.

If you wish, you can also hire an architect in other ca-
pacities. For example, he or she will prepare the plan and
supervise the job, charging a percentage of the cost—anywhere from 12 to 16 percent. So, for example, if the job was
priced at $100,000, the architect would get an additional
$12,000 to $16,000.

BUILDER/DESIGNER

This is normally a general contractor who will design your
addition and build it. That is, he will create the design with
the help of an architect or engineer on his staff. The architect
will approve the plans for submission to the building department.

A builder/designer can charge anywhere from $400 to
$800. If you take his plans and he builds the job, that's it.
If you don't, and want to buy the plan from him, he might
double the cost. One contractor, we learned, charged $900
for addition plans. If you wanted to buy them but not have
the job done, they would cost an additional $900—$1,800.

Dan Miller, president of the International Remodeling
Contractors Association, thought this "unconscionable. He
can create those plans in about an hour on the computer."
Knowing this, perhaps you can negotiate a better price—or
might want to think twice about hiring someone who would
charge this much. What else will he try to overcharge on?

Designer. Here, we mean a kitchen and bath designer, such
as a member of the National Kitchen and Bath Association.
These people strictly design baths and kitchens. They may
be combination dealers and designers, or designers only. They
will provide anything from consultations to working plans
and specifications for the job. Francis Jones, ex-president
of NKBA, estimates this charge could range from $300
to $500. If they supervise the job, the cost will be a lot
higher.

WHAT DO YOU NEED?

On all but the biggest renovation-style jobs—where house structure is modified—the average person will probably only require an architect's plans. Those with bigger jobs may want the full services of an architect.

An architect can and will help you specify materials, but some contractors caution that "you have to watch them," as one contractor said. "Some of these guys design something so that it can resist even direct mortar fire. They have champagne tastes—and the client may be on a beer budget."

Before hiring an architect, you should check out three or four of his or her jobs to ensure that he designs the kind of job you need. Look carefully at the job and talk it over with the owners. Did the job reach their expectations? Would they hire this person again?

The American Institute of Architects can give you some local names. Also, people in the neighborhood who have had work done may have had it done by an architect.

If you have a big job to do, you will want to talk to a few builder/designers. As you check them out, you will get ample opportunity to look at their designs.

KITCHENS AND BATHS

If you are only doing a bath or kitchen improvement that involves replacing things, then a kitchen/bath designer would not be required. If you are getting into reallocating space, say creating an open kitchen, a larger bath, or a new bath, then you definitely need the services of a designer.

Before calling anyone in, you should have a good idea of what you want. You can check other jobs, pore through magazines, check out videos. There are many sources for ideas for a plan.

And do put your ideas on paper. The more you know, the more you can show, the better off you'll be.

CHAPTER 3

Where to Get
the Money

It's good to have your financing in place, or know where it's coming from, before you contact any contractors. There is nothing like telling the contractor you know where the money's coming from to tickle his interest.

Of course you won't know exactly how much you need before you call the contractors in, but it is possible to get a rough idea. Part 2 gives costs of jobs, and there are also charts showing how much jobs cost throughout the country.

"To whatever figure you arrive at," says remodeling attorney Reynolds Graves, "add 20 percent. People almost always spend more than they plan to, and you should have the money ready." Matt Mahoney, a contractor and president of Mahoney Construction in Huntington, New York, says that "improving their homes is like sex to some people. The more they get, the more they want."

SHOP AROUND

As mentioned in chapter 1, studies have shown that only one out of three people who need a loan shop around for it.

They should. The money saved can be enormous, and there are other benefits to getting the right loan for your particular situation.

One example: If you borrowed $100,000 and the interest rate on it was 10 percent and the term was thirty years, you would pay about $878 per month, or a little more than three times the loan, or $315,720, over the thirty years.

If you pay 14 percent interest, you would pay $1185 per month, or $307 per month more and over the thirty years, $426,553—four times the amount of the loan and costing over $110,846 more—two or three years' salary for many people.

All loans can be divided into one of two types: secured or unsecured. The former means that collateral, such as a house or car, serves as security for the loan. If the person defaults on the loan, the property can be seized. (In some cases—if the borrower is fiscally strong, for example—banks will take liens on property.)

Unsecured means that there is nothing backing up the loan. All the lender is counting on is the borrower's past credit history and income. Such loans are generally more expensive than secured loans.

Following is a potpourri of loans, with advantages and disadvantages of each:

Home Equity Loan. This is generally regarded as a very desirable loan, particularly for large projects, because 100 percent of the interest charged is tax deductible as long as the sum of one's total debt on one or more homes doesn't exceed $1.1 million (which will not be a problem for most of us).

On a home equity loan one borrows on the equity in the house. That is, the market value of the house less the amount owed on the mortgage. For example, if $25,000 was still owed on the mortgage and the market value of the house was $200,000, then $175,000 would theoretically be available for borrowing.

Theoretical is the operative word. In practice banks usually do not want the homeowner's monthly debts—car, mortgage, and so on—to exceed more than 37 percent of monthly income.

The rate of interest you pay on a home equity loan is dependent on what the prime rate is—the prime being the rate that banks charge preferred customers. So, for example, if the prime were 10 percent, the bank might lend you the money at two "points," or percentage points, above that, or 12 percent.

But it depends on the bank. Different banks have vastly different rates—three and four percentage points—which, as detailed above, can translate to many thousands of dollars over the life of the loan, which is normally five to thirty years, depending on what you can pay and how long you want to pay.

The rate can be either fixed or adjustable, with the rate going up or down according to the prime rate. A fluctuating rate can be quite high—you are at the mercy of the prime rate—so it is something to consider carefully.

Home Equity Line. Another usually desirable type of loan for larger projects is the home-equity-line type. This is an approved credit line: You can borrow as much as a home equity loan, but you get a checkbook and can write checks for what you need as you need it, instead of getting a loan—a lump sum—as in a home equity loan.

This is advantageous interest-wise because you only pay interest on what you actually write a check for. It's a plus if you are involved in paying a contractor for a job that will take several months. You pay him, say $5,000 one week, another $5,000 two weeks later, and so forth. Interest is charged only on the amounts you write.

The downside of both home equity lines and loans is the fees one pays. In essence you'll pay more or less the same fees you would if you were refinancing your mortgage: a few hundred dollars for a title search, $60 for a credit check plus points, each point being 1 percent of the face amount of the loan (three points on a $30,000 loan would be $900).

Such fees vary from bank to bank (costs can range between hundreds of dollars) and should be carefully compared when shopping for the loan.

Home equity lines can be adjustable- or fixed-rate, and these can also vary widely—at this writing from 12 to 18 percent. When shopping for the loan, make sure you ask what the "cap" rate is, that is, the fixed rate the loan cannot rise above no matter what the prime is. You don't want interest rates going through the roof—as they did in the early 1980s—and getting choked by them.

BALLOON PAYMENTS: A BAD IDEA

Some banks offer so-called balloon payments, where you only pay back interest over a relatively short period of time, then the "balloon"—the principal on the loan—all at once.

This is a very risky loan, because equity in your home may fall over the next ten years—and you won't have enough in it to make the balloon payment. Or the market for refinancing may be so tight that you can't get the loan and can be foreclosed.

Be aware, too, of possible come-on deals, where the interest is low for the first few months of the loan, then rises. Some banks will charge you 7 or 8 percent for three months, then jack it up after that to an interest rate that is unwise. It's a common gambit.

As mentioned, banks vary in the rates they charge for home equity loans. Credit unions also offer home equity loans, and the rates are usually better. If you are a member, check them out.

Banks will usually offer low fees and high interest or high fees and lower interest. For a short-term project, the lower fees will usually be the better deal. For projects where more time is required, the lower interest rate is better.

Home equity loans usually have a minimum one can borrow, currently $5,000. And check out rates around tax-paying time. Some banks offer lower rates then than at other times of the year: Borrowers find the tax write-off attractive.

Refinance Mortgage. Refinancing a mortgage means borrowing a certain amount to pay off the old mortgage and then borrowing up to 80 percent on the equity. Interest is also 100 percent tax deductible, as long as the old mortgage was made after October 13, 1987. If not, then the write-off will be less.

CLOSING COSTS

Lending Institution	Appraisal Application Fee	Points	Origination Fee	Bank Attorney Fee	Total Costs on 50K
Home Equity Loans Fidelity New York (516) 488-2400	-0-	-0-	-0-	-0-	1500–1600
DIME (516) 351-1550	225	-0-	-0-	-0-	1100
NATWEST 1-800-NAT-WEST	-0-	-0-	-0-	-0-	1200
Reliance (516) 222-9300 (3 months together)	-0-	-0-	-0-	-0-	1392.00
Central Federal (516) 271-2000 (516) 873-3000	250	-0-	-0-	-0-	Less than 2%

Interest rates in general are usually lower than those rates available for home equity loans. But refinancing loans, despite lower interest rates, may be more expensive because of high fees.

Home-Improvement Loans. These loans, which may be had from a minimum of $1,000 to a maximum of $20,000, are normally for five to seven years, and with interest rates now ranging from 15 to 18 percent. The disadvantage is the relatively short payback period, which results in high monthly payments.

Fees are slight, however—usually just the $50 or $60 for a credit check—and the loan is 100 percent tax deductible if secured by the house.

Unsecured Personal Loan. If the loan is unsecured, it gets even worse. The payback period is three to five years, and there is no tax deductibility. Rates are three to five points higher than for a secured home-improvement loan.

Total Costs on 70K	Introductory Offer Percentage	% Over Prime	Lifetime Ceiling Cap	Annual Cap	Years Line of Credit is Available	Additional Years to Pay off Loan
1700–19000	10.5	1.50	15.5%	No	10 Years	15 Years
1300	9% for 3 months	1.50	14.9%	No	10 Years	20 Years
1500	10.5%	1.75	17.0%	No	10 Years	15 Years
1688 (on 75K)	11.5 1st yr	1.50	14.75%	No	10 Years	20 Years
Less than 2%	11.5 1st Yr	1.50	13.90	No	10 Years	15 Years

6. It's good to record the costs of various different loans. The one shown was devised by Huntington, New York, homeowner Al Visco and is for example only.

HUD. The Federal Housing Administration, under its FHA Title I program, also makes loans up to $17,500. These are given by a variety of banks and may be used for essential home improvements such as remodeling baths and kitchens, but not for luxuries, such as a sauna. The advantage of such loans is the term of the loan—up to fifteen years (five years minimum). Rates are around the same as for a secured home-improvement loan. Fees consist only of charges for a credit check.

401 (k). Under this law many companies let you borrow on profit-sharing monies, with the interest rate just a little above prime and with no fees.

Life Insurance. If you have whole life insurance, this is another source to consider. The interest is tax deductible, rates are low—up to around 8 percent—and you can borrow up to 100 percent of the cash value of your policy.

Contractor-Arranged Loans. Many big contractors have many loan dealings with certain banks, but it's the same story: Check out the interest rate and fees—don't let someone else do it for you.

If you have the cash, it's usually the best way of all to pay for the project, even though you haven't anything to deduct for taxes as you could with other types of loans.

To sum up, then, when considering a loan, focus on three things: tax deductibility, interest, and fees. Make liberal use of a sharp pencil or calculator, and pick the blend that works out best for you.

CHAPTER 4

Finding
Contractors

Getting a good contractor for the job is a process, a series of tests you put contractors through until there is only one standing at the end. There is no single thing that says a contractor is good; it is more like a survival test, which eliminates the least fit.

It starts with a list of names. Consumer protection departments around the country do not agree on everything, but on two points everyones agrees: Get multiple bids on any job you contract for and, as your first source for names of contractors "ask friends and neighbors for references," as a consumer brochure from Iowa suggests.

The logic here is implicit: To find the best contractor, you have to start by getting a pool of candidates from people who, as much as possible, have no vested interest in your hiring a particular person.

A caution: If the contractor is a friend or relative of the person you know, the situation is ripe for problems. If something goes awry, there's not much you can do without possibly damaging your relationship with the person who made the referral.

It is even worse to have someone do the work whom you're directly friendly with or related to. Sue Grant, former con-

sumer watchdog of Massachusetts, says, "Doing that is a
very good way to ruin a friendship."

Consider, for example, the following scenario:

THE PERILS OF ERNIE

Your cousin Ernie is "handy" and you need a new roof. Ernie
puts it on—and it leaks. Never mind that Ernie is sincere
and diligent and that he comes back time and again to try
to correct the problem. It may turn out that he doesn't have
the know-how or skill to do this, so you're stuck with a leaky
roof and no place to go. All you can do is call in a professional
and get the job done, at additional expense, correctly. You
don't want to proceed against Ernie, do you?

Of course you could protect yourself by having a written
contract with Ernie, but this in itself might be regarded as
insulting to some people, and perhaps it is.

This is not to say that such "marriages" (the term contractors give to the relationship between homeowner and
contractor) can't work. They can work out well. But by the
book—this book—it is the wrong road to travel.

The next best possible contractor source is people in your
area who are having jobs done. Contractors usually hang
their signs outside homes where they're working. Just drop
by and speak with the homeowner when the contractor's not
there. If the homeowner starts speaking in tongues, you
know the contractor isn't too great! But the homeowner
might recommend him and give you a name for your list.

Another possible source—and usually a good one even
though there could be a vested interest—is lumberyards or
building-supply yards. Clerks will ordinarily refer you to
their best contractor customers, but this isn't a negative
thing. Good contractors have a lot of work. More than this,
clerks don't want the homeowner returning with blood in her
eye because the contractor fouled up. You might also try hardware stores, real estate agents, banks (particularly the one
you're borrowing money from), or the chamber of commerce.

Contractor associations are another possible source. Many
consumer affairs departments glibly recommend them, but

they have to be approached with the same caution as other sources. Membership does not necessarily confer sainthood, though it is probably true that such associations have members who are generally more reliable than are the people who are not in associations, simply because two goals of associations are to promote professionalism and to promote image. Life is easier when you're known as a bunch of responsible professionals rather than a wolfpack of thieves and incompetents—so the people who join are usually partly or wholly motivated by these things. (One motivation, too, is that membership sounds good in a sales presentation.)

To keep themselves sanitary, associations are supposed to police themselves; that is, drum out the bad guys whom customers constantly complain about. But some contractor associations do a very poor job at this.

CONFLICT OF INTEREST

Listen, for example, to what one contractor said about one association he left: "I quit because they allowed suppliers to be members. That defeated our purpose of policing the ranks. If a contractor was bad, they wouldn't throw him out, because they didn't want to offend him. He was their bread and butter. We had guys in the organization who had *hundreds* of consumer complaints. I told them to shove the association."

There are generally two kinds of organizations. One kind contains a hodgepodge of home improvers: general contractors, as well as specialty contractors, people who do siding, roofing, and so forth. The National Association of the Remodeling Industry (NARI) and the Remodelors Council of the National Association of Home Builders (NAHB) are examples of these.

The other kind are made up exclusively of specialty contractors, such as the National Association of Tile Contractors. All these organizations have national headquarters as well as local chapters. Check the telephone directory.

It is suggested that you contact someone who specializes in the job you're interested in. For example, if you're interested in tilework, contact the National Tile Contractors Association. The assumption here is that a specialist is better than a generalist, just as a skin doctor would be better able to handle a wart than a GP. For bigger jobs NARI or the NAHB could provide names.

If you need something done that is strictly electrical or strictly plumbing, you can contact any of the sources listed in back. Because their work directly impacts on the preservation of life, electricians and plumbers are closely monitored and regulated by governmental bodies.

Beneath the association contractors I would put anyone who advertises. It's not that companies who advertise are incompetents or thieves, just that a greater number of bad apples come from this group. As the Connecticut Department of Consumer Protection says in one of its consumer brochures, "Surveys in other states seem to indicate that homeowners who have hired contractors based on radio, TV or print ads, the yellow pages . . . have more problems with their home improvements."

The yellow pages aways struck me as a crazy place from which to hire a contractor. One would hardly get a heart surgeon, or even an endodontist, from the yellow pages. Then why hire a person who could easily do work that costs thousands of dollars—and cause you a kind of heart ache that no heart surgeon can cure?

SOURCES TO AVOID

At the bottom of the heap, as it were, are people who come at you directly by phone or door-to-door.

For example, someone may call you with a proposal, such as to have your house resided, the chimney cleared, the house painted because they are "in the neighborhood" and therefore "can give you a substantial discount." Or someone knocks on your door who says he's a "student on summer vacation" or who says he's in the area and has "some materials left over" from another job and will give you a "good deal" on it; or a sad-eyed, out-of-work dad "trying to make a few dollars"; or "I was just passing by and noticed that you badly need. . . ."

And then of course there are the "others," as the North Dakota consumer manual warns, "[who] will pose as inspectors who have come to inspect your wiring, furnace, insulation, plumbing or some other item. You can rest assured that they will find something wrong and offer to repair or replace it [you pay the bill]."

Then there are the slicksters who offer to do your work free or almost free in order to attract other folks. Indeed. Remember the picture *Tin Men?* There you could see that ploy played out to perfection.

One group of scamsters that has been around for years is the phony termite inspectors. They will inspect your house and find termites or wormy wood—the termites or wormy wood they brought into the house with them. Most of these folks are *polished*. They are actors, con men, psychologists ready to play your fear, sympathy, whatever like a violin. So if anyone comes to you, you go the other way. It's a golden rule in more ways than one.

I have one friend who played his own trick on a door-to-door vinyl-siding salesman. "Come on in and let's talk," he said to the salesman, "but once you're inside, don't make any sudden moves. I own a couple of high-strung pit bull terriers."

The salesman demurred.

HOW MANY CONTRACTORS?

How many names should you compile?

There is nothing chiseled in stone here, and it perhaps relates to the time and energy you have more than anything else. But starting with eight to ten seems good. It may sound like a lot—but it's not.

Once you have names, the survival test begins. First check with the consumer affairs department in your city, state, or local community as well as with the Better Business Bureau, if your state has one. (Surprisingly, four states do not.) The addresses and numbers are included at the end of this chapter.

You should understand, however, that consumer affairs departments and the BBB are generally overrated on what they can and cannot do vis-à-vis contractors. People invest them with magical powers they simply don't have. In essence they can't tell you if a contractor is good or bad; they are just part of the pruning process, but an important part.

What they can tell you, first, is whether the contractor has any complaints—resolved or unresolved—against him. Both kinds of organizations record such complaints.

The feedback you get can be limited because not all complaints may be listed—it takes a while for complaints to get on file—and bad contractors regularly go in and out of business under different names. What was formerly known as Joe Blow Super Duper Remodelers, with a veritable seething throng of complaints on file, last week may have gone out of business and reemerged with a pristine record and a new name, say Mother Teresa Remodeling Experts, Inc., this week.

You should also ask just how long the company has been in business. A contractor who's been in business more than five years and has a local address has a couple of things on his side. If you can't find out from the governmental body, ask the contractors the same question when they come to your house.

Whatever, the feedback is something. It can eliminate the obvious bad actors. But if a contractor has one or two complaints, so what? Ask him about them, if he seems otherwise okay, when he comes in to bid. He might have a solid explanation.

As one contractor told me, "Yeah, I've had a few problems. I don't walk on water."

More than this, some customers are "truly nuts," as one

7. If required by law in your locale, it is very important that a contractor have a license.

contractor said, "and some are mean-spirited rip-off artists themselves. I had one guy who just wanted to hurt me because I wouldn't help him hose his insurance company," said another contractor.

Then again, there may have been a simple misunderstanding. Misunderstandings occur all the time: The homeowner understood one thing, the contractor another. But when the homeowner complains, the contractor has no way of defending himself; the one-sided complaint is punched into the computer and that's it.

Also, the law of averages may militate against a contractor. One reliable Long Island contractor has, at any given time, 150 big jobs going. What odds would you give him against not getting a complaint or two, or three, or more.

And not that the consumer is always right. Bill Baessler and Bob Klein, who worked with the Suffolk Department of Consumer Affairs, agree that "of 100 percent of the complaints we get, 20 percent are valid, 20 percent invalid, and around 60 percent somewhere in the middle."

Indeed. Contracting expert Walt Stoeppelwerth believes that because of their inability to be satisfied, or because of a larcenous streak, "one in five customers will not allow a contractor to make money."

However, if you see a batch of complaints, cross that contractor off the list. (Incidentally, if you have trouble getting through to consumer affairs or the BBB, drop them a line. They'll respond. Just make sure you give them full information regarding the contractor's company name and complete address.) It depends on the policy of individual BBBs or consumer affairs departments: Some will give you the nature of the complaints, but you have to ask. And you should.

MOST-IMPORTANT FUNCTIONS

Perhaps even more important than acting as a screen for contractors, consumer affairs departments (though not the BBB) can tell you if a contractor is licensed or registered, something many jurisdictions require.

In actuality all being licensed may mean is that a con-

tractor paid a fee for being registered or licensed and proved
that he had liability insurance. In few states does it measure
competence or honesty. (In California, though, to be licensed,
you have to have, among other things, four years' appren-
ticeship in your trade.)

Sue Nichols, formerly of the Connecticut Department of
Consumer Affairs, thinks licensing can work against consumers: "It gives consumers a false sense of security. They
think that since a contractor's licensed, he's okay."

On the other hand it can lend some credibility to a contractor because he took the time to be registered or licensed,
and he will be in the minority: All states who responded to
surveys we conducted reported many more unlicensed contractors than licensed ones.

It may also mean, and it varies from jurisdiction to jurisdiction, that the contractor is not only insured but bonded.
Though bond amounts vary, being bonded means that the
contractor has a sort of job insurance. If he doesn't complete
the job, he could forfeit the bond. For example, California
has a bond requirement of $10,000. Bonding, incidentally,
can be very difficult to get. As an assistant attorney general
of Washington state, says, "They start by getting you to put
up your firstborn as collateral."

Aside from questions of credibility and bonding, hiring
someone who is not licensed or registered can hurt you in
other important ways. If there is a dispute with the contractor, the consumer affairs agency will have no way of
twisting the contractor's arm, such as threatening to suspend
his license or, in some states, fining him to resolve the dispute. Action can only be taken if he's done something criminal—and many contractors who do something criminal are
long gone from the scene when law enforcement gets to them.

Also important, even crucial: *a number of states and counties have refund plans.* You can collect money from a general
fund licensed or registered contractors contribute to if the
contractor cannot refund your money himself. In some cases
all you must do is simply apply to the consumer affairs department. In other cases you have to go through civil court
and obtain a judgment. But the great thing is that it means
the money is there even if the contractor has fled the scene
or has gone out of business and is insolvent.

But no jurisdiction I know of will award you a nickel if the contractor is unlicensed or unregistered.

The refund sums are meaningful.

In New York City, for example, you can get up to $20,000 per complaint.

In Suffolk and Nassau counties, Long Island, the amounts are $5,000 per complaint.

In Hawaii they'll give you up to $12,500 (and send McGarrett after the contractor).

In Maryland you can get up to $10,000.

In Virginia you can get more than $20,000.

Finally, if a contractor is not licensed or registered, it probably means he has no insurance. So if the contractor or someone who works for him hurts himself on your property, you could be the victim of a lawsuit, which hopefully your homeowner's insurance (or umbrella insurance) would cover. If it doesn't, you're out in the cold.

CALL CONTRACTORS

After contacting consumer affairs and the BBB, contact the contractors who are left. Just call each and tell them (best times are usually at around 7:00 A.M. and between 6:30 and 8:30 P.M.—they go to bed early!) that you got their name from such-and-such and are interested in getting such-and-such job done. Would they be interested in taking a look at it?

Your list, which will probably have shrunk already, will likely become a little shorter. Some contractors may not be interested, some may not return your calls (cross off anyone who doesn't return your call), and you may not be interested in some if it will be a very long time before they come. (One contractor we talked to jokingly said, "If you get an answering machine and it asks you to leave your name, number, a brief message, and, most important, the *year* that you called—get someone else!")

If the contractor gives you an instant bid on the phone, also say bye-bye. How can he? How careful could he be?

You don't need to tell him that you are having other contractors come in to bid. Most contractors will assume you are, but some will ask. Don't volunteer information, but don't lie. You have enough to keep straight without trying to remember to whom you told what. More than that, making up stories sets up a subtle adversarial approach that most people can live without. Honesty—without giving away your game plan—is the best route.

One other thing, when you contact consumer affairs, as well as the BBB, ask to get their literature on home improvements. You should keep it and everything else related to the job in one place in a folder or the like.

Finally, it will take a while before contractors start to show up. Call two to three months before you expect to see most people to check on their schedules, though sometimes contractors do show up on time.

DON'T BE PRESSURED

It's important to allow enough time to find and select a good contractor. After all, it requires patience, research, and attention to detail. If you need to get the job done last Thursday, you are apt to make a contractor selection that doesn't serve you well. You should accept that getting everything checked out, set up, and arranged simply takes time and on some jobs, sometimes many months.

In some localities finding a good contractor can be hard, but if you give yourself enough time you're much more likely to be successful and happy with your choice. In the end—again depending on the market—you might end up picking one who is not perfect, but the best of the lot. That's okay. As long as you keep in mind the general principles—including the seminally important one of controlling the money—you'll be fine.

STATE, COUNTY AND CITY GOVERNMENT CONSUMER PROTECTION OFFICES

ALABAMA

State Office
Mr. Dennis Wright, Chief
  Director
Consumer Affairs Division
Office of Attorney General
11 South Union Street
Montgomery, AL 36130
(334) 242-7334
1 (800) 392-5658 (toll free in
  AL)

ALASKA

The Consumer Protection
  Section in the Office of
  Attorney General has been
  closed. Consumers with
  complaints are being referred
  to the Better Business
  Bureau (see page 76), small
  claims court and private
  attorneys.

AMERICAN SAMOA

Ms. Jennifer Joneson
Assistant Attorney General
Consumer Protection Bureau
P.O. Box 7
Pago Pago, AS 96799
011 (684) 633-4163
011 (684) 633-1838 (fax)

ARIZONA

State Offices
Ms. Sydney K. Davis, Chief
  Counsel
Consumer Protection
Office of the Attorney General
1275 West Washington Street,
  Room 259
Phoenix, AZ 85007
(602) 542-3702
(602) 542-5763
(consumer information and
  complaints)
1 (800) 352-8431 (toll free in
  AZ)
(602) 542-5002 (TDD)

Ms. Noreen Matts
Assistant Attorney General
Consumer Protection
Office of the Attorney General
400 West Congress South
  Building,
Suite 315
Tucson, AZ 85701
(602) 628-6504

County Offices
Mr. Stephen Udall, County
  Attorney
Apache County Attorney's
  Office
P.O. Box 637
St. Johns, AZ 85936
(520) 337-4364, ext. 240
(520) 337-2427 (fax)

Mr. Alan Polley, County
  Attorney
Cochise County Attorney's
  Office
P.O. Drawer CA
Bisbee, AZ 85603
(520) 432-9377
(520) 432-4208 (fax)

Mr. Terence C. Hance, County
  Attorney
Coconino County Attorney's
  Office
Coconino County Courthouse
100 East Birch
Flagstaff, AZ 86001
(520) 779-6518
(520) 779-5618 (fax)

Mr. Jerry B. DeRose, County
  Attorney
Gila County Attorney's Office
1400 East Ash Street
Globe, AZ 85501
(520) 425-3231
(520) 425-3720 (fax)

Mr. Jack M. Williams, County
  Attorney
Graham County Attorney's
  Office
Graham County Courthouse
800 West Main
Safford, AZ 85546

(520) 428-3620
(520) 428-7200 (fax)

Mr. Dennis L. Lusk, County
   Attorney
Greenlee County Attorney's
   Office
P.O. Box 1717
Clifton, AZ 85533
(520) 865-4108
(520) 865-4665 (fax)

Mr. Steven P. Suskin, County
   Attorney
La Paz County Attorney's
   Office
1320 Kofa Avenue
P.O. Box 709
Parker, AZ 85344
(520) 669-6118
(520) 669-2019 (fax)

Mr. William Ekstrom, County
   Attorney
Mohave County Attorney's
   Office
315 North 4th Street
P.O. Box 7000
Kingman, AZ 86420-7000
(520) 752-0719
(520) 753-2669 (fax)

Mr. Melvin Bowers, County
   Attorney
Navajo County Attorney's
   Office
P.O. Box 668
Holbrook, AZ 86025
(520) 524-6161, ext. 303
(520) 524-4244 (fax)

Mr. Stephen D. Neely, County
   Attorney
Pima County Attorney's Office
1400 Great American Tower
32 North Stone
Tucson, AZ 85701
(520) 740-5733
(520) 791-3946 (fax)

Mr. Gilberto V. Figueroa
Pinal County Attorney
P.O. Box 887
Florence, AZ 85232
(520) 868-6271
(520) 868-6521 (fax)

Ms. Jan Smith Florez, County
   Attorney

Santa Cruz County Attorney's
   Office
2100 N. Congress Drive,
   Suite 201
Nogales, AZ 85621
(520) 281-4966

Mr. Charles Hastings, County
   Attorney
Yavapai County Attorney's
   Office
Yavapai County Courthouse
Prescott, AZ 86301
(520) 771-3344
(520) 771-3110 (fax)

Mr. David S. Ellsworth, County
   Attorney
Yuma County Attorney's Office
168 South Second Avenue
Yuma, AZ 85364
(520) 329-2270
(520) 329-2284 (fax)

City Office
Mr. Ronald M. Detrick
Supervising Attorney
Consumer Affairs Division
Tucson City Attorney's Office
110 East Pennington Street,
   2nd Floor
P.O. Box 27210
Tucson, AZ 85726-7210
(520) 791-4886

ARKANSAS

State Office
Ms. Kay Dewitt, Director
Consumer Protection Division
Office of Attorney General
200 Tower Building
323 Center Street
Little Rock, AR 72201
(501) 682-2341
1 (800) 482-8982
(toll free voice/TDD in AR)
(501) 682-6073 (TDD)

CALIFORNIA

State Offices
Mr. James Conran, Director
California Department of
   Consumer Affairs
400 R Street, Suite 1040
Sacramento, CA 95814

(916) 522-1700 (TDD)
1 (800) 344-9940 (toll free in
CA)

Office of Attorney General
Public Inquiry Unit
P.O. Box 944255
Sacramento, CA 94244-2550
(916) 322-3360
1 (800) 952-5225 (toll free in
CA)
1 (800) 952-5548 (toll free TDD
in CA)

Mr. Martin Keller, Chief
Bureau of Automotive Repair
California Department of
Consumer Affairs
10240 Systems Parkway
Sacramento, CA 95827
(916) 445-7960
(916) 322-1700 (TDD)
1 (800) 952-5210
(toll free in CA—auto repair
only)

County Offices
Ms. Aldene Croswell,
Commissioner
Alameda County Consumer
Affairs Commission
4400 MacArthur Boulevard
Oakland, CA 94619
(510) 535-6444

Mr. Gary Yancey, District
Attorney
Contra Costa County District
Attorney's Office
725 Court Street, 4th Floor
P.O. Box 670
Martinez, CA 94553
(510) 646-4500
(510) 646-2116 (fax)

Mr. Alan Yengoyan
Senior Deputy District Attorney
Business Affairs Unit
Fresno County District
Attorney's Office
1250 Van Ness Avenue,
2nd Floor
Fresno, CA 93721
(209) 488-3156
(209) 495-1315 (fax)

Mr. Edward R. Jagels, District
Attorney

Criminal Division
Kern County District Attorney's
Office
1215 Truxtun Avenue,
4th Floor
Bakersfield, CA 93301
(805) 861-2421
(805) 861-2797 (fax)

Mr. Monty H. Hopper, Director
Kern County Department of
Weights and Measures
1116 E. California Avenue
Bakersfield, CA 93307
(805) 861-2418
(805) 324-0668 (fax)

Mr. Pastor Herrera, Jr., Director
Los Angeles County
Department of Consumer
Affairs
500 West Temple Street,
Room B-96
Los Angeles, CA 90012
(213) 974-1452 (Public)
(213) 974-9750 (Private)

Marin County Mediation
Services
Marin County Civic Center,
Room 278
San Rafael, CA 94903
(415) 499-7454

Mr. Robert Nichols
Deputy District Attorney
Consumer Protection Division
Marin County District Attorney's
Office
Hall of Justice, Room 183
San Rafael, CA 94903
(415) 499-6450
(415) 499-3719 (fax)

Ms. Susan Massini, District
Attorney
Mendocino County District
Attorney's Office
P.O. Box 1000
Ukiah, CA 95482
(707) 462-4211
(707) 463-4687 (fax)

Mr. Dean D. Flippo
Monterey County District
Attorney
Consumer Protection Division
P.O. Box 1369

Salinas, CA 93902
(408) 755-5073
(408) 755-5608 (fax)

Mr. Daryl A. Roberts
Deputy District Attorney
Consumer Affairs Division
Napa County District Attorney's
  Office
931 Parkway Mall
P.O. Box 720
Napa, CA 94559
(707) 253-4211
(707) 253-4041

Mr. Robert C. Gannon, Jr.
Supervising Deputy District
  Attorney
Consumer/Environmental
  Protection Unit
405 W. 5th Street, Suite 606
Santa Ana, CA 92701
(714) 568-1240
(714) 568-1250 (fax)

Mr. Jay Orr
Deputy District Attorney
Economic Crime Division
Riverside County District
  Attorney's Office
4075 Main Street
Riverside, CA 92501
(909) 275-5400
(909) 275-5470 (fax)

Mr. M. Scott Prentice
Supervising Deputy District
  Attorney
Consumer and Environmental
  Protection Division
Sacramento County District
  Attorney's Office
P.O. Box 749
Sacramento, CA 95812-0749
(916) 440-6174

Mr. Anthony Samson, Director
Consumer Fraud Division
San Diego County District
  Attorney's Office
P.O. Box X-1011
San Diego, CA 92112-4192
(619) 531-3507 (fraud
  complaint message line)

Mr. Robert H. Perez, Attorney
Consumer and Environmental
  Protection Unit

San Francisco County District
  Attorney's Office
732 Brannan Street
San Francisco, CA 94103
(415) 552-6400 (public
  inquiries)
(415) 553-1814 (complaints)
(415) 552-7038 (fax)

Ms. Lorrie Rogers
Consumer Mediator
San Joaquin County District
  Attorney's Office
222 East Weber, Room 412
P.O. Box 990
Stockton, CA 95202
(209) 468-2481
(209) 468-0314 (fax)

Ms. Leigh Lawrence
Director, Economic Crime Unit
Consumer Fraud Department
County Government Center
1050 Monterey Street,
  Room 235
San Luis Obispo, CA 93408
(805) 781-5856

Mr. John E. Wilson, Deputy in
  Charge
Consumer Fraud and
  Environmental Protection
  Unit
San Mateo County District
  Attorney's Office
401 Marshall Street
Hall of Justice and Records
Redwood City, CA 94063
(415) 363-4656
(415) 363-4873 (fax)

Mr. Allan Kaplan, Senior
  Deputy District Attorney
Consumer Protection Unit
Santa Barbara County District
  Attorney's Office
1105 Santa Barbara Street
Santa Barbara, CA 93101
(805) 568-2300
(805) 568-2398 (fax)

Mr. Al Bender
Consumer Fraud Unit
Santa Clara County District
  Attorney's Office
70 West Hedding Street, West
  Wing

San Jose, CA 95110
(408) 299-8478
(408) 279-8742 (fax)

Ms. Patricia McRae,
Coordinator
Santa Clara County Consumer
Protection Unit
70 West Hedding Street
West Wing, Lower Level
San Jose, CA 95110-1705
(408) 299-4211

Ms. Robin McFarland Gysin
Ms. Gloria Lorenzo
Ms. Barbara Davis
Coordinators, Division of
Consumer Affairs
Santa Cruz County District
Attorney's Office
701 Ocean Street, Room 200
Santa Cruz, CA 95060
(408) 454-2050
(408) 454-2227 (fax)

Ms. Criselda B. Gonzalez
Deputy District Attorney
Consumer Protection Unit
Solano County District
Attorney's Office
600 Union Avenue
Fairfield, CA 94533
(707) 421-6860
(707) 421-7986 (fax)

Mr. Thomas Quinlan
Deputy District Attorney
Consumer Fraud Unit
Stanislaus County District
Attorney's Office
P.O. Box 442
Modesto, CA 95353-0442
(209) 525-5550
(209) 525-5545 (fax)

Mr. Greg Brose, Deputy District
Attorney
Consumer and Environmental
Protection Division
Ventura County District
Attorney's Office
800 South Victoria Avenue
Ventura, CA 93009
(805) 654-3110

Mr. Mark Jerome Jones
Chief Deputy District Attorney
Special Services Unit—

Consumer/Environmental
Yolo County District Attorney's
Office
P.O. Box 245
Woodland, CA 95776
(916) 666-8424
(916) 666-8423 (fax)

City Offices
Mr. Donald Kass
Supervising Deputy City
Attorney
Consumer Protection Division
Los Angeles City Attorney's
Office
200 North Main Street
1600 City Hall East
Los Angeles, CA 90012
(213) 485-4515
(213) 237-0402 (fax)

Ms. Kimery A. Shelton
Deputy City Attorney
Ms. Teresa Bransfield
Consumer Affairs Specialist
Consumer Protection, Fair
Housing & Public Rights Unit
1685 Main Street, Room 310
Santa Monica, CA 90401
(310) 458-8336
(310) 458-8370 (Spanish
hotline)
(310) 395-6727 (fax)

COLORADO

State Office
Consumer Protection Unit
Office of Attorney General
1525 Sherman St., 5th Floor
Denver, CO 80203-1760
(303) 866-5189

County Offices
Mr. Gregory G. Lyman, District
Attorney
Archuleta, LaPlata and San
Juan Counties
District Attorney's Office
P.O. Drawer 3455
Durango, CO 81302
(970) 247-8850
(970) 259-0200 (fax)

Mr. Alex Hunter, District
Attorney

Boulder County District
  Attorney's Office
P.O. Box 471
Boulder, CO 80306
(303) 441-3700
(303) 441-4703 (fax)

Mr. Philip A. Parrott, Chief
  Deputy District Attorney
Mr. Gilberto Espinosa, Chief
  Deputy
Ms. Clair Villano, Director of
  Consumer Services
Denver District Attorney's
  Economic Crimes Division
303 West Colfax Avenue,
  Suite 1300
Denver, CO 80204
(303) 640-3555 (administration)
(303) 640-3557 (complaints)
(303) 640-3180 (fax)

Mr. David Zook
Chief Deputy District Attorney
Economic Crime Division
El Paso and Teller Counties
  District Attorney's Office
326 South Tejon
Colorado Springs, CO 80903-
  2083
(719) 520-6002
(719) 520-6185 (fax)

Mr. Gus Sandstrom, District
  Attorney
Pueblo County District
  Attorney's Office
Courthouse
215 West Tenth Street
Pueblo, CO 81003
(719) 546-6030

Mr. A.M. Dominguez, Jr.,
  District Attorney
Mr. Tony Molocznik, Chief
  Investigator
Weld County District Attorney's
  Office
P.O. Box 1167
Greeley, CO 80632
(970) 356-4010
(970) 352-8023 (fax)

CONNECTICUT

State Offices
Mr. Mark A. Shiffrin,
  Commissioner
Department of Consumer
  Protection
165 Capitol Avenue
Hartford, CT 06106
(203) 566-2534
1 (800) 842-2649 (toll free in
  CT)
(203) 566-1531 (fax)

Mr. Steven M. Rutstein
Assistant Attorney General
Antitrust/Consumer Protection
Office of Attorney General
110 Sherman Street
Hartford, CT 06105
(203) 566-5374
(203) 523-5536 (fax)

City Office
Mr. Philip P. Cacciola, Director
Middletown Office of Consumer
  Protection
City Hall
Middletown, CT 06457
(203) 344-3491
(203) 344-0136 (fax)
(203) 344-3521 (TDD)

DELAWARE

State Offices
Ms. Mary McDonough, Director
Consumer Protection Unit
Department of Justice
820 North French Street,
  4th Floor
Wilmington, DE 19801
(302) 577-3250
(302) 577-6499 (fax)

Mr. Eugene M. Hall, Deputy
  Attorney General
Fraud and Consumer
  Protection Unit
Office of Attorney General
820 North French Street
Wilmington, DE 19801
(302) 577-2505

DISTRICT OF COLUMBIA

Mr. Hampton Cross, Director
Department of Consumer and
    Regulatory Affairs
614 H Street, N.W.
Washington, DC 20001
(202) 727-7120
(202) 727-8073 (fax)
(202) 727-7842 (fax)

FLORIDA

State Offices
Mr. James P. Kelly, Director
Department of Agriculture and
    Consumer Services
Division of Consumer Services
407 South Calhoun Street
Mayo Building, 2nd Floor
Tallahassee, FL 32399-0800
(904) 488-2221
(904) 487-4177 (fax)
1 (800) 435-7352 (toll free in
    FL)

Mr. Jack A. Norris, Jr., Chief
Consumer Litigation Section
4000 Hollywood Blvd.,
    Suite 505-South
Hollywood, FL 33021
(305) 985-4780
(305) 985-4496 (fax)

Ms. Mona Fandel, Bureau
    Chief
Economic Crimes Division
Office of Attorney General
4000 Hollywood Blvd.,
    Suite 505-South
Hollywood, FL 33021
(305) 985-4780
(305) 985-4496 (fax)

County Offices
Mr. Stanley A. Kaufman,
    Director
Broward County Consumer
    Affairs Division
115 S. Andrews Avenue
Annex Room A460
Fort Lauderdale, FL 33301
(305) 765-5355

Mr. Leonard Elias, Consumer
    Advocate
Metropolitan Dade County
Consumer Protection Division

140 West Flagler Street,
    Suite 902
Miami, FL 33130
(305) 375-4222

Mr. Frederic A. Kerstein, Chief
Dade County Economic Crime
    Unit
Office of State Attorney
1350 N.W. 12th Avenue,
    5th Floor
Graham Building
Miami, FL 33136-2111
(305) 547-0671

Ms. Jeanette LaRussa Fenton,
    Director
Hillsborough County
    Commerce Dept.
Consumer Protection Unit
P.O. Box 110
Tampa, FL 33601
(813) 272-6750

Mr. Larry F. Blalock, Chief
Orange County Consumer
    Fraud Unit
250 North Orange Avenue
P.O. Box 1673
Orlando, FL 32802
(407) 836-2490

Citizens Intake
Office of the State Attorney
401 N. Dixie Highway,
    Ste. #1600
West Palm Beach, FL 33401
(407) 355-7108

Mr. Lawrence Breeden,
    Director
Palm Beach County Division of
    Consumer Affairs
3323 Belvedere Road,
    Building 503
West Palm Beach, FL 33406
(407) 233-4820

Mr. Alfred Leslie
Consumer Investigator
Pasco County Consumer
    Affairs Division
7530 Little Road
New Port Richey, FL 34654
(813) 847-8110

Ms. Sheryl Lord, Director
Pinellas County Office of
    Consumer Protection

P.O. Box 17268
Clearwater, FL 34622-0268
(813) 464-6200

City Offices
Mr. Dana A. Fernety
Chief of Consumer Affairs
City of Jacksonville
Division of Consumer Affairs
421 W. Church Street,
  Suite 404
Jacksonville, FL 32202
(904) 630-3667

Mr. Al Dezure, Chairperson
Lauderhill Consumer Protection
  Board
1176 N.W. 42nd Way
Lauderhill, FL 33313
(305) 321-2456
(305) 321-2455 (TDD)

GEORGIA

State Office
Mr. Barry W. Reid,
  Administrator
Governors Office of Consumer
  Affairs
2 Martin Luther King, Jr. Drive,
  S.E.
Plaza Level-East Tower
Atlanta, GA 30334
(404) 651-8600
(404) 656-3790
1 (800) 869-1123 (toll free in
  GA)
(404) 651-9108 (fax)

HAWAII

State Offices
Mr. Russell Blair, Executive
  Director
Office of Consumer Protection
Department of Commerce and
  Consumer Affairs
828 Fort St. Mall, Suite 600B
P.O. Box 3767
Honolulu, HI 96813
(808) 586-2636
(808) 586-2640 (fax)

Mr. Gene Murayama,
  Investigator
Office of Consumer Protection
Department of Commerce and
  Consumer Affairs

75 Aupuni Street
Hilo, HI 96720
(808) 933-4433

Ms. Pamela LaVarre,
  Investigator
Office of Consumer Protection
Department of Commerce and
  Consumer Affairs
54 High Street
Wailuku, HI 96793
(808) 243-5387

IDAHO

State Office
Mr. Brett De Lange
Deputy Attorney General
Office of the Attorney General
Consumer Protection Unit
700 West Jefferson, Room 119
Boise, ID 83720-0010
(208) 334-2424
1 (800) 432-3545 (toll free in
  ID)
(208) 334-2830 (fax)

ILLINOIS

State Offices
Mr. Jim Ryan, Attorney General
Governors Office of Citizens
  Assistance
222 South College
Springfield, IL 62706
(217) 782-0244
1 (800) 642-3112 (toll free in
  IL)
(Only handles problems related
  to state government)

Ms. Patricia Kelly, Chief
Consumer Protection Division
Office of Attorney General
100 West Randolph, 12th Floor
Chicago, IL 60601
(312) 814-3000
(312) 793-2852 (TDD)

Mr. Charles Gil Fergus, Bureau
  Chief
Consumer Fraud Bureau
100 West Randolph, 13th Floor
Chicago, IL 60601
(312) 814-4714
(312) 814-3374 (TDD)
1 (800) 252-8666 (toll free)

Regional Offices
Assistant Attorney General
Carbondale Regional Office
Office of Attorney General
1001 E. Main Professional Park
East
Carbondale, IL 62901
(618) 457-3505
(618) 457-4421 (TDD)

Assistant Attorney General
Champaign Regional Office
34 East Main Street
Champaign, IL 61820
(217) 333-7691 (voice/TDD)

Ms. Deborah Hagan
Assistant Attorney General and
Chief
Consumer Fraud Bureau
Office of Attorney General
500 South Second Street
Springfield, IL 62706
(217) 782-9020
1 (800) 252-8666 (toll free in
IL)

County Offices
Mr. Raymond Threlkeld,
Supervisor
Consumer Fraud Division-303
Cook County Office of State's
Attorney
303 Daley Center
Chicago, IL 60602
(312) 443-4600

Mr. William Haine, State's
Attorney
Madison County Office of
State's Attorney
157 N. Main, Suite 402
Edwardsville, IL 62025
(618) 692-6280

City Offices
Ms. Caroline O. Shoenberger
Commissioner
Chicago Department of
Consumer Services
121 North LaSalle Street,
Room 808
Chicago, IL 60602
(312) 744-4006
(312) 744-9385 (TDD)

Mr. Robert E. Hinde,
Administrator

Des Plaines Consumer
Protection Commission
1420 Miner Street, Room 502
Des Plaines, IL 60016
(708) 391-5363

INDIANA

State Office
Mrs. Lisa Hayes
Chief Counsel and Director
Consumer Protection Division
Office of Attorney General
Indiana Government Center
South, 5th Floor
402 West Washington Street
Indianapolis, IN 46204
(317) 232-6330
1 (800) 382-5516 (toll free in
IN)

County Office
Mr. Scott C. Newman
Marion County Prosecuting
Attorney
560 City-County Building
200 East Washington Street
Indianapolis, IN 46204-3363
(317) 327-5338
(317) 327-5409 (fax)

IOWA

State Office
Mr. William Branch
Assistant Attorney General
Consumer Protection Division
Office of Attorney General
1300 East Walnut Street,
2nd Floor
Des Moines, IA 50319
(515) 281-5926
(515) 281-6771 (fax)

KANSAS

State Office
Mr. C. Steven Rarrick
Deputy Attorney General
Consumer Protection Division
Office of Attorney General
301 West 10th
Kansas Judicial Center
Topeka, KS 66612-1597
(913) 296-3751

1 (800) 432-2310 (toll free in KS)
(913) 291-3699 (fax)

County Office
Consumer Fraud Division
Johnson County District
  Attorney's Office
Johnson County Courthouse
P.O. Box 728
Olathe, KS 66051
(913) 764-8484, ext. 5318
(913) 764-8184, ext. 5334 (fax)

City Office
Mr. Brenden Long
Assistant City Attorney
Topeka Consumer Protection
  Division
City Attorney's Office
215 East Seventh Street
Topeka, KS 66603
(913) 295-3883
(913) 295-3901 (fax)

KENTUCKY

State Offices
Mr. Robert V. Bullock, Director
Consumer Protection Division
Office of Attorney General
209 Saint Clair Street
Frankfort, KY 40601-1875
(502) 564-2200
1 (800) 432-9257 (toll free in KY)

Mr. Robert L. Winlock,
  Administrator
Consumer Protection Division
Office of Attorney General
107 South 4th Street
Louisville, KY 40202
(502) 595-3262
1 (800) 432-9257 (toll free in KY)
(502) 595-4627 (fax)

LOUISIANA

State Office
Ms. Tamera R. Velasquez,
  Chief
Consumer Protection Section
Office of Attorney General
1 America Place
P.O. Box 94095

Baton Rouge, LA 70804-9095
(504) 342-9638
(504) 342-9637 (fax)

County Office
Mr. Albert H. Olsen, Chief
Consumer Protection Division
Jefferson Parish District
  Attorney's Office
5th Floor, Gretna Courthouse
  Annex
Gretna, LA 70053
(504) 364-3644
(504) 364-3636 (fax)

MAINE

State Offices
Mr. William N. Lund, Director
Office of Consumer Credit
  Protection
State House Station
Augusta, ME 04333-0035
(207) 624-8527
1 (800) 332-8529 (toll free in ME)
(207) 582-7699 (fax)

Mr. Stephen Wessler, Chief
Consumer and Antitrust
  Division
Office of Attorney General
State House Station No. 6
Augusta, ME 04333
(207) 626-8849 (9 a.m.–1 p.m.)

MARYLAND

State Offices
Mr. William Leibovici, Chief
Consumer Protection Division
Office of Attorney General
200 St. Paul Place, 16th Floor
Baltimore, MD 21202-2021
(410) 528-8662 (consumer
  hotline)
(410) 576-6372 (TDD in
  Baltimore area)
(410) 576-6566 (fax)

Mr. Jack Joyce, Director
Licensing & Consumer
  Services
Motor Vehicle Administration
6601 Ritchie Highway, N.E.
Glen Burnie, MD 21062
(410) 768-7535
(410) 768-7167 (fax)

Ms. Emalu Myer
Consumer Affairs Specialist
Eastern Shore Branch Office
Consumer Protection Division
Office of Attorney General
201 Baptist Street, Suite 30
Salisbury, MD 21801-4976
(410) 543-6620

Mr. Larry Munson, Director
Western Maryland Branch
  Office
Consumer Protection Division
Office of Attorney General
138 East Antietam Street,
  Suite 210
Hagerstown, MD 21740-5684
(301) 791-4780

County Offices
Mr. Stephen D. Hannan,
  Administrator
Howard County Office of
  Consumer Affairs
6751 Columbia Gateway Drive
Columbia, MD 21046
(410) 313-6420
(410) 313-6424 (fax)
(410) 313-6401 (TDD)

Ms. Barbara B. Gregg,
  Executive Director
Montgomery County Office of
  Consumer Affairs
100 Maryland Avenue,
  3rd Floor
Rockville, MD 20850
(301) 217-7373
(301) 217-7367 (fax)

Ms. Sandra Peaches,
Prince George's County Office
  of Business and Regulatory
  Affairs
County Administration Building,
  Suite L15
Upper Marlboro, MD 20772
(301) 952-5232
(301) 925-5167 (TDD)
(301) 952-4709 (fax)

MASSACHUSETTS

State Offices
Mr. George Weber, Chief
Consumer and Antitrust
  Division

Department of Attorney
  General
1 Ashburton Place
Boston, MA 02108
(617) 727-2200
(information and referral to
  local consumer offices that
  work in conjunction with the
  Department of Attorney
  General)
(617) 727-5765 (fax)

Ms. Priscilla H. Douglas,
  Secretary
Executive Office of Consumer
  Affairs and Business
  Regulation
One Asburton Place,
  Room 1411
Boston, MA 02108
(617) 727-7780
(information and referral only)
(617) 227-6094 (fax)

Mr. Thomas J. McCormick
Assistant Attorney General
Western Massachusetts
  Consumer Protection
  Division
Department of Attorney
  General
436 Dwight Street
Springfield, MA 01103
(413) 784-1240
(413) 784-1244 (fax)

County Offices
Mr. Paul Finnegan, Case
  Coordinator
Consumer Fraud Prevention
North Western District
  Attorney's Office
238 Main Street
Greenfield, MA 01301
(413) 774-5102
(413) 773-3278 (fax)

Mr. Stephen Gary-Saindon,
  Director
Consumer Fraud Prevention
Hampshire County District
  Attorney's Office
1 Court Square
Northampton, MA 01060
(413) 586-9225
(413) 584-3635 (fax)

Ms. Carol Balberelli, Director
Consumer Council of
  Worcester County
484 Main Street, 2nd Floor
Worcester, MA 01608-1690
(508) 754-1176 (9:30 a.m.–
  4 p.m.)
(508) 754-0203 (fax)

City Offices
Ms. Donna M. Mueller, Director
Mayor's Office of Consumer
  Affairs and Licensing
Boston City Hall, Room 817
Boston, MA 02201
(617) 635-4165
(617) 635-4174

Ms. Jean Courtney, Director
Consumer Information Center
Springfield Action Commission
P.O. Box 1449 Main Office
Springfield, MA 01101
(413) 263-6516
(Hamden and Hampshire
  Counties)
(413) 263-6514 (fax)

MICHIGAN

State Offices
Mr. Frederick H. Hoffecker
Assisant in Charge
Consumer Protection Division
Office of Attorney General
P.O. Box 30213
Lansing, MI 48909
(517) 373-1140

Mr. Rodger James, Director
Bureau of Automotive
  Regulation
Michigan Department of State
Lansing, MI 48918-1200
(517) 373-4777
1 (800) 292-4204 (toll free in
  MI)
(517) 485-5530 (TDD)
(517) 373-0964 (fax)

County Offices
Ms. Juliane M. Tanner, Chief
  Investigator
Bay County Consumer
  Protection Unit
Bay County Building
Bay City, MI 48708-5994
(517) 895-4139

Ms. Margaret DeMuynck,
  Director
Consumer Protection
  Department
Macomb County
Office of the Prosecuting
  Attorney
Macomb Court Building,
  6th Floor
Mt. Clemens, MI 48043
(810) 469-5350
(810) 466-8714 (TDD)
(810) 469-5609 (fax)

Ms. Charleen Berels, Director
Washtenaw County Consumer
  Protection
4133 Washtenaw Avenue
P.O. Box 8645
Ann Arbor, MI 48107-8645
(313) 971-6054
1 (800) 649-3777 (TDD)

City Office
Ms. Esther K. Shapiro, Director
City of Detroit
Department of Consumer
  Affairs
1600 Cadillac Tower
Detroit, MI 48226
(313) 224-3508
(313) 224-2796 (fax)

MINNESOTA

State Office
Mr. Curt Loewe, Director
Consumer Services Division
Office of Attorney General
1400 NCL Tower
445 Minnesota Street
St. Paul, MN 55101
(612) 296-3353

County Office
Hennepin County Citizen
  Information Hotline
Office of the Hennepin County
  Attorney
C-2000 County Government
  Center
Minneapolis, MN 55487
(612) 348-4528
(612) 348-9712 (fax)

City Office
Mr. James Moncur, Director

Minneapolis Department of
Licenses & Consumer
Services
One C City Hall
Minneapolis, MN 55415
(612) 673-2080
(612) 673-3399 (fax)

MISSISSIPPI

State Offices
Ms. Leslie Staehle
Special Assistant Attorney
General
Director, Office of Consumer
Protection
P.O. Box 22947
Jackson, MS 39225-2947
(601) 359-4230
(601) 359-4198 (fax)
(601) 359-4231 (fax)
1 (800) 281-4418 (toll free in
MS)

Mr. Joe B. Hardy, Director
Bureau of Regulatory Services
Department of Agriculture and
Commerce
121 North Jefferson Street
P.O. Box 1609
Jackson, MS 39201
(601) 354-7063
(601) 354-6502 (fax)

MISSOURI

State Office
Mr. Doug Ommen, Chief
Counsel
Consumer Protection Division
Office of Attorney General
P.O. Box 899
Jefferson City, MO 65102
(314) 751-3321
1 (800) 392-8222 (toll free in
MO)
(314) 751-7948 (fax)

MONTANA

State Office
Ms. Annie Bartos, Chief Legal
Council
Consumer Affairs Unit
Department of Commerce
1424 Ninth Avenue
Box 200501

Helena, MT 59620-0501
(406) 444-4312
(406) 444-2903 (fax)

NEBRASKA

State Office
Mr. Paul N. Potadle
Assistant Attorney General
Consumer Protection Division
Department of Justice
2115 State Capitol
P.O. Box 98920
Lincoln, NE 68509
(402) 471-2682
(402) 471-3297 (fax)

NEVADA

State Offices
Ms. Patricia Morse Jarman
Commissioner of Consumer
Affairs
Department of Business and
Industry
State Mail Room Complex
Las Vegas, NV 89158
(702) 486-7355
1 (800) 992-0900 (toll free in
NV)
(702) 486-7901 (TDD)
(702) 486-7371 (fax)

Mr. Ray Trease, Supervisory
Compliance Investigator
Consumer Affairs Division
Department of Business and
Industry
4600 Kietzke Lane, B-113
Reno, NV 89502
(702) 688-1800
1 (800) 992-0900 (toll free in
NV)
(702) 486-7901 (TDD)
(702) 688-1803 (fax)

County Office
Mr. John Long, Investigator
Consumer Fraud Division
Washoe County District
Attorney's Office
P.O. Box 11130
Reno, NV 89520
(702) 328-3456

NEW HAMPSHIRE

State Office
Chief
Consumer Protection and
   Antitrust Bureau
Office of Attorney General
State House Annex
Concord, NH 03301
(603) 271-3641
(603) 271-2110 (fax)

NEW JERSEY

State Offices
Mr. Mark S. Herr, Director
Division of Consumer Affairs
P.O. Box 45027
124 Halsey Street, 7th Floor
Newark, NJ 07101
(201) 504-6534
(201) 648-3538 (fax)

Ms. Lauren F. Carlton
Deputy Attorney General
New Jersey Division of Law
P.O. Box 45029
124 Halsey Street, 5th Floor
Newark, NJ 07101
(201) 648-7579
(201) 648-3879 (fax)

County Offices
Mr. William H. Ross III, Director
Atlantic County Consumer
   Affairs
1333 Atlantic Avenue, 8th Floor
Atlantic City, NJ 08401
(609) 345-6700

Mr. John Wassberg, Director
Bergen County Office of
   Consumer Protection
21 Main Street, Room 101-E
Hackensack, NJ 07601-7000
(201) 646-2650
(201) 489-6095 (fax)

Mrs. Renee L. Borstad,
   Director
Burlington County Office of
   Consumer Affairs
49 Rancocas Road
Mount Holly, NJ 08060
(609) 265-5098

Ms. Patricia M. Tuck, Director
Consumer Protection/Weights
   and Measures

Jefferson House
Lakeland Road
Blackwood, NJ 08012
(609) 374-6161
(609) 232-0748 (fax)

Mr. E. Robert Spiegel, Director
Cape May County Consumer
   Affairs
4 Moore Road
Cape May Court House, NJ
   08210
(609) 463-6475

Mr. Louis G. Moreno, Director
Cumberland County
   Department of Consumer
   Affairs and Weights and
   Measures
788 East Commerce Street
Bridgeton, NJ 08302
(609) 453-2203
(609) 453-2206 (fax)

Ms. Estaher Chernofski, Senior
   Contact Person
Essex County Consumer
   Services
15 South Munn Avenue,
   2nd Floor
East Orange, NJ 07018
(201) 678-8071
(201) 678-8928

Mr. Joseph Silvestro, Director
Gloucester County Department
   of Consumer
   Protection/Weights &
   Measures
152 North Broad Street
Woodbury, NJ 08096
(609) 853-3349
(609) 853-3358
(609) 848-6616 (TDD)

Ms. Barbara Donnelly, Director
Hudson County Division of
   Consumer Affairs
595 Newark Avenue
Jersey City, NJ 07306
(201) 795-6295
(201) 795-6462 (fax)

Ms. Helen Mataka, Director
Hunterdon County Consumer
   Affairs
P.O. Box 283

Lebanon, NJ 08833
(908) 236-2249

Ms. Donna Giovannetti,
Division Chief
Mercer County Consumer
Affairs
640 South Broad Street,
Room 229
P.O. Box 8068
Trenton, NJ 08650-0068
(609) 989-6671
(609) 989-6032 (fax)

Mr. Lawrence Cimmino,
Director
Middlesex County Consumer
Affairs
10 Corporate Place South
Piscataway, NJ 08854
(908) 463-6000
(908) 463-6008 (fax)

Ms. Dorothy H. Avallone,
Director
Monmouth County Consumer
Affairs
50 East Main Street
P.O. Box 1255
Freehold, NJ 07728-1255
(908) 431-7900
(908) 294-5965 (fax)

Mr. Kenneth J. Leake, Director
Ocean County Consumer
Affairs
P.O. Box 2191
County Administration Building
Room 107-1
Toms River, NJ 08754-2191
(908) 929-2105
(908) 506-5330 (fax)

Ms. Mary Ann Maloney,
Director
Passaic County Consumer
Affairs
309 Pennsylvania Avenue
Paterson, NJ 07503
(201) 881-4547, 4499
(201) 881-0012 (fax)

Ms. Marianne Mattei
Somerset County Consumer
Affairs
County Administration Building
P.O. Box 3000
Somerville, N.J. 08876-1262

(908) 231-7000, ext. 7400
(908) 707-4127 (fax)

Mrs. Ollie Jones, Director
Union County Consumer Affairs
300 North Avenue East
P.O. Box 186
Westfield, NJ 07091
(201) 654-9840

City Offices
Cinnaminson Consumer Affairs
P.O. Box 2100
1621 Riverton Road
Cinnaminson, NJ 08077
(609) 829-6000

Ms. Theresa Ward, Director
Clark Consumer Affairs
430 Westfield Avenue
Clark, NJ 07066
(908) 388-3600
(908) 382-2940 (fax)

Ms. Mary Ann Pizzello, Director
Elizabeth Consumer Affairs
City Hall
50-60 Winfield Scott Plaza
Elizabeth, NJ 07201
(908) 820-4183
(908) 820-0112 (fax)

Mr. Joseph J. Licata, Director
Fort Lee Consumer Protection
Board
309 Main Street
Fort Lee, NJ 07024
(201) 592-3654

Ms. Bernadine Jacobs, Director
Livingston Consumer Affairs
357 South Livingston Avenue
Livingston, NJ 07039
(201) 535-7976

Ms. Mary Mosley, Director
Maywood Consumer Affairs
459 Maywood Avenue
Maywood, NJ 07607
(201) 845-2900
(201) 845-5749
(201) 909-0673 (fax)

Ms. Genevieve Ross, Director
Middlesex Borough Consumer
Affairs
1200 Mountain Avenue
Middlesex, NJ 08846
(908) 356-8090

Ms. Mildred Pastore, Director
Mountainside Consumer Affairs
1455 Coles Avenue
Mountainside, NJ 07092
(908) 232-6600

Mr. Max Moses, Deputy Mayor
Director Consumer Affairs
Municipal Building
North Bergen, NJ 07047
(201) 392-2157
(201) 330-7291
(201) 330-7292

Ms. Annmarie Nicolette,
    Director
Nutley Consumer Affairs
Public Safety Building
228 Chestnut Street
Nutley, NJ 07110
(201) 284-4936

Ms. Mina Ramos, Director
Perth Amboy Public Information
City Hall
1 Olive Street
Perth Amboy, NJ 08861
(908) 826-1690, ext. 16, 17
(908) 826-1519 (fax)

Ms. Priscilla Castles, Director
Plainfield Action Services
510 Watchung Avenue
Plainfield, NJ 07060
(908) 753-3519
(908) 753-3540 (fax)

Mr. Michael B. Bukatman,
    Director
Secaucus Department of
    Consumer Affairs
Municipal Government Center
Secaucus, NJ 07094
(201) 330-2019

Ms. Marion Cramer, Director
Union Township Consumer
    Affairs
Municipal Building
1976 Morris Avenue
Union, NJ 07083
(908) 688-6763
(908) 688-2554 (fax)

Mr. Charles A. Stern, Director
Wayne Township Consumer
    Affairs
475 Valley Road

Wayne, NJ 07470
(201) 694-1800, ext. 3290

Mr. John Weitzel, Director
Weehawken Consumer Affairs
400 Park Avenue
Weehawken, NJ 07087
(201) 319-6005
(201) 319-0113 (fax)

Ms. Lourdes Rodriguez,
    Director
West New York Consumer
    Affairs
428 60th Street
West New York, NJ 07093
(201) 861-2522
(201) 669-1715 (fax)

Mr. Herb Gilsenberg
Woodbridge Consumer Affairs
Municipal Building
One Main Street
Woodbridge, NJ 07095
(908) 634-4500, ext. 6058

NEW MEXICO

State Office
Consumer Protection Division
Office of Attorney General
P.O. Drawer 1508
Santa Fe, NM 87504
(505) 827-6060
1 (800) 678-1508 (toll free in
    NM)

NEW YORK

State Offices
Ms. Rachel Kretser
Assistant Attorney General
Bureau of Consumer Frauds
    and Protection
Office of Attorney General
State Capitol
Albany, NY 12224
(518) 474-5481
1 (800) 788-9898 (TDD)

Ms. Catherine W. Dudley
Deputy Executive Director
New York State Consumer
    Protection Board
99 Washington Avenue
Albany, NY 12210-2891
(518) 474-8583
(518) 474-2474

Ms. Shirley F. Sarna
Assistant Attorney General
Bureau of Consumer Frauds
   and Protection
Office of Attorney General
State Capitol
Albany, NY 12224
(518) 474-5481

Mr. John W. Corwin
Assistant Attorney General in
   Charge
Bureau of Consumer Frauds
   and Protection
Office of Attorney General
120 Broadway
New York, NY 10271
(212) 416-8345

Regional Offices
Mr. Michael Hanuszczak
Assistant Attorney General in
   Charge
Central New York Regional
   Office
44 Hawley Street, 17th Floor
State Office Building
Binghamton, NY 13901
(607) 721-8779

Mr. Michael A. Battle
Assistant Attorney General in
   Charge
Buffalo Regional Office
Office of Attorney General
65 Court Street
Buffalo, NY 14202
(716) 847-7184
1 (800) 771-7755 (toll free)

Mr. Alan J. Burczak
Assistant Attorney General in
   Charge
Plattsburgh Regional Office
Office of Attorney General
70 Clinton Street
Plattsburgh, NY 12901
(518) 563-8012

Mr. J. Gardner Ryan
Acting Attorney General in
   Charge
Poughkeepsie Regional Office
Office of Attorney General
235 Main Street
Poughkeepsie, NY 12601
(914) 485-3920
1 (800) 771-7755 (toll free)

Mr. Charles Genese
Assistant Attorney General in
   Charge
Rochester Regional Office
Office of Attorney General
144 Exchange Boulevard
Rochester, NY 14614
(716) 546-7430
(716) 327-3249 (TDD)
1 (800) 771-7755 (toll free)

Ms. Lynda Nicolino
Assistant Attorney General in
   Charge
Suffolk Regional Office
Office of Attorney General
300 Motor Parkway
Hauppauge, NY 11788
(516) 231-2400

Mr. Michael L. Hanuszczak
Assistant Attorney General in
   Charge
Syracuse Regional Office
Office of Attorney General
615 Erie Boulevard West,
   Suite 102
Syracuse, NY 13204-2465
(315) 448-4848
1 (800) 771-7755 (toll free)

Ms. Aniela J. Carl
Assistant Attorney General in
   Charge
Utica Regional Office
Office of Attorney General
207 Genesee Street
Utica, NY 13501
(315) 793-2225
(315) 793-2228 (fax)
1 (800) 771-7755 (toll free)

County Offices
Mr. Thomas M. Jablonowski
Director of Consumer Affairs
Broome County Bureau of
   Consumer Affairs
Governmental Plaza, P.O. Box
   1766
Binghamton, NY 13901
(607) 778-2168

Mr. Nelson Kranker, Director
Dutchess County Department
   of Consumer Affairs
38-A Dutchess Turnpike
Poughkeepsie, NY 12603

(914) 486-2949
(914) 486-2947 (fax)

Ms. Candace K. Vogel
Assistant District Attorney
Consumer Fraud Bureau
Erie County District Attorney's
  Office
25 Delaware Avenue
Buffalo, NY 14202
(716) 858-2424

Mr. James E. Picken,
  Commissioner
Nassau County Office of
  Consumer Affairs
160 Old Country Road
Mineola, NY 11501
(516) 571-2600

Mr. John McCullough,
  Executive Director
New Justice Conflict
  Resolution Services Inc.
1153 West Fayette Street,
  Suite 301
Syracuse, NY 13202
(315) 471-4676

Mr. Edward J. Brown,
  Commissioner
Orange County Department of
  Consumer Affairs and
  Weights and Measures
99 Main Street
Goshen, NY 10924
(914) 294-9291, ext. 1762

Mr. Francis D. Phillips II,
  District Attorney
Orange County District
  Attorney's Office
255 Main Street
County Government Center
Goshen, NY 10924
(914) 294-5471

Ms. Johanna R. Farley,
  Commissioner
Rockland County Office of
  Consumer Protection
County Office Building
18 New Hempstead Road
New City, NY 10956
(914) 638-5280

Mr. Dennis S. Abbey, Director
Steuben County Department of

Weights, Measures and
  Consumer Affairs
3 East Pulteney Square
Bath, NY 14810
(607) 776-9631
(607) 776-9631 ext. 2409
  (voice/TDD)

Ms. Mary A. Fallon, Director
Suffolk County Executive's
  Office of Citizen Affairs
North County Complex, Bldg.
  340
Veterans Memorial Highway
Hauppauge, NY 11788
(516) 853-4600

Mr. Jon Van Vlack, Director
Ulster County Consumer Fraud
  Bureau
285 Wall Street
Kingston, NY 12401
(914) 339-5680, ext. 240

Mr. Frank D. Castaldi, Jr.
Chief, Frauds Bureau
Westchester County
District Attorney's Office
111 Grove Street
White Plains, NY 10601
(914) 285-8303

Mr. Richard Linkowski, Deputy
  Director
Westchester County
  Department of Consumer
  Protection
112 East Post Road, 4th Floor
White Plains, NY 10601
(914) 285-2155
(914) 285-3115 (fax)

City Offices
Mr. James A. Adkinson,
  Director
Babylon Consumer Protection
  Board
Town Hall Office Annex
281 Phelps Lane
North Babylon, NY 11703
(516) 422-7636

Town of Colonie Consumer
  Protection
Memorial Town Hall
Newtonville, NY 12128
(518) 783-2790

Mr. Stephen Pedone,
Commissioner
Mr. Vernon Office of Consumer
Affairs
City Hall
Mt. Vernon, NY 10550
(914) 665-2433
(914) 665-2496 (fax)

Mr. Alfred Cerullo III, Acting
Commissioner
New York City Department of
Consumer Affairs
42 Broadway
New York, NY 10004
(212) 487-4403
(212) 487-4465 (TDD)
(212) 487-4497 (fax)

Bronx Neighborhood Office
New York City Department of
Consumer Affairs
851 Grand Concourse
Room 913
Bronx, NY 10451
(718) 590-6006

Ms. Isabel Butler, Director
Queens Neighborhood Office
New York City Department of
Consumer Affairs
120-55 Queens Boulevard,
Room 301A
Kew Gardens, NY 11424
(718) 286-2990

Mr. Joseph Kapuscinski,
Director
City of Oswego Office of
Consumer Affairs
City Hall
West Oneida Street
Oswego, NY 13126
(315) 342-8150
(315) 342-8100 (fax)

Schenectady Bureau of
Consumer Protection
City Hall, Room 204
Jay Street
Schenectady, NY 12305
(518) 382-5061

Mr. Ralph A. Capozzi, Director
Yonkers Office of Consumer
Protection, Weights and
Measures
201 Palisade Avenue

Yonkers, NY 10703
(914) 377-6807

NORTH CAROLINA

State Office
Mr. Alan S. Hirsch
Special Deputy Attorney
General
Consumer Protection Section
Office of Attorney General
Raney Building
P.O. Box 629
Raleigh, NC 27602
(919) 733-7741
(919) 715-0577 (fax)

NORTH DAKOTA

State Offices
Ms. Heidi Heitkamp
Office of Attorney General
600 East Boulevard
Bismarck, ND 58505
(701) 224-2210
1 (800) 472-2600 (toll free in
ND)

Mr. Tom Engelhardt, Director
Consumer Fraud Section
Office of Attorney General
600 East Boulevard
Bismarck, ND 58505
(701) 224-3404
1 (800) 472-2600 (toll free in
ND)

County Office
Mr. Kent Keys, Executive
Director
Quad County Community
Action Agency
27½ South Third Street
Grand Forks, ND 58201
(701) 746-5431

OHIO

State Offices
Mr. Mark T. D'Alessandro
Consumer Frauds and Crimes
Section
Office of Attorney General
30 East Broad Street
State Office Tower, 25th Floor
Columbus, OH 43266-0410
(614) 466-4986 (complaints)

(614) 466-1393 (TDD)
(800) 282-0515 (toll free in
   OH)

Mr. William A. Spratley
Office of Consumers' Counsel
77 South High Street, 15th
   Floor
Columbus, OH 43266-0550
(614) 466-9605 (voice/TDD)
1 (800) 282-9448 (toll free in
   OH)

County Offices
Mr. William J. Owen, Director
Corrupt Activities Prosecution
   Unit
Franklin County Office of
   Prosecuting Attorney
369 South High Street
Columbus, OH 43215
(614) 462-3555

Mr. Robert A. Skinner
Assistant Prosecuting Attorney
Montgomery County Fraud and
   Economic Crimes Division
301 West 3rd Street
Dayton Montgomery County
   Courts Building
Dayton, OH 45402
(513) 225-4747

Mr. Victor Vigluicci, Prosecuting
   Attorney
Portage County Office of
   Prosecuting Attorney
466 South Chestnut Street
Ravenna, OH 44266-0671
(216) 296-4593

Mrs. Maureen O'Connor,
   Prosecuting Attorney
Summit County Office of
   Prosecuting Attorney
53 University Avenue
Akron, OH 44308-1680
(216) 643-2800

City Offices
Department of Neighborhood
   Services
Division of Human Services
City Hall, Room 126
801 Plum Street
Cincinnati, OH 45202
(513) 352-3971

Mr. Anthony C. Julian, Director
Youngstown Office of
   Consumer Affairs and
   Weights and Measures
26 South Phelps Street
City Hall
Youngstown, OH 44503-1318
(216) 742-8884

OKLAHOMA

State Offices
Ms. Jane Wheeler
Assistant Attorney General
Office of Attorney General
Consumer Protection Division
4545 N. Lincoln Blvd.,
   Suite 260
Oklahoma City, OK 73105
(405) 521-4274
(405) 512-2929 (consumer
   hotline)
(405) 528-1867 (fax)

Mr. John L. McClure,
   Administrator
Department of Consumer
   Credit
4545 N. Lincoln Boulevard,
   Suite 104
Oklahoma City, OK 73105-
   3408
(405) 521-3653
(405) 521-6740 (fax)

OREGON

State Office
Mr. Peter Sheperd, Attorney in
   Charge
Financial Fraud Section
Department of Justice
1162 Court St. N.E.
Salem, OR 97310
(503) 378-4732
(503) 373-7067 (fax)

PENNSYLVANIA

State Offices
Mr. Joseph Goldberg, Director
Bureau of Consumer Protection
Office of Attorney General
Strawberry Square, 14th Floor
Harrisburg, PA 17120
(717) 787-9707

1 (800) 441-2555 (toll free in PA)

Mr. Irwin A. Popowsky, Consumer Advocate
Office of Consumer Advocate-Utilities
Office of Attorney General
1425 Strawberry Square
Harrisburg, PA 17120
(717) 783-5048 (utilities only)

Mr. Michael Butler, Deputy Attorney General
Bureau of Consumer Protection
Office of Attorney General
1251 South Cedar Crest Blvd.
Suite 309
Allentown, PA 18103
(610) 821-6690

Mr. Mitchell Miller, Director
Bureau of Consumer Services
Pennsylvania Public Utility Commission
P.O. Box 3265
Harrisburg, PA 17105-3265
(717) 783-1470 (out-of-state calls only)
1 (800) 782-1110 (toll free in PA)

Mr. Jesse Harvey, Deputy Attorney General
Bureau of Consumer Protection
Office of Attorney General
919 State Street, Room 203
Erie, PA 16501
(814) 871-4371
(814) 871-4848 (fax)

Mr. E. Barry Creany
Senior Deputy Attorney General
Bureau of Consumer Protection
Office of the Attorney General
171 Lovell Avenue, Suite 202
Ebensburg, PA 15931
(814) 949-7900
1 (800) 441-2555 (toll free in PA)

Mr. John E. Kelly, Deputy Attorney General
Bureau of Consumer Protection
Office of Attorney General
21 South 12th Street, 2nd Floor
Philadelphia, PA ´9107

(215) 560-2414
1 (800) 441-2555 (toll free in PA)

Ms. Stephanie L. Royal
Deputy Attorney General
Bureau of Consumer Protection
Office of Attorney General
Manor Complex, 5th Floor
564 Forbes Avenue
Pittsburgh, PA 15219
(412) 565-5394
1 (800) 441-2555 (toll free in PA)

Mr. J.P. McGowan
Deputy Attorney General
Bureau of Consumer Protection
Office of Attorney General
214 Samters Building
101 Penn Avenue
Scranton, PA 18503-2025
(717) 963-4913
(717) 963-3410 (fax)

County Offices
Mr. Sidney Elkin, Director
Beaver County Alliance for Consumer Protection
699 Fifth Street
Beaver, PA 15009-1997
(412) 728-7267

Mr. A. Courtney Yelle, Director/Chief Sealer
Bucks County Consumer Protection, Weights and Measures
50 North Main Street
Doylestown, PA 18901
(215) 348-7442
(215) 348-4570 (fax)

Mr. Robert Taylor, Director
Chester County Weights and Measures/Consumer Affairs
Government Services Center, Suite 390
601 Westtown Road
West Chester, PA 19382-4547
(610) 344-6150
1 (800) 692-1100 (toll free in PA)

Consumer Mediator
Cumberland County Consumer Affairs
One Courthouse Square

Carlisle, PA 17013-3387
(717) 240-6180

Ms. Evelyn Yancoskie, Director
Delaware County Office of
Consumer Affairs, Weights
and Measures
Government Center Building
Second and Olive Streets
Media, PA 19063
(610) 891-4865

Mrs. Helen Dunigan, Director
Montgomery County Consumer
Affairs Department
County Courthouse
Norristown, PA 19404
(610) 278-3565
(610) 278-5228 (fax)

City Office
Mr. Bruce Sagel, Chief
Economic Crime Unit
Philadelphia District Attorney's
Office
1421 Arch Street
Philadelphia, PA 19102
(215) 686-8750

PUERTO RICO

Mr. Jóse Antonio Alicia Rivera,
Secretary
Department of Consumer
Affairs (DACO)
Minillas Station, P.O. Box
41059
Santurce, PR 00940-1059
(809) 721-0940

Mr. Pedro R. Pierluisi,
Secretary
Department of Justice
P.O. Box 192
San Juan, PR 00902
(809) 721-2900

RHODE ISLAND

State Offices
Mr. Steve Bucci, President
Consumer Credit Counseling
Services
99 Bald Hill Road
Cranston, RI 02920
(401) 463-6070
(401) 463-6663 (fax)
1 (800) 781-2227 (toll free)

Ms. Christine S. Jabour, Esq.
Consumer Protection Division
Department of Attorney
General
72 Pine Street
Providence, RI 02903
(401) 274-4400
(401) 277-1331 (fax)
(401) 274-4400, ext. 2354
(TDD)
1 (800) 852-7776 (toll free in
RI)

SOUTH CAROLINA

State Offices
Mr. Ken Moore, Deputy
Attorney General
Consumer Fraud and Antitrust
Section
Office of Attorney General
P.O. Box 11549
Columbia, SC 29211
(803) 734-3970

Mr. Steve Hamm, Administrator
Department of Consumer
Affairs
P.O. Box 5757
Columbia, SC 29250-5757
(803) 734-9452
(803) 734-9455 (TDD)
1 (800) 922-1594 (toll free in
SC)

Mr. W. Jefferson Bryson, Jr.
State Ombudsman
Office of Executive Policy and
Program
1205 Pendleton Street,
Room 308
Columbia, SC 29201
(803) 734-0457
(803) 734-1147 (TDD)

SOUTH DAKOTA

State Office
Division of Consumer
Protection
Office of Attorney General
500 East Capitol
State Capitol Building
Pierre, SD 57501-5070
(605) 773-4400
(605) 773-6585 (TDD)

1 (800) 300-1986 (toll free)
(605) 773-4106 (fax)

TENNESSEE

State Offices
Mr. Mark Williams
Division of Consumer
  Protection
Office of Attorney General
500 James Robertson Parkway
Nashville, TN 37243-0600
(615) 741-3491
(615) 741-4737 (fax)

Ms. Elizabeth Owen, Director
Division of Consumer Affairs
500 James Robertson Parkway
Nashville, TN 37243-0600
(615) 741-4737
1 (800) 342-8385 (toll free in
  TN)

TEXAS

State Offices
Mr. Joe Crews
Assistant Attorney General and
  Chief
Consumer Protection Division
Office of Attorney General
P.O. Box 12548
Austin, TX 78711
(512) 463-2070

Mr. Robert E. Reyna
Assistant Attorney General
Consumer Protection Division
Office of Attorney General
714 Jackson Street, Suite 800
Dallas, TX 75202-4506
(214) 742-8944

Mrs. Valli Jo Acosta
Assistant Attorney General
Consumer Protection Division
Office of Attorney General
6090 Surety Drive, Room 113
El Paso, TX 79905
(915) 772-9476

Mr. Richard Tomlinson
Assistant Attorney General
Consumer Protection Division
Office of Attorney General
1019 Congress Street,
  Suite 1550

Houston, TX 77002-1702
(713) 223-5886

Mr. Ron McLaurin
Assistant Attorney General
Consumer Protection Division
Office of Attorney General
916 Main Street, Suite 806
Lubbock, TX 79401-3997
(806) 747-5238
(806) 747-6307 (fax)

Mr. Ric Mardrigal
Assistant Attorney General
Consumer Protection Division
Office of Attorney General
3201 North McColl Rd., Suite B
McAllen, TX 78501
(210) 682-4547
(210) 682-1957 (fax)

Mr. Aaron Valenzuela
Assistant Attorney General
Consumer Protection Division
Office of Attorney General
115 East Travis Street,
  Suite 925
San Antonio, TX 78205-1607
(512) 225-4191

Office of Public Insurance
  Counsel
333 Guadalope, Suite 3-120
Austin, TX 78701
(512) 322-4143
(512) 322-4148 (fax)

County Offices
Mrs. Kim Gilles
Assistant District Attorney and
  Chief of Dallas County
  District Attorney's Office
Specialized Crime Division
133 North Industrial Boulevard,
  LB 19
Dallas, TX 75207-4313
(214) 653-3820
(214) 654-3845 (fax)

Mr. Russel Turbeville
Assistant District Attorney and
  Chief
Harris County Consumer Fraud
  Division
Office of District Attorney
201 Fannin, Suite 200
Houston, TX 77002-1901
(713) 755-5836

City Office
Ms. Adela Gonzalez, Director
Dallas Consumer Protection
  Division
Health and Human Services
  Department
320 East Jefferson Boulevard,
  Suite 312
Dallas, TX 75203
(214) 948-4400
(214) 670-5216
(214) 948-4374 (fax)

UTAH

State Office
Ms. Francine A. Giani, Director
Division of Consumer
  Protection
Department of Commerce
160 East 300 South
P.O. Box 45804
Salt Lake City, UT 84145-0804
(801) 530-6001
(801) 530-6601 (fax)
1 (800) 721-7233 (toll free in
  UT)

VERMONT

State Offices
Mr. Jojn Hansen
Assistant Attorney General
  and Chief Public Protection
  Division
Office of Attorney General
109 State Street
Montpelier, VT 05609-1001
(802) 828-3171

Mr. Bruce Martell, Supervisor
Consumer Assurance Section
Department of Agriculture,
  Food and Market
120 State Street
Montpelier, VT 05620-2901
(802) 828-2436

VIRGIN ISLANDS

Mr. Clement Magras,
  Commissioner
Department of Licensing and
  Consumer Affairs
Property and Procurement
  Building

Subbase #1, Room 205
St. Thomas, VI 00802
(809) 774-3130

VIRGINIA

State Offices
Mr. Frank Seales, Jr., Chief
Antitrust and Consumer
  Litigation Section
Office of Attorney General
900 East Main Street
Richmond, VA 23219
(804) 786-2116
1 (800) 451-1525 (toll free in
  VA)

Ms. Betty W. Blakemore
  Sulzbach
Director, Office of Consumer
  Affairs
Department of Agriculture and
  Consumer Services
Room 101, Washington
  Building
P.O. Box 1163
Richmond, VA 23209
(804) 786-2042
(804) 371-6344 (TDD)
(804) 371-7479 (fax)

County Offices
Office of Citizen and Consumer
  Affairs
#1 Court House Plaza,
  Suite 314
2100 Clarendon Boulevard
Arlington, VA 22201
(703) 358-3260

Mr. Ronald B. Mallard, Director
Fairfax County Department of
  Consumer Affairs
12000 Government Center
  Parkway
Suite 433
Fairfax, VA 22035
(703) 222-8435 (fax)
(Mail complaints only)

City Offices
Mr. Prescott Barbash,
  Administrator
Alexandria Office of Consumer
  Affairs
City Hall

P.O. Box 178
Alexandria, VA 22313
(703) 838-4350
(703) 838-5056 (TDD)

Mr. Robert L. Gill, Coordinator
Division of Consumer Affairs
City Hall
Norfolk, VA 23501
(804) 664-4888
(804) 441-2000 (TDD)

Ms. Dolores Daniels
Assistant to the City Manager
Roanoke Consumer Protection
  Division
364 Municipal Building
215 Church Avenue, S.W.
Roanoke, VA 24011
(540) 981-2583

Ms. Cathy Townsend Parks,
  Director
Consumer Affairs Division
Office of the Commonwealth's
  Attorney
Municipal Center
Virginia Beach, VA 23456
(804) 426-5836
(804) 427-8779 (fax)

WASHINGTON

State Offices
Mr. Larry D. Keyes, Supervisor
Consumer Protection Division
Office of the Attorney General
P.O. Box 40118
Olympia, WA 98504-0118
(360) 753-6210

Ms. Sally Sterling
Director of Consumer Services
Consumer and Business
Fair Practices Division
Office of the Attorney General
900 Fourth Avenue, Suite 2000
Seattle, WA 98164
(206) 464-6684
1 (800) 551-4636 (toll free in
  WA)

Mr. Owen Clarke, Chief
Consumer and Business
Fair Practices Division
Office of the Attorney General

West 1116 Riverside Avenue
Spokane, WA 99201
(509) 456-3123

Ms. Cynthia Lanphear, Contact
  Person
Consumer and Business
Office of the Attorney General
1019 Pacific Avenue, 3rd Floor
Tacoma, WA 98402-4411
(206) 593-2094

City Offices
Ms. Kristie Anderson, Director
Department of Weights and
  Measures
3200 Cedar Street
Everett, WA 98201
(206) 259-8810

Mr. C. Patrick Sainsbury
Chief Deputy Prosecuting
  Attorney
Fraud Division
900 4th Avenue, #1002
Seattle, WA 98164
(206) 296-9010

Mr. Dale H. Tiffany, Director
Seattle Department of Licenses
  and Consumer Affairs
600 4th Avenue, #103
Seattle, WA 98104-1893
(360) 684-8484

Mr. Dick Selander
Weights & Measures
  Supervisor
Seattle Department of Licenses
  & Consumer Affairs
805 S. Dearborn Street
Seattle, WA 98134
(360) 386-1298

Mr. R. Keith Stoner
Consumer Affairs Inspector
Seattle Department of Licenses
  & Consumer Affairs
600 4th Avenue, #102
Seattle, WA 98104-1893
(360) 684-8405

WEST VIRGINIA

State Offices
Ms. Jill Miles, Deputy Attorney
   General
Consumer Protection Division
Office of Attorney General
812 Quarrier Street, 6th Floor
Charleston, WV 25301
(304) 558-8986
1 (800) 558-0184 (toll free in
   WV)

Mr. Karl H. Angell, Jr. Director
Division of Labor
Weights and Measures
   Selection
570 MacCorkle Avenue
St. Albans, WV 25177
(304) 348-7890
(304) 722-0605 (fax)

WISCONSIN

State Offices
Ms. Patricia Allen,
   Administrator
Division of Trade and
   Consumer Protection
Department of Agriculture,
   Trade and Consumer
   Protection
2811 Agriculture Drive
P.O. Box 8911
Madison, WI 53708
(608) 224-4939
1 (800) 422-7128 (toll free in
   WI)

Ms. Margaret Quaid, Regional
   Supervisor
Division of Trade and
   Consumer Protection
Department of Agriculture,
   Trade and Consumer
   Protection
927 Loring Street
Altoona, WI 54720
(715) 839-3848
1 (800) 422-7128 (toll free in
   WI)
(715) 839-3867 (fax)

Regional Supervisor
Division of Trade and
Consumer Protection
Department of Agriculture,
   Trade and Consumer
   Protection
200 North Jefferson Street,
   Suite 146A
Green Bay, WI 54301
(414) 448-5111
1 (800) 422-7128 (toll free in
   WI)
(414) 608-2245 (TDD)

Regional Supervisor
Consumer Protection Regional
   Office
Department of Agriculture,
   Trade and Consumer
   Protection
3333 N. Mayfair Road,
   Suite 114
Milwaukee, WI 53222-3288
(414) 266-1231

Mr. Jerry Hancock
Assistant Attorney General
Office of Consumer Protection
   and Citizen Advocacy
Department of Justice
P.O. Box 7856
Madison, WI 53707-7856
(608) 266-1852
1 (800) 362-8189 (toll free)
(608) 267-8902 (fax)

Mr. Nadim Sahar
Assistant Attorney General
Office of Consumer Protection
Department of Justice
Milwaukee State Office Building
819 North 6th Street,
   Room 520
Milwaukee, WI 53203-1678
(414) 266-1231
1 (800) 362-8189 (toll free)

County Offices
Mr. Frederic Matestic
Assistant District Attorney
Milwaukee County District
   Attorney's Office
Consumer Fraud Unit
821 West State Street,
   Room 412
Milwaukee, WI 53233-1485
(414) 278-4585
(414) 223-1955 (fax)

Mr. James A. Dehne
Consumer Fraud Investigator
Racine County Sheriffs
  Department
717 Wisconsin Avenue
Racine, WI 53403
(414) 636-3125
(414) 636-3346 (fax)

WYOMING

State Office
Mr. Mark Moran
Assistant Attorney General
Office of Attorney General
123 State Capitol Building
Cheyenne, WY 82002
(307) 777-7874
(307) 777-6869 (fax)

BETTER BUSINESS BUREAU

National Headquarters
Council of Better Business
  Bureaus, Inc.
4200 Wilson Boulevard
Arlington, VA 22203
(703) 276-0100

Local Bureaus

ALABAMA

BIRMINGHAM, AL 35205
1210 S. 20th Street
P.O. Box 55268 (35255)
(205) 558-2222

FLORENCE, AL 35630
102 Court Street, Suite 512
(800) 239-1642 (24 hrs.)

HUNTSVILLE, AL 35801-5549
501 Church Street, N.W.
P.O. Box 383 (35804)
(205) 533-1640

MOBILE, AL 36602-3295
100 N. Royal Street
(334) 433-5494
So. AL (800) 544-4714

MONTGOMERY, AL 36104-3559
60 Commerce Street, Suite 806
(334) 262-5606

ALASKA

ANCHORAGE, AK 99503-3819
2805 Bering Street, Suite 2
(907) 562-0704

FAIRBANKS, AK 99707
P.O. Box 74675
(907) 451-0222

KENAI, AK 99611
P.O. Box 1229
(907) 283-4880

MAT-SU VALLEY, AK 99654
Palmer-Wasilla Hwy., Ste. 107
(907) 376-4324

ARIZONA

PHOENIX, AZ 85014-4585
4428 North 12th Street
(602) 240-3973 ($3.80/all) CC#
(900) 225-5222
(95¢/min., 24 hrs.)

TUCSON, AZ 85719
3620 N. 1st Ave., Ste. 136
Inq. (520) 888-5353
Comp. (520) 888-5454;
(800) 696-2827
So. AZ only

ARKANSAS

LITTLE ROCK, AR 72204-2605
1415 South University
(501) 664-7274
(800) 482-8448 AR only

CALIFORNIA

BAKERSFIELD, CA 93301-4882
705 Eighteenth Street
(805) 322-2074

COLTON, CA 92324-0814
290 N. 10th St., Ste. 206
P.O. Box 970
(900) 225-5222
(95¢/min., 24 hrs.)
(909) 426-0813
($2.75/call) CC#

CYPRESS, CA 90630-3966
6101 Ball Road, Suite 309
($2.75/call) CC#
(909) 426-0813
(900) 225-5222
(95¢/min., 24 hrs.)

FRESNO, CA 93711
2519 W. Shaw #106
(209) 222-8111

LOS ANGELES, CA 90020-2538
3727 West 6th St., Suite 607
(909) 426-0813
($2.75/call) CC#

(900) 225-5222
(95¢/min., 24 hrs.)

MONTEREY, CA 93940-2717
494 Alverado Street, Suite C
(408) 372-3149

OAKLAND, CA 94612-1584
510 16th Street, Suite 550
(510) 238-1000 (24 hrs.)

SACRAMENTO, CA 95814-6997
400 S Street
(916) 443-6843

SAN DIEGO, CA 92123
5050 Murphy Canyon, Ste. 110
(619) 496-2131 (24 hrs.)

SAN FRANCISCO, CA 94104
114 Sansome St., Suite 1108
(415) 243-9999

SAN JOSE, CA 95125
1530 Meridian Ave., Suite 100
(408) 445-3000

SAN MATEO, CA 94402-1706
400 S. El Camino Real,
 Suite 350
P.O. Box 294 (94401-0294)
(415) 696-1240

SANTA BARBARA, CA 93102
213 Santa Barbara St.,
P.O. Box 129 (93101)
(805) 963-8657

STOCKTON, CA 95203
509 W. Weber, Ste. 202
(209) 948-4880

COLORADO

COLORADO SPRINGS, CO 80907-5454
3022 North El Paso
P.O. Box 7970 (80933-7970)
(719) 636-1155

DENVER, CO 80222-4350
1780 S. Bellaire, Suite 700
(303) 758-2212; (24 hrs.) Inq.
(303) 758-2100 Comp.
(303) 758-4786 TDD (24 hrs.)

FORT COLLINS, CO 80525-1073
1730 S. College Avenue, Suite
 303

(303) 484-1348
Cheyenne (307) 778-2809

PUEBLO, CO 81003-3119
119 W. 6th Street, Suite 203
(719) 542-6464

CONNECTICUT

FAIRFIELD, CT 06432-1410
2345 Black Rock Turnpike
P.O. Box 1410 (06430-1410)
(203) 374-6161
Danbury (203) 798-7300;
Norwalk (203) 853-0659
Stamford (203) 359-9892;
Waterbury (203) 597-1177

WALLINGFORD, CT 06492-2420
821 North Main Street Ext.
(203) 269-2700

DELAWARE

WILMINGTON, DE 19808-5532
2055 Limestone Road,
 Suite 200
(302) 996-9200

DISTRICT OF COLUMBIA

WASHINGTON, DC 20005-3410
1012 14th St., NW, 9th Floor
(202) 393-8000

FLORIDA

CLEARWATER, FL 34620
5830-142nd Ave. N., Suite B,
P.O. Box 7950 (34618-7950)
(all 24 hrs.)
 Pasco City
(813) 842-5459
Pinellas Cty. (813) 535-5522;
Hills/Tampa (813) 854-1154
Hernando (800) 525-1447;
Sarasota/Manatee
(813) 957-0093

FORT MEYERS, FL 33901
2710 Swamp Cabbage Ct.
(305) 625-0307 (95¢/min.)
 CC#
(900) 225-5222
(95¢/min., 24 hrs.)

JACKSONVILLE, FL 32211
7820 Arlington Expressway,
   Suite 147
(904) 721-2288

MIAMI, FL 33014-6709
16291 N.W. 57th Avenue
(305) 625-0307
(95¢/min.) CC#
(900) 225-5222
(95¢/min., 24 hrs.)

PENSACOLA, FL 32503-2533
P.O. Box 1511 (32597-1511)
(904) 494-0222

PORT ST. LUCIE, FL 34954-5579
1950 Port St. Lucie Blvd.,
   Suite 211
(407) 878-2010
(407) 337-2083

WEST PALM BEACH, FL 33409
580 Village Blvd., Suite 340
(407) 686-2200
Martin City (407) 337-2083

WINTER PARK, FL 32789-1736 (Orlando)
1011 N. Wymore Rd., Ste. 204
(407) 621-3300 (24 hrs.)

GEORGIA

ALBANY, GA 31701
611 N. Jefferson St.,
   P.O. Box 808 (31702)
(912) 883-0744

ATLANTA, GA 30303-3075
100 Edgewood Ave.,
   Suite 1012
(404) 688-4910
(615) 266-6144
No. GA (Chattanooga)

AUGUSTA, GA 30901
310 7th Street
P.O. Box 2085 (30903-2085)
(706) 722-1574

COLUMBUS, GA 31901
208 13th St., P.O. Box 2587
   (31901)
(706) 324-0712,13

MACON, GA 31211-2199
1765 Shurling Drive
(912) 742-7999

SAVANNAH, GA 31405
6806 Abercom Street,
   Suite 108-C
P.O. Box 13956 (91416-0956)
(912) 354-7521,22

HAWAII

HONOLULU, HI 96814-3801
1600 Kapiolani Blvd., Suite 201
(808) 942-2355

IDAHO

BOISE, ID 83702-5320
1333 West Jefferson
(208) 342-4649

IDAHO FALLS, ID 83404-5926
1575 South Blvd.
(208) 523-9754

ILLINOIS

CHICAGO, IL 60606-1217
211 West Wacker Drive
(312) 346-3315 ($3.80/call)
   CC#
(900) 225-5222
(95¢/min., 24 hrs.)

PEORIA, IL 61615-3770
3024 West Lake
(309) 688-3741

ROCKFORD, IL 61104-1001
810 E. State Street, 3rd Floor
(815) 963-8967
   ($3.80/call) CC#
(900) 225-5222
(95¢/min., 24 hrs.)

INDIANA

ELKHART, IN 46514-2988
722 W. Bristol Street, Suite H-2
P.O. Box 405 (46515-0405)
(219) 262-8996

EVANSVILLE, IN 47715-2265
4004 Morgan Ave., Suite 201
(812) 473-0202, 1425

FORT WAYNE, IN 46802-3493
1203 Webster Street
(219) 423-4433
(800) 552-4631 IN only

GARY, IN 46408
4189 Cleveland Street

(219) 980-1511
(219) 769-8053;
(800) 637-2118 No. IN only
INDIANAPOLIS, IN 46204-3584
Victoria Ctr., 22 E. Washington
St., Ste 200
(317) 488-2222

SOUTH BEND, IN 46637-3360
207 Dixie Way North, Suite 130
(219) 277-9121
(800) 439-5313
No. IN only

IOWA

BETTENDORF, IA 52722-4100
852 Middle Road, Suite 290
(319) 355-6344

DES MOINES, IA 50309-2375
505 5th Ave., Suite 615
(515) 243-8137

SIOUX CITY, IA 51101
505 Sixth Street, Ste. 417
(712) 252-4501

KANSAS

TOPEKA, KS 66607-1190
501 Southeast Jefferson,
Suite 24
(913) 232-0454

WICHITA, KS 67211
328 Laura
(316) 263-3146

KENTUCKY

LEXINGTON, KY 40507-1616
410 W. Vine Street, Suite 280
(606) 259-1008

LOUISVILLE, KY 40203-2186
844 S. Fourth Street
(502) 583-6546 (24 hrs.)
(800) 388-2222
(24 hrs.) S. IN & KY only

LOUISIANA

ALEXANDRIA, LA 71301-6875
1605 Murray Street, Suite 117
(318) 473-4494

BATON ROUGE, LA 70806-1546
2055 Wooddale Boulevard
(504) 926-3010

HOUMA, LA 70360-6354
1626 Barrow Street
(504) 868-3456

LAFAYETTE, LA 70506
100 Huggins Rd., P.O. Box
30297 (70593-0297)
(318) 981-3497

LAKE CHARLES, LA 70605
3941-L Ryan St., P.O. Box
7314 (70606-7314)
(318) 478-6253

MONROE, LA 71201-7380
141 Desiard Street, Suite 808
(318) 387-4600

NEW ORLEANS, LA 70130-5843
1539 Jackson Ave., Ste 400
(504) 581-6222 (24 hrs.)
(501) 528-9277

SHREVEPORT, LA 71105-2122
3612 Youree Drive
(318) 861-6417

MAINE

PORTLAND, ME 04103-2648
812 Stevens Avenue
(207) 878-2715

MARYLAND

BALTIMORE, MD 21211-3215
2100 Huntingdon Avenue
(410) 347-3990
($3.80/call) CC#
(900) 225-5222
(95¢/min., 24 hrs.)

MASSACHUSETTS

BOSTON, MA 02116-4344
20 Park Plaza, Suite 820
(617) 426-9000
(800) 422-2811 802 area only

SPRINGFIELD, MA 01103-1402
293 Bridge Street, Suite 320
(413) 734-3114

WORCESTER, MA 01608-1900

32 Franklin St., P.O. Box
  16555 (01601-6555)
(508) 755-2548

MICHIGAN

GRAND RAPIDS, MI 46503-3001
40 Pearl, NW, Ste. 354
(616) 744-8236
(800) 684-3222
W.MI only (24 hrs.)

SOUTHFIELD, MI 48076-7751 (Detroit)
30555 Southfield Rd., Ste 200
(810) 644-9100 (24 hrs.)

MINNESOTA

MINNEAPOLIS-St. PAUL 55116-2600
2706 Gannon Road
(612) 699-1111
(800) 646-6222 Comp.

MISSISSIPPI

JACKSON, MS 39206
4915 I-55 North, P.O. Box
  12745 (39236-2745)
(601) 987-8282

MISSOURI

KANSAS CITY, MO 64106-2418
306 E. 12th Street, Suite 1024
(816) 421-7800

ST. LOUIS, MO 63110-1400
5100 Oakland, Suite 200
(314) 531-3300 (24 hrs.)

SPRINGFIELD, MO 65806-1326
205 Park Central East, Suite
  509
(417) 862-4222
(800) 497-4222 S.W. MO only

NEBRASKA

LINCOLN, NE 68510-1670
3633 'O' Street, Suite 1
(402) 476-8855

OMAHA, NE 68134-6022
2237 N. 91st Court
(402) 391-7612

NEVADA

LAS VEGAS, NV 89104-1515
1022 E. Sahara Avenue
(702) 735-6900

RENO, NV 89502
991 Bible Way, P.O. Box
  21269 (89515-1269)
(702) 322-0657

NEW HAMPSHIRE

CONCORD, NH 03301-3483
410 S. Main St., Ste. 3
(603) 224-1991;
(603) 228-3789, 3844

NEW JERSEY

PARSIPPANY, NJ 07054 (Newark)
2 Sylvan Way, 3rd Floor
(201) 539-8222

TOMS RIVER, NJ 08753-8239
1721 Route 37 East
(908) 270-5577

TRENTON, NJ 08690-3596
1700 Whitehorse-Hamilton Sq.,
  #D-5
(609) 588-0808

WESTMONT, NJ 08108-0303
16 Maple Ave., P.O. Box 303
(609) 854-8467

NEW MEXICO

ALBUQUERQUE, NM 87110-3657
2625 Pennsylvania NE,
  Suite 2050
(505) 884-0500
(800) 873-2224 NM only

FARMINGTON, NM 87401-5855
308 North Locke
(505) 326-6501

LAS CRUCES, NM 88001-3548
201 N. Church, Suite 330
(505) 524-3130

NEW YORK

BUFFALO, NY 14202
346 Delaware Ave.

(716) 856-7180
($3.80/call) CC#
(900) 225-5222
(95¢/min., 24 hrs.)

FARMINGDALE, NY 11735
266 Main Street
(212) 533-6200
($3.80/call) CC#
(900) 225-5222
(95¢/min., 24 hrs.)

NEW YORK, NY 10010
257 Park Ave., South
(212) 533-6200
($3.80/call) CC#
(900) 225-5222
(95¢/min., 24 hrs.)

SYRACUSE, NY 13202
847 James Street, Suite 200
($3.80/call) CC#
(716) 856-7180
(95¢/min., 24 hrs.)
(900) 225-5222

WHITE PLAINS, NY 10603
30 Glenn Street
(212) 533-6200
($3.80/call) CC#
(900) 225-5222
(95¢/min., 24 hrs.)

NORTH CAROLINA

ASHEVILLE, NC 28801-3418
1200 BB&T Building
(704) 253-2392

CHARLOTTE, NC 28209-3650
5200 Park Rd., Ste. 202
(704) 527-0012 (24 hrs.)

GREENSBORO, NC 27410-4895
3608 W. Friendly Ave.
(910) 852-4240 (24 hrs.)

RALEIGH, NC 27604-1080
3125 Poplarwood Ct.,
   Suite 308
(919) 872-9240
(800) 222-0950 East NC only

SHERRILLS FORD, NC 28673
Eden Place, 8366 Drena Drive
P.O. Box 69 (28673-0069)
(704) 478-5622

WINSTON-SALEM, NC 27101-2728

500 W. 5th Street, Suite 202
(910) 725-8348

OHIO

AKRON, OH 44303-2111
222 W. Market Street
(216) 253-4590

CANTON, OH 44703-3135
1434 Cleveland Ave., N.W.
P.O. Box 8017 (44711-8017)
(216) 454-9401
(800) 362-0494 OH only

CINCINNATI, OH 45202-2097
898 Walnut Street
(513) 421-3015

CLEVELAND, OH 44115-1299
2217 East 9th St., Ste. 200
(216) 241-7678

COLUMBUS, OH 43215-1000
1335 Dublin, Suite 30A
(614) 486-6336

DAYTON, OH 45402-1828
40 West Fourth St., Suite 1250
(513) 222-5825

LIMA, OH 45802-0269
112N, N. West St. (45801),
   P.O. Box 269
(419) 223-7010
(800) 462-0468

TOLEDO, OH 43604-1055
425 Jefferson Ave., Ste. 909
(419) 241-6276

YOUNGSTOWN, OH 44501-1495
600 Mahoning Bank Bldg.,
   P.O. Box 1495
(216) 744-3111
Lisbon (216) 424-5522;
Warren (216) 394-0628

OKLAHOMA

OKLAHOMA CITY, OK 73102-2400
17 South Dewey
(405) 239-6081 Inq.

TULSA, OK 74136-3327
6711 South Yale, Suite 230
(918) 492-1266

OREGON

PORTLAND, OR 97205-3690
610 SW Alder Street, Suite 615
(503) 226-3981
OR/SW WA only
(800) 488-4166

PENNSYLVANIA

BETHLEHEM, PA 18018-5789
528 North New Street
(610) 866-8780
Berks Cty. (610) 372-2005

LANCASTER, PA 17602-2852
29 E. King Street, Ste. 322
(215) 448-3870
($3.80/call) CC#
(900) 225-5222
(95¢/min., 24 hrs.)

PHILADELPHIA, PA 19103-0297
1930 Chestnut Street
P.O. Box 2297
(215) 448-3870
CC# ($3.80/call)
(900) 225-5222
(95¢/min., 24 hrs.)

PITTSBURGH, PA 15222-2511
300 Sixth Avenue, Ste. 100-UL
(412) 456-2700

SCRANTON, PA 18503-2204
129 N. Washington Avenue
P.O. Box 993 (18501-0993)
(717) 342-9129
(717) 655-0445

PUERTO RICO

SAN JUAN, PR 00936-3488
1608 Bori St. (00927-6100),
P.O. Box 363488
(809) 756-5400

RHODE ISLAND

WARWICK, RI 02887-1300 (Providence)
Bureau Park, Box 1300
(401) 785-1212 Inq.
(401) 785-1213 Comp.

SOUTH CAROLINA

COLUMBIA, SC 29202-8326
2330 Devine St. (29205),
P.O. Box 8326
(803) 254-2525

GREENVILLE, SC 29605-4077
113 Mills Avenue
(803) 242-5052

MYRTLE BEACH, SC 29577-1601
1601 North Oak St., Ste. 403
(803) 626-6881

TENNESSEE

BLOUNTVILLE, TN 37617-1178
P.O. Box 1178 TCA, #121
(615) 323-6311

CHATTANOOGA, TN 37402-2614
1010 Market Street, Suite 200
(615) 266-6144

KNOXVILLE, TN 37919
2633 Kingston Pike, Suite 2
P.O. Box 10327 (37939-0327)
(615) 522-2552

MEMPHIS, TN 38120
6525 Quail Hollow, Suite 410
P.O. Box 17036 (38187-0036)
(901) 759-1300
(24 hrs.)

NASHVILLE, TN 37219-1778
NationsBank Plaza, 414 Union
Street, Ste. 1830
(615) 242-4222 (24 hrs.)

TEXAS

ABILENE, TX 79605-6052
3300 South 14th Street,
Suite 307
(915) 691-1533

AMARILLO, TX 79101-3408
1000 South Polk, P.O. Box
1905 (79105-1905)
(806) 379-6222

AUSTIN, TX 78741-3854
2101 South IH35, Suite 302
(512) 445-2911 (24 hrs.)

BEAUMONT, TX 77701-2011
476 Oakland Ave., P.O. Box
2988 (77704-2988)
(409) 835-5348

BRYAN, TX 77802-4413
4346 Carter Creek Pkwy.
(409) 260-2222

CORPUS CHRISTI, TX 78401
216 Park Avenue
(512) 887-4949

DALLAS, TX 75201-3093
2001 Bryan St., Ste. 850
(214) 740-0348
($3.80/call) CC#
(900) 225-5222
(95¢/min., 24 hrs.)

EL PASO, TX 79901
State Nat'l Plaza, Ste. 1101
(915) 577-0191

FORT WORTH, TX 76102-5978
1612 Summit Ave., Suite 260
(817) 332-7585 (24 hrs.)

HOUSTON, TX 77008-1085
2707 N. Loop West, Ste. 400
(713) 867-4946
($3.80/call) CC#
(900) 225-5222
(95¢/min., 24 hrs.)

LUBBOCK, TX 79401-3410
916 Main Street, Suite 800
(806) 763-0459 (24 hrs.)

MIDLAND, TX 79711-0206
10100 County Rd., 118 West
P.O. Box 60206
(915) 563-1880
(800) 592-4433 TX only

SAN ANGELO, TX 76904
3121 Executive Drive
P.O. Box 3366 (76902-3366)
(915) 949-2989

SAN ANTONIO, TX 78217-5296
1800 Northeast Loop 410,
Ste 400
(210) 828-9441

TYLER, TX 75701
3600 Old Bullard Road,
Suite 103A
P.O. Box 6652 (75711-6852)
(903) 581-5704

WACO, TX 76710
6801 Sanger Avenue,
Suite 125

P.O. Box 7203 (76714-7203)
(817) 772-7530

WESLACO, TX 78599-0069
609 International Blvd.,
P.O. Box 69
(210) 968-3678

WICHITA FALLS, TX 76308-2830
4245 Kemp Blvd., Ste. 900
(800) 388-1778

UTAH

SALT LAKE CITY, UT 84115-5382
1588 South Main Street
(801) 487-4656 (24 hrs.)
(800) 456-3907 UT only

VERMONT

See **BOSTON, MA 02116-4344**
(800) 422-2811 (802) area only

VIRGINIA

FREDERICKSBURG, VA 22408
11903 Main Street
(540) 373-9872

NORFOLK, VA 23509-1499
3608 Tidewater Drive
(804) 627-5651
Peninsula area (804) 722-9101

RICHMOND, VA 23219-2332
701 East Franklin, Suite 712
(804) 648-0016 (24 hrs.)

ROANOKE, VA 24011-1301
31 West Campbell Avenue
(703) 342-3455

WASHINGTON

KENNEWICK, WA 99336-3819
101 N. Union #105
(509) 783-0892

SEATAC, WA 98188
4800 South 188th St., Ste. 222
P.O. Box 68926 ($4 Flat fee,
24 hrs.)
(206) 431-2222
($4 Flat fee) CC#

(900) 225-4222 ($4 flat fee 24 hrs.)

SPOKANE, WA 99207-2356
East 123 Indiana, Suite 106
(509) 328-2100

YAKIMA, WA 98901
222 Washington Mutual Bldg.
P.O. Box 1584 (98907-1584)
(509) 248-1326

WISCONSIN

MILWAUKEE, WI 53203-2478
740 North Plankinton Ave.
(414) 273-1600 Inq.
(414) 273-0123 Comp.

INTERNATIONAL BUREAUS

NATIONAL HEADQUARTERS
FOR CANADIAN BUREAUS

MARKHAM, ONTARIO L3R 6C9
115 Apple Creek Blvd.,
   Suite 209

ALBERTA

CALGARY, AB T2H 2H8
7330 Fisher Street, SE,
   Suite 357
(403) 531-8780

EDMONTON, AB T5K 2L9
514 Capital Pl, 9707-110th
   Street
(403) 482-2341

BRITISH COLUMBIA

VANCOUVER, BC V6B 2M1
788 Beatty Street, Suite 404
(604) 682-2711

VICTORIA, BC V8W 1V7
201-1005 Langley Street
(604) 386-6348

MANITOBA

WINNIPEG, MB R3B 2K3
301-365 Hargrave Street,
   Room 301
(204) 943-1486

NEWFOUNDLAND

ST. JOHNS, NF A1E 2B6
360 Topsail Road, P.O. Box
   516 (A1C 5K4)
(709) 364-2222

NOVA SCOTIA

HALIFAX, NS B3J 3J8
1888 Brunswick St., Suite 601
(902) 422-6581 Inq.
(902) 422-6582 Comp.

ONTARIO

HAMILTON, ON L8N 1A8
100 King Street, East
(905) 526-1112

KITCHENER, ON N2G 4L5
354 Charles Street, East
(519) 579-3080

LONDON, ON N6A 5C7
200 Queens Avenue, Suite 616
P.O. Box 2153 (N6A 4E3)
(519) 673-3222

OTTAWA, ON K1P 5N2
130 Albert Street, Suite 603
(613) 237-4856

ST. CATHARINES, ON L2R 3H6
101 King Street
(905) 687-6688

WINDSOR, ON N9A 5K6
500 Riverside Drive West
(519) 258-7222

QUEBEC

MONTREAL, PQ H3A 1V4
2055 Peel Street, Suite 460
(514) 286-9281

QUEBEC CITY, PQ G1R 1K2
485 rue Richelieu
(418) 523-2555

SASKATCHEWAN

REGINA, SA S4P 1Y3
302-2080 Broad Street
(306) 352-7601

CC# = Call charged to consumer's credit card

CHAPTER 5

Bids

Contractors will give you bids on the job a few ways, depending on its complexity. In some cases they will give a bid over the phone. If so, cross them off your list. If a contractor can't spend the time to analyze and then bid on a job, how scrupulous do you think he'll be with the job itself?

The other way is to come in person. The contractor will come to the house, look at the job, and if the job is easy to bid on, he will do it right then and there.

An example would be roofing or siding. These are measured in terms of "squares," or 100-square-foot areas. It might just be a matter of the contractor measuring it out, multiplying it by the cost per installed square, and giving you a figure. Or there may be some preparation involved, such as removing existing siding. Whatever, it is possible to get this type of bid right away, or the contractor will get back to you, either by phone or by mail.

Windows would also be simple to do—assuming you know what you want—as would painting, building a driveway, anything where the contractor knows his unit cost (say a square or a yard of installed concrete, cost per window, etc.).

More difficult to estimate is something involving modifying house structure, or adding a room. The reason is that there are many more elements involved—roofing, siding, windows, a foundation, wall material, plumbing, electrical, and so on. He knows his unit cost perhaps, but he has to blend it all together, get prices from his subcontractors, if any, and so forth. It gets complicated. On such a complex project formal plans can shine. The contractor knows exactly what you want.

On a big job don't expect to get the bid right away. A contractor will noodle it over for days, perhaps weeks, and then either return in person or mail it to you.

If the company is large, you may not see the contractor, only a salesman. But the salesman is more than just a seller, which is of course his primary function. He will also know construction, products and materials, and design. He can advise you knowledgeably.

If the company is small, perhaps just one person, you will see the contractor himself.

PRESENTING . . . THE COMPANY!

Before you get a bid, you will get a presentation, which has only one purpose: to make the company look solid, good, and wonderful to you and get them the job. The presentation to you will be either slick or simplistic, or perhaps somewhere in between.

Some contractors or salesmen will present a company history, testimonial letters, before-and-after pictures of jobs they've done, sample contract and paperwork, a copy of their license, and perhaps pictures of their children and/or grandchildren.

Says longtime contractor Fred Gorman, "Above all, the salesman wants to come across as a 'nice guy.' Nice guys sell jobs."

SMALL VERSUS LARGE

Large companies will huckster their ability to give service, their fiscal stability (they're not going to run out on you halfway through the job because cash flow has dried up), and the speed with which they can do the job (they flood a job with people and bang it out, rather than drag it on because only one or possibly two people are working).

The smaller contractor might tell you that his price will be lower because he has less overhead and no salesman taking a 9 or 10 percent commission, that the quality of his work is high because it's him working and not a subcontractor who couldn't care less, or a bunch of workers, "20 percent who are good, 60 percent fair, and 20 percent bad apples," as Walt Stoeppelwerth says.

While all of these things are generally true, you have to make a decision based on specifics, so it is suggested that you record this information for later analysis and thought, weighing the relative importance of each thing.

For example, how important is speed? How important is it to have a single person working around the house? How important is money versus time? Will you be willing to be charged more to save, say, five or six weeks?

KEEP A RECORD

You should keep a written record of everything each contractor says.

One of the best forms for this, reproduced on p. 90, was created by my writer friend Barbara Lagowski. She needed a roofing-and-siding job done, so she thoroughly researched the jobs—just as she would one of her books—and compiled a list of relevant questions about warranties, guarantees, whether the contractor could do the job by a certain date and straight through, price, extras, materials used, and so on. In sum, she jotted down the answers of five contractors, and the form was extraordinarily handy in evaluating them and selecting the one she wanted.

If you do your homework, you can create your own form for your job. If it's siding or roofing, feel free to purloin from Barbara's form as you wish.

Barbara's efforts, by the way, paid off handsomely. She got good jobs at fair prices.

Some contractors, you should know, are not accustomed to using materials selected by the consumer. They usually like the consumer to select from materials and products they display for a variety of reasons, from ease of workability to sheer greed; some items, such as vinyl windows, are high profit; they are marked up big and go in easily.

To this end they will have books showing endless arrays of products and materials and will probably have product samples such as siding, roofing, flooring, and even miniature windows, if that's what your job involves.

But there is *no* logical reason for them to reject what you want, unless it is esoteric and virtually impossible to get.

Of course they may champion their own products and materials over what you picked. Listen carefully—and take notes. If you've done your homework, what they say to you will be meaningful.

Naturally one can get intimidated by someone spewing out product "facts." But you do have a system of checks and balances: namely, other contractors. If one contractor has raised questions you want answered, ask the other contractors who come to bid. That's one of the advantages of having four, five, or six contractors bid on a job.

For example, one may say that on this particular siding job the existing siding had to come off. But double-check that. What do the other contractors think?

You should know that some contractors and salespeople will try deliberately to change the materials or products used on a job. They know that other contractors are bidding and will try to create an apples-to-grapefruit situation. For example, you may want vinyl siding and the salesman will tell you it's not that good, you should get wood siding. If you are talked into this, then you have no way of comparing wood versus vinyl in any meaningful way. To get the best quality and price on wood, you'll have to ask the other contractors to rebid the job.

ROOFING AND SIDING INFORMATION SHEET

Company name: _____ Phone: _____

Physical Address: _____

Any complaints per Monmouth County Consumer Affairs? _____

Any complaints per Better Business Bureau? _____

Issues to clarify: _____

How many roofing crews does co. have? _____ Siding crews? _____

Does company subcontract? _____

Can co. provide addresses where work is in progress? _____

Are co. trucks on site fitted with permanent or temporary signs? _____

Will co. guarantee in writing they do not subcontract? _____

Will they agree to a penalty if subs are used? _____

References Can co. provide list of references? _____

Do references include jobs in progress? _____

Decking: What kind of wood will be used? _____

How much will it cost? _____

Can gutters be boxes in? _____

Roofing: Thickness (235 lb) and type of roofing? (Co. name) _____

Guarantee of materials? _____

Guarantee of workmanship? _____

Does price include drip cap? _____ Flashing where roofs meet? _____

Must attic contents be moved? _____ Can samples be kept? _____

Siding: Gauge, type and brand of siding preferred by company? _____

Why? _____

Type of insulation preferred by company? _____

Why? _____

Guarantee on siding? _____ Workmanship? _____

Can siding/insulation samples be kept? _____ _____

Can leftover siding, shingles be kept by customer? _____

Roofing estimate: _____Siding Estimate: _____Total:

Additional cost to do garage. Roofing: _____Siding: _____

Will company arrange for necessary permits? ($5 per thousand, per city of LB).

Does company arrange for dumpster? _____Dumping fees? _____

Does estimator have any comments on other companies? _____

8. Some sort of form, such as this one shown for roofing and siding jobs, is useful for taking bid information. You should research the job first so that relevant questions can be devised.

DOES ALL THE FOLLOWING APPEAR IN CONTRACT?

Physical address?
Name/home phone number of owner.
Type, gauge and brand of siding. Insulation? Decking? Roofing?
Price of job, including siding? Roofing? Garage?
Specific tasks to be included in price, including drip cap.
Flashing? Boxing in gutters? Any other specifics discussed?
Any agreements re permits, dumpsters, dumping fees?
Guarantees on siding, insulation, decking, roofing and workmanship?
Guarantees regarding subcontracting practices?
Payment schedule: (preferably small binder, ⅓ to supplier on delivery of materials, ⅓ on completion of roofing, remainder at completion of siding). ⅓ on start, ⅓ on ½ way pt., ⅓ on comp.
Job commencement date. Roofing begins 5 wks hence.
Job completion date. siding @ 8–10 days. NO STOPS guaranteed

PENALTY CLAUSE FOR LATE COMPLETION DUE TO WEATHER

CONDITIONS?

HEARSAY AND NOTABLE GOSSIP RE:COMPANY

OTHER COMMENTS/ISSUES:

WRITTEN BIDS

Bids for any job should be in writing, even assuming you are taking notes. The more information you get, the better. In some instances the written bid submitted will also be the contract, particularly if it's a relatively small job, such as siding or roofing.

Whatever, you should never sign a contract right away. If someone pressures you to sign with a statement like "This price is good for the next week, but that's all," eliminate him as a candidate. He's a con man.

Unfortunately there is no magic formula to use in selecting a contractor, because beyond questions of competence, reliability, and honesty, there are price and other factors, not to mention the subtleties of human interaction. Do you get along with this guy, or is he a macho jerk who will have you frothing at the mouth before he gets out of his giant-wheeled truck?

It is absolutely essential that you feel you can get along with the contractor, because on ALL jobs things will go wrong. If you can't have a civilized conversation, then, if he intimidates you, where are you?

Never, ever hire someone you're afraid of. Better, walk away from the improvement. There's nothing cast in stone that says you have to hire someone by, say, last Thursday, unless you are having an extreme emergency.

One thing is *for sure:* The bids you get will be surprisingly diverse, both high and low and somewhere in the middle. On her siding-and-roofing job Barbara got a high bid of $16,000 and a low bid of $7,500. Another person I know had bids on an addition that varied as much as $25,000!

And this is also for sure: The bids will stun you.

MIDDLE BID BEST?

It is a truism among people in the remodeling field that the middle bid is usually the best one to take, with some people saying it is the upper-middle bid that usually comes from the best contractor. (Barbara Lagowski went for the middle bid.)

Maybe, but if a bid is very low, ask the contractor why. For example, on a siding bid he may have misunderstood and not included trim in the bid, which can add 20 percent to the cost.

On the other hand, it may be very low because the contractor is desperate for the job, for whatever reason. He may have come with great recommendations, and he may have been great, but life situations change—fast. "Shit happens" (one of the truest things I have ever heard), and yesterday's good guy might be today's bad guy.

A public relations person in Wisconsin, for example, told me a story of how her boss—an interior designer—recommended a kitchen remodelor to her, someone her boss had been using for years. The person turned out to be a disaster. When he showed up, he was fine. The problem is that he hardly ever showed up, and when he did, the woman said, "He looked terrible. Dark rings under his eyes and so forth. I don't know what was going on in his life."

Neither do I. But it might have been cocaine, or the loss of a spouse to another man, or finding out his kid is a drug dealer—or worse. Things change. More checking is required.

To do this, you need two things from him. Job references and the place (or places) where he is currently working. Job references should not be just a few people. Most people can come up with someone who will recommend them highly.

Ask for fifteen or twenty names. He shouldn't object. Indeed, in his book Walt Stoeppelwerth talks about one New Jersey contractor who will provide a customer with five thousand names! Many can supply hundreds simply by printing out some pages on a computer.

Also ask to see his license and ask him if he has liability and workman's compensation insurance, if he will have someone working with him, and get the name of his insurance agent. If a bond is required, ask to see it.

Eventually all the stars will be in their proper order and you will likely lean toward one contractor. But don't tell anyone anything yet. It is a time to check him out thoroughly in order to nail things to the wall, appropriately enough.

SUBCONTRACTORS: HOW GOOD?

In general it is accepted in the home-improvement field that people who work as part of a regular crew make better workers than do subcontractors. People who are part of a crew depend on one specific GC for their livelihood, whereas subs usually don't. The job they do for the general contractor is a side job, and they may not have a big stake in doing a good job.

In itself the fact that a GC employs subs is not enough reason to reject him. But it is a negative factor that probably should have some impact.

THE LANGUAGE OF BALONEY

We all have our ways of selling ourselves in this world, and though I do not have unassailable proof of this, I think that one way some contractors do it is by buffaloing consumers, specifically by inundating them with facts and terms that they don't understand. Once someone can get you nodding and feeling like a low-level goofball, there's a tendency to go along with, or agree with whatever that person says rather than look stupid by asking potentially stupid questions.

Here, again, the importance of educating yourself about the job comes through. Once you know what "up to code" and "deck" and "underlayment" and all those other terms mean, no one will be able to bowl you over.

And remember this too: Plumbers aren't rocket scientists, and neither are carpenters or masons or siding installers. They do not practice inscrutable arts. Once you understand the arts they do practice, you'll be that much better off.

CHAPTER 6

Check the
Contractor Out

To check out the contractor you like, start by selecting two or three recent jobs from the list of references furnished. Call the people up and tell them that you are thinking of hiring the particular contractor and would like to see his work.

At the job look at the workmanship. While you may not be a contractor, workmanship is workmanship, and if you look at something, you can probably get an idea of the job. Even better, if you've pored over the material in part 2, you'll have some sense of what to look for.

Gently question the people, but keep it *conversational.*

"How was he to work with?" "Did he work straight through?" "Did he respond to problems quickly?" "Was he clean and neat?"

And the crucial question: Would the person who had the job done recommend him?

Go to a second job, and a third if you think it's necessary. But if you get two positive readings from what were random selections, that's a very good sign.

VISIT A JOB IN PROGRESS

Also visit a job in progress. This can be very illuminating. Does the work seem to be getting done in an orderly manner?

Does it appear to be quality work? For example, if pipes are exposed, do they go through holes in framing members, or have notches been cut out for them? Making notches is the speedier way to do things, but this can weaken framing members.

What about the joints of framing members. Are they neat?

How about cleanliness? Does it look as if people are picking up after themselves?

CHECK THE CONTRACTOR'S CREDIT

One long-time contractor suggests that you have a credit check done by the financial institution who will be lending you the money but you can do so only if the contractor agrees. "You want to get an idea of how he pays his bills," the contractor says. The bank can also check him out at Dun & Bradstreet.

Another way of doing this is to check his supplier. Visit the place or places where he deals and ask to see the manager. Ask him how the contractor pays his bills. Timely bill paying can be crucial because it relates to the lien law. If the contractor doesn't pay his bills, someone can end up wanting you to pay them for him.

Of course the supplier may be reluctant to reveal this— but he may not be, and his reaction may tell you all you need to know.

VISIT HIS PLACE OF BUSINESS

Another measure is to visit his place of business. You want to make sure that it isn't the glove compartment of a car.

Big-time contractors will say that every contractor should

have a place of business—it shouldn't be a room in his house. But I have no problem with someone operating out of his house. *What you are mainly concerned with is that he has a permanent address* so that you know where to reach him if you have to.

You might also look at the house and grounds. Does he take care of them? This, too, can tell you something about him.

If the contractor survives all these tests, then it is highly likely that you have found someone who is good and trustworthy, but, alas, vigilance is still required, and you have to write up a contract to protect yourself in every way possible.

At the core of that contract is the payment schedule.

CHAPTER 7

Payment Schedule

One interview for this book I particularly remember, was with Fred Gorman, a general contractor who had been in the business for over fifty years and who was giving me the benefit of his experience to help ensure that people didn't get ripped off or otherwise hurt by contractors.

The interview had gone on for a while when Fred asked me a question: "What's the most important thing the homeowner has in protecting himself when working with a contractor?"

I hesitated. I was very interested, to say the least. Across the table from me was decades of experience in the field. This man had probably known thousands of contractors throughout his life.

"Just one word," Fred prompted.

My research had given me a lot of important ideas, but perhaps the word *attitude* covered it all.

"Paranoia," I said, not so jokingly.

Fred shook his head.

"Money," he said, "that's the most important thing."

When I thought about it, I realized Fred was right. Money is the most important thing, and the bottom line, as it were, is this: As long as you never let the contractor get ahead of you on the money, you can't get burned badly. If he gets ahead—has money in his pocket for work not yet done—then to that degree you can get scorched.

This single premise, then, which I believe to be true and which many *contractors* affirm, seriously questions the job-payment schedules suggested by many consumer affairs departments across the country.

The most common suggestion is that one-third the price of the job should be paid up front. As I got deeper in my research, however, I began to think of this as risky. One-third up front can be a substantial amount of money. For example, if a $45,000 extension is contracted for, one-third of that is $15,000. That is, you write a $15,000 check for nothing.

Why, I asked one consumer specialist, did her state—and a lot of others—suggest this?"

"It's standard in the industry."

"That still doesn't answer why."

"Well, the contractor has to pay his supplier for materials."

Therein lies the usual reason why. But I don't think it's valid; it can be dangerous, and the people who are first to agree are again, other contractors, and people on consumer protection boards, such as Bill Baessler of Suffolk County, who used to be a contractor.

"I don't want any money up front," says Bill Garthe of Adamson Construction. "I don't need it."

"If a contractor can't work without getting paid first, you shouldn't hire him," says Fred Gorman.

The danger is that, for whatever reason, the contractor may not start the job, or he may start the job and then leave and not come back. If you've given him $10,000 and he's done $3,000 worth of work, that leaves you $7,000 in the hole.

Some consumers say, "I can sue."

Yes, they can. But as remodeling attorney Reynolds Graves says, "they can sue and they can win a judgment. But as so many lawyers say, a judgment is just a piece of paper. You still have to collect."

THAT SAVAGE LIEN LAW

An even more malevolent aspect to paying up front is the lien law. Some people, for example, will say it's okay to pay a contractor for the materials when they are dropped at the site. What could be safer? There are the materials, here's the money.

The danger is that the contractor likely has credit at the supplier. What happens if you give him $10,000 or $15,000 for lumber and he doesn't pay the supplier? What if he's fighting a desperate struggle to turn his business around, and neither you nor the supplier, who put the lumber on his tab, know this?

You could both be out of the money, but under the lien law the supplier has a much more vulnerable and viable place to get his money back: *from you.* Your house is sitting there, so all he has to do is slap a lien on it. And as many people have discovered—and as I've emphasized in this book—liens work.

WHAT ABOUT SPECIAL ORDERS?

In most cases a contractor can return products or materials to suppliers if they're not used. So, for example, if a consumer backed out of a job, the contractor wouldn't get burned too badly. And he has that lien law at his disposal.

What about special orders, materials that lumberyards won't take back, such as special moldings, custom-made windows, and the like?

For example, Reynolds Graves reports one horror story where a contractor installed some fifty custom-made windows in a posh new house. There was only one problem: The windows were white and they should have been brown. The homeowner rejected them, and therein began a war that was costly and dispiriting for all.

I think that the following is fair. The homeowner should give nothing up front, unless it can be assured that the money is going to the supplier or if he or she is otherwise protected in one of the following ways:

- The check is made out directly to the supplier for the materials delivered, or to the contractor *and* the supplier. In other words, a check that requires two signatures to cash.
- A bond is posted that exceeds or equals the amount of money advanced for the job. A bond is where a third party guarantees *completion* of a job by a contractor. If the contractor doesn't finish it, the bonding company must pay the owner the cost of the job. A bond is not easy to get.
- A lien release is given to the homeowner by the *supplier*—not the contractor. A release from the contractor at the beginning of a job is worthless: Those lien rights belong to his supplier, and subcontractors—not him.

In other words, I don't see anything wrong with giving a chunk of money up front for special orders, as long as you are protected against its loss. Good faith representation from the contractor is not enough.

The alternative is to give the contractor the money and hope that everything turns out all right. That's a bad alternative, and the contractor should be able to see your point of view: You'll pay the money, you just don't want to be vulnerable.

Incidentally, in many states you will be served with lien notices at the beginning of a job by suppliers and subcontractors. This means nothing. It's just the law. But it does constitute a potent reminder of what could be.

PAYMENT SCHEDULE

A payment schedule, aside from being established so that the consumer can protect himself, should also be viewed as a carrot. Adults work, at least in part, for money, and when all the money has been paid and there's work still to be done, what is the natural human tendency? Not to work, because we've already gotten the carrot. There's no reward, other than the reward of finishing a job and being proud of it, waiting for us.

What, then, should the payment schedule be?

It can be anything you want it to be, but the abiding principle should be followed: Never let the contractor get ahead of you.

On a big job, many payments are better than chunks. For a $60,000 room addition you could pay a few hundred dollars up front, then $6,000 upon *completion* of each phase of the construction—say after foundation, framing, plumbing, electrical, and so forth (You could also pay for supplies—as long as, as detailed above, you *know* the supplier is getting the money). The appendix of this book contains an actual contract showing a payment schedule.

On specialty jobs, such as roofing and siding, the same might pertain, but since the job does not have so many components, it might be set up as follows: half the money when half the job is done and most of the rest of the money when the job is done.

Some final payment should be held back for ten to thirty days to allow problems to show up—and be corrected. For example, a ten-day wait is appropriate for a roofing job, and a thirty-day wait is appropriate for an addition. If the contractor has all the money, there will be a natural inclination among most not to return right away. (Though one big contractor told me he built his business on return calls. If a customer with a completed job called with a problem, he would drop everything and service that customer. "Word got around," he said. "Last year we did three million dollars in business.")

Incidentally, before a contractor leaves a job, he and you should walk through the job and list what, if anything, needs to be done (contractors call this the punch list), and he should not leave until all the items have been handled.

The question is, though, how much should be held back? Most consumer affairs departments suggest 10 percent, but this may not be enough unless it is a substantial job.

For example, if the overall job is $50,000 and you hold back 10 percent, that's $5,000—a substantial amount of money. But if you hold back 10 percent on a $3,200 roofing job, that's $320. Suppose it starts to leak after two weeks?

The contractor might know right away that if he returns, it will likely cost him much more than $320, and he might not return. But if there was double that owed to him—$640—he might be more inclined to return and make the repairs.

Of course one could argue that contractors guarantee their work. It varies, but it is typically for a year. And he may come back. But when? Meanwhile you're trying to live with the problem. However, if you have his money, that may well be a different story.

On the subject of the end payment, then, there is no rule cast in bronze. It should just be enough so that it will give you protection. I would say 15% to 20%.

Many contractors will be able to understand this (some don't want *any* money until the *end* of the job), and some won't. But it is good business practice, and if the contractor cannot understand that, you are better off folding your cards and going elsewhere.

Or, again, running needless risks.

THE POWER OF MONEY

During the years following the publication of this book I have given a number of talks at various places on hiring contractors. At one, a woman provided a prime example of the power of money and the importance of its control over the contractor.

"On the day he finished," she said, "I gave the bath remodeling contractor the entire final payment. What a mistake! That night I was down in the basement and heard water trickling. To my horror, I discovered a pipe in the bathroom was leaking water into the basement.

"Panicked, I called the contractor and told him the problem. He said that it was no sweat—that he'd be there . . . in thirty days.

"But you have to come tomorrow."

"I can't," he said, "I'm booked up."

"In that case," I said, "I'll be at the bank tomorrow morning at nine o'clock to stop payment on the check I gave you today."

Around eight o'clock the next morning the contractor was working on the leak.

CHAPTER 8

A Written Contract

Sue Johnson is a sophisticated, smart professional person who works in New York City. But Sue and her husband were also trusting and had no written agreement with a man they hired to install some kitchen cabinets in their home in South-hold, New York. As she tells it, "We bought the cabinets for twelve hundred dollars and hired him to install them at fifty dollars an hour. High, but he told us orally that the job would only take a day and a half or so.

"Three and a half weeks later he was still working on them and, when he was finished, presented us with a bill for over ten thousand dollars!

"We went to court, and it cost us what we had agreed on plus the cost of our lawyer, which wasn't that much. We were lucky.

"I don't know how we got into it. We were just so trusting. We could never believe that when we sat down at that old battered kitchen table in our Southhold house and drank some wine and orally agreed to this with this nice man that it would come to this.

"It never will be that way again. I don't trust anyone anymore."

Sue and her husband also learned another lesson: Have

everything in writing. Have a contract. It reduces the possibility of misunderstandings, and if you have to present a case to someone, you will have what lawyers call a trail of paper.

And without the paper why should the authorities believe you rather than the contractor?

STATES REQUIRE A WRITTEN CONTRACT

How important is a written contract? Many states consider it so important that it's illegal not to have one.

To be truly effective, the contract must be detailed: The files of consumer protection agencies are riddled with complaints by homeowners who got into trouble because of not having a written contract, or having a poorly written one.

"Poorly written contracts are one of our biggest problems," says Sue Nichols formerly of Connecticut's Department of Consumer Affairs. "The contract should contain not only what the contractor will do, but what he won't do."

A number of areas must be covered in detail. How much detail? Jane Devine, former commissioner of Consumer Affairs in Suffolk County, Long Island, reflects the sentiments of many other consumer protection specialists when she says, "No contract can have too much detail."

The contract actually consists of a number of papers, including the central agreements, plans, and material specifications, all the permits and paperwork from the town, a notice of recision (see below), and more.

The central agreement is the key, and the question arises as to whose should be used.

Contractors commonly have their own contracts, but many of the ones I've seen are inadequate for the task at hand. On a major addition, for example, I've seen one-page contracts with space for writing details in very short supply. Also, many of the points that should be covered for the consumer's protection are not covered.

A contract cannot cover everything in a few pages. To spell everything out, more pages would be needed.

NOTICE OF RIGHT TO CANCEL

Your Right to Cancel

You are entering into a transaction that will result in a mortgage/lien on your home. You have a legal right under federal law to cancel this transaction, without cost, within three business days from whichever of the following events occurs last:

  (1) the date of the transaction, which is _____; or
  (2) the date you received your Truth in Lending disclosures; or
  (3) the date you received this notice of your right to cancel.

If you cancel the transaction, the mortgage/lien is also canceled. Within 20 calendar days after we receive your notice, we must take the steps necessary to reflect the fact that the mortgage/lien on your home has been canceled, and we must return to you any money or property you have given to us or to anyone else in connection with this transaction.

You may keep any money or property we have given you until we have done the things mentioned above, but you must then offer to return the money or property. If it is impractical or unfair for you to return the property, you must offer its reasonable value. You may offer to return the property at your home or at the location of the property. Money must be returned to the address below. If we do not take possession of the money or property within 20 calendar days of your offer, you may keep it without further obligation.

How to Cancel

If you decide to cancel this transaction, you may do so by notifying us in writing, at

_____
(NAME OF CREDITOR)

_____
(ADDRESS)

You may use any written statement that is signed and dated by you and states your intention to cancel, or you may use this notice by dating and signing below. Keep one copy of this notice because it contains important information about your rights.

If you cancel by mail or telegram, you must send the notice no later than midnight of _____
                              (RECISION DATE)
(or midnight of the third business day following the latest of the three events listed above). If you send or deliver your written notice to cancel some other way, it must be delivered to the above address no later than that time.

I WISH TO CANCEL

_____   _____
(BUYER'S SIGNATURE)   (DATE)

The above Notice of Right to Cancel applies to the Retail Instalment Obligation or Home Improvement Installment Contract dated _____ between you as Buyer(s) and _____ as Contractor (Seller).
Each of you hereby acknowledges receipt of two fully completed copies of the above Notice of Right to Cancel.

_____   _____
(DATE)   (BUYER)

_____   _____
(DATE)   (BUYER)

NOTE: TWO COPIES MUST BE DELIVERED TO EACH BUYER. THE RECISION DATE TO BE ENTERED IS 3 DAYS FOLLOWING THE TRANSACTION DATE EXCLUSIVE OF SUNDAY AND LEGAL PUBLIC HOLIDAYS, AS NEW YEAR'S DAY, WASHINGTON'S BIRTHDAY, MEMORIAL DAY, INDEPENDENCE DAY, LABOR DAY, COLUMBUS DAY, VETERANS DAY, THANKSGIVING DAY, AND CHRISTMAS DAY.

---

9. Notice of recision. Federal law gives you the right to cancel a contract within three days of signing. (California State Contractors Board)

The American Institute of Architects sells a wide variety of agreements covering various contractor/consumer and architect/consumer relationships, which are quite long and detailed.

The question naturally arises as to whether or not one should hire a lawyer. Consumer protection departments do not supply definitive advice. They usually say something like, "It may be a good idea to have a lawyer look over your contract."

In light of what I learned in researching this book, my advice would be as follows:

If the particular improvement involves an addition, or an alteration of the house, definitely hire a lawyer. Such projects cost a lot of money and are complex. There's more potential for misunderstanding. So it's worth hiring a lawyer.

For smaller projects that are not complex, such as roofing, siding, a new driveway, new windows—one basic product— I think the average person can handle it himself. Or, write the contract, but before signing have a lawyer look it over. Incidentally, you might want to use the contractor's contract as a boiler-plate document. If it doesn't have all the detail you need, add extra pages.

Or tell the contractor that either he will have to use your contract or you can't assign him the job.

If you have a lawyer prepare the contract on a big project, it could cost you $1,000 or more. If he just looks over one you've worked up, it might just be a charge for an hour's worth of his time—$100 or $150. Whichever, I think it's money well spent.

Of course you cannot just hire *any* lawyer. Get one who is familiar with home remodeling and has written such contracts before. Ideally you would find a lawyer who is also an architect. Such people exist.

To find a lawyer, check with friends or relatives or people who have had work done. Or contact your local bar association and ask for the names of three lawyers who specialize in home remodeling, and go from there. Other lawyers suggest that anyone you hire should have malpractice insurance. If he makes a mistake that costs, the payment will come from the insurance company—and not you.

CLAUSES TO INCLUDE

There are a number of clauses that a good contract should contain. Some states, such as New York, Maine, and Massachusetts, have model contracts, but while all cover important points, not all cover everything. The following is, you might say, a roundup of clauses that should be included:

1. *Name, address, number, and license or registration number, if any.* The address should not be a post office box number but a street address. You want to reach the contractor if you have to. If, when checking him out, you went to his place of business or home, this shouldn't be a problem.

2. *A date when the job will begin—and be done.* Very important. If you don't have starting and completion dates, you could be sitting around twiddling your thumbs waiting for the job to start—and gnashing your teeth waiting for it to end.

3. *Detailed description of products and materials to be used.* Most contracts fail woefully (see box in this chapter) to do this properly. It is not enough to say "white vinyl windows" or "Certain-Teed white siding" or "birch door" or "2 by 4s." Names, models, colors, and so on must be included. The key is this: The descriptions of the products and materials should be *detailed enough to order from.*

4. *Payment schedule.* This should be adhered to, as suggested in chapter 6, with payments made after each phase of construction is completed, making sure never to let the contractor get ahead of you.

5. *Final payment clause.* It should state that final payment (see chapter 7) is not due until a certain period after the work is completed and that the homeowner will not pay if defective work is not remedied. Final payment also depends on the contractor providing the homeowner with filled-out waivers of lien forms from suppliers and subcontractors that will state that they have been paid in full and have no legal claims against the homeowner.

6. *Statement on warranties.* Many products carry warranties. This clause should spell out who is responsible for servicing them, and copies of the warranties should be attached and become part of the contract.

7. *Contractor guarantee.* Contractors routinely give guarantees on their work, usually a year. The clause should state what the guarantee provides and when it expires.

8. *Permits and fees.* On some home improvement jobs a variety of permits will be required. This clause should state that all necessary permits have been obtained, and copies should be attached to the contract.

9. *Insurance.* It is the responsibility of the contractor to obtain insurance that will cover personal injury, property damage, and workmen's compensation. Copies of those coverages should be attached. (Incidentally, you can get "umbrella insurance" if you are not satisfied with either your insurance or the contractor's insurance. So-called umbrella

policies provide millions in protection for practically nothing.)

10. *Injury*. It should be stipulated that the contractor is liable for all damage or injury caused by the contractor or the subcontractor or their agents or employees.

11. *Contract changes*. It often happens that changes are made in a job—the homeowner doesn't like what's put in or sees something else he or she likes. These are known as change orders, and it should be stated in the contract that such changes will be *written down, with costs clearly stated, and become part of the contract.*

Here, not so incidentally, don't forget what lawyer Reynolds Graves calls "deducts." If you change something for something else—say, one sink for another—make sure that the price of the original item is deducted from the price of the job. Graves said that many people forget to do this and lose hundreds, even thousands, of dollars for products that are never used.

12. *Cleanup*. The contractor is responsible for cleaning up all debris and unwanted materials when the work is completed and is to leave the property "broom clean."

13. *Unused products and materials*. These can be returned to suppliers and can be credited to the homeowner. Unused materials that can't be returned can be sold to the contractor or gotten rid of at the discretion of the homeowner.

14. *Notice of recision*. Under federal law a contractor is

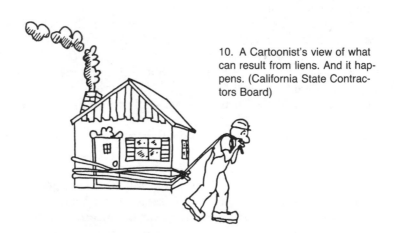

10. A Cartoonist's view of what can result from liens. And it happens. (California State Contractors Board)

required to furnish you with a notice of recision, which states that you have three days from the time you signed the contract to cancel it. To do so, you have to mail your notice to the contractor within those three days or else deliver it or have it delivered to him within that time. If you have emergency work that needs to be done, this recision clause can be waived. Also, it is only valid if the contract is signed at your home, not the contractor's place of business.

15. *Arbitration clause.* This clause would state that in the event of a dispute, it will be settled by the American Arbitration Association. This is an organization that has offices all over America and will be *much cheaper* to use for settling disputes than private attorneys. Some BBB's will also settle disputes by arbitration.

16. *Dated and signed by both the homeowner and the contractor.* A number of consumer agencies warn that no contract should have any blank spaces in it. And if anything is changed at a later date, both the contractor and consumer should initial the changes.

Do keep all your paperwork related to the job in one place. Having a separate folder for it is a good idea.

LIEN LAWS

All states have lien laws. They vary in the way they're written and implemented, though the thrust, as suggested in a number of places in this book, is the same: If the general contractor doesn't pay his suppliers or subcontractors, these people can lien—make a claim against—the homeowner for the money, and no "hold harmless" or other written documents from the contractor can protect the homeowner from the subs and suppliers.

In some states suppliers and subcontractors will serve a notice of lien on the homeowner before they begin a job. This is just a notice and doesn't mean anything more than that, except that the homeowner can't sell or transfer the property while the lien is on it.

In other states, however, no such notice is required: The homeowners will not know they can be liened.

If the GC doesn't pay his bills, the supplier or sub generally has a certain amount of time to "perfect" a lien against the homeowner's house or property. If he doesn't, then he loses his legal rights after that time (60 or 90 days is usual).

Assuming he dots all his *i*'s and crosses all his *t*'s, and that the homeowner doesn't respond, he will get his money. Many people have had their homes foreclosed by suppliers and subs, ending up with nothing but heartache. For example, if a home is worth $125,000 but is foreclosed, it might be sold for $30,000 on the courthouse steps. The lien is paid off from the proceeds of the sale, and the homeowner gets the balance—and loses tens of thousands of dollars in the process.

As you can see, it pays to become conversant with lien laws. They vary in severity, but all are dangerous.

In the state of Washington, for example, and many other states, if the supplier or subcontractor has dotted all his *i*'s and crossed all his *t*'s in "liening," it is very difficult to get out from under: You'll end up paying—or losing your property.

In New York reasonableness prevails. As lawyer Reynolds Graves says, "Good faith permeates the law. If the homeowner acted in good faith, then he's not going to have to pay."

But good faith, Graves points out, includes responding to the lien notice that the subcontractor or materials man files against him. "If he does not respond, then he can lose out." In other words, responding is tantamount to good faith.

At least one state, Michigan, protects its consumers wonderfully. There, according to a spokesperson, the state will pay off liens of a homeowner up to $75,000. Why? "We just don't want them to have to pay," says the spokesperson.

But, she adds, the contractor whom the homeowner dealt with must be *licensed*.

It is suggested that, to protect yourself, you have someone explain the lien law in your state. You could call the attorney general's office or contact a lawyer who specializes in remodeling contracts, as suggested in chapter 8. Of course, if you are hiring an attorney to write the contract, then he or she should know what you need to know.

Two other points: While a job is progressing, it won't hurt to ask subs or the crew members if they're being paid by the GC. The sooner you know, the better.

And, at the end of the job you must receive lien release forms from the subs and supplier before making final payment. Again, a GC can't give you a final release for subs or suppliers. Those are not the GC's rights to give.

WHAT'S WRONG WITH THESE CONTRACT SPECS?

As we have suggested throughout this book, contract specifications for materials and products usually don't have enough detail. In essence *they should have enough detail so that a clerk in a lumberyard or building-supply yard could read them and fill the order without further questions.* But that mostly isn't the case.

Why is this so?

I think, usually, because an inadequate list gives the contractor the option of using cheaper grades of product and materials. What he's written seems good, but only to someone who doesn't know any better.

If an architect has made out the list and it is not sufficiently specific, it can also be because he has the legal heebie-jeebies. In this day and age, when people sue you if you blink at them, architects like a degree of vagueness, both in materials and products and in plans, to let things be open to a little interpretation so that they can always claim, if things go wrong, "That's not what I meant." They're off the hook.

Following is a look at contract specs for a $100,000 plus extension, and where and why such specs would be deficient. Look for problems in these specs, and then check your knowledge with the itemized critique that follows. Next, check out the specs in the contract in the appendix of this book. Taken together, they should give you a good idea of what *detailed* really means.

The items in the contract are numbered 1 to 30.

SPECIFICATIONS

Work: Demolish existing 30-by-20-foot structure on the side and erect in its place 30-by-20-foot two-story addition following plans and specifications and add new 20-by-8-foot porch entry.

1. **Permits.** Obtained and fees paid by XYZ Corporation, Long Spear, Idaho.
2. **Debris.** Remove and cart away all debris from existing 30-by-20 foot structure. Chimney, foundations, and floor slabs to remain.
3. **Decks for floor.** Install new decks using 2-by-8-inch lumber on 16-inch centers on top of which is ⅓-inch plywood subflooring. Insulate lower deck only with batt R-19 insulation.
4. **Walls, exterior.** All exterior walls will be framed with 2-by-4-inch studs coverd with ¾-inch CDX plywood sheathing

and a layer of 15-pound felt and all walls insulated with R-13 insulation. Front and side of addition will be covered with wood shakes to match original. Rear will be covered with vinyl siding and brick veneer.

5. Ceilings. Constructed with 2-by-8-inch joists, 16 inches on center. Ceiling insulated with R-30 insulation.

6. Overhangs. Faced to match original with vinyl and aluminum.

7. Gutters. Install new gutters and leaders to match the existing gutters and leaders.

8. Windows. Install Andersen double-insulated vinyl-clad white windows as per plan and as follows: 5 Model # 3456 picture windows; 4 Model #3425 picture windows; 2 Model # 2345 casement windows; and 1 Model # C4432 casement window.

9. Patio doors. Install 2 Andersen white, vinyl-clad doors: 2 Model # 2345.

10. Entry door to addition: Install 3-foot-by-6-foot-8-inch white vinyl-clad door following plan. Also install fixed side windows as per plan. Remove existing door and close opening.

11. Deck. Construct 20-foot-by-5-inch cantilevered deck with 2-inch by 8-inch joists on 16-inch centers and supported with steel columns.

12. Stairs. Install new oak stairs as per plan. Option: Sheetrock with oak cap.

13. Interior doors. Install flush birch doors with 2¼ inch trim.

14. Fireplace. Install 42-inch-wide zero-clearance fireplace following plan using brick facing and slate hearth.

15. Existing entry. Close up using existing brick as required.

16. Walls and ceilings: Install ½ inch plasterboard (Sheetrock) for all new walls and ceilings and demolish and remove walls of living and dining room and install ½-inch Sheetrock. All Sheetrock will be taped and have three coats of spackle and the rear wall of living room 3⅜ inches of insulation.

17. Wall trim. All trim will be 2¼-inch clear pine, either clamshell profile.

18. Closets. Construct three closets as per plan.

19. Washer and dryer: Move as indicated on plan, completely hooked up and with washer placed on metal; or fiberglass drain.

20. Install American Standard lavatory on first floor, American Standard porcelain wash basin in laundry area. Install client's medicine cabinet and accessories. Formica vanity.

21. Full bathroom: Install American Standard tub, lavatory and toilet plus 36-inch-by-48-inch shower (fiberglass) with sliding glass (tempered) door. Install client's medicine cabinet and accessories.
22. Electrical facilities for addition: Increase electric service to 150 amps; install new breaker panels. Install 10 regular switches, one three-way switch, 18 duplex outlets, 2 GFCI's and 10 metal boxes for lights.
23. Bow window. Install Andersen double insulated glass window, vinyl-clad, and casement sidelight windows with screens.
24. Whole house fan. Cut vents and install 36-inch whole house fan above stairs on second floor.
25. Basement insulation: Install 6-inch batt insulation in basement ceiling.
26. Family room flooring. Install oak strip flooring (sanding and finishing not included).
27. Entry stoop. Install new concrete entry platform topped with slate. Construct overhang over entry following plans and redwood railings.
28. Kitchen. "Gut" existing room, remove all debris, and install all new appliances of client and "Marcus" oak cabinets following plan and with Formica post-formed top. Remove wall between kitchen and dining area, install 3-by-3-foot-5-inch casement window following plan. Install 22-by-25-inch stainless steel sink with Moen single-lever faucet and spray. Make all appliance hookups required. Electrical: Install high hat lights (75 watt) as per plan with 2 dimmer switches. Install metal (with foam core) rear entry door with double insulated glass.
29. Dining room. Remove existing walls and new walls as per plan. Construct floor so it is level with garage floor using oak flooring as per code. Install 2 duplex wall outlets.
30. Exclusions. Painting, heating, air conditioning, light fixtures, faucet sets, medicine cabinets and accessories, sheet goods and finishing floors not included in overall price quoted.

Accepted by:

_____   _____
                                        Owner

                                        _____
                                        Owner

Following is a list of the problems with each specification on pgs. 113–115.

1. Which permits? Which fees? What were they and how much did they cost?
2. Okay.
3. What kinds of 2 by 8s? Lumber varies in grade.
4. What kinds of studs? They vary in grade.
   "Vinyl siding"—what grade? It varies tremendously, from good stuff to garbage. What kind of brick veneer? This varies too. What about trim back there? Is this vinyl too?
5. Need more detail on framing lumber and what kind of asphalt/fiberglass roof shingles. They differ greatly in quality.
6. What grade of vinyl, what aluminum: .019, .024? What?
7. Seems okay, but why not specify? Maybe the matching gutter won't really be that close a match, or that good. Gutter varies in quality too.
8. Okay. The kind of information one could order with.
9. Okay.
10. Which "insulating metal exterior entry door"? They vary greatly in quality. Stanley? Gadgo? Which? What's the model number?
11. Maybe the lumber here is specified in the plans. But there is not a clue as to whether he's using redwood, cedar, pressure-treated, or whatever stock. Quality and look vary significantly, as does price.
12. How thick is the Sheetrock? What grade is the oak? Oak is good wood, but its grade matters.
13. "Flush birch doors"—what kind of flush doors? Hollow core, solid, what? The difference is like that between night and day. And what are the sizes?
14. Which brand fireplace?
15. Okay.
16. What is the R-value of 3⅝-inch insulation? Thickness does not tell you how effective insulation is; R-value factor does.
17. How much trim is involved here? Does the homeowner understand exactly what the contractor is thinking?
18. I can't see the plan, so I don't know if it's okay.
19. "Metal or fiberglass pan with drain"—whose, and what model? They vary in quality.

20. How thick is the Formica? It makes a difference. The thicker the better. Which American Standard lavatory? They vary in quality (and price).
21. Just whose "4-piece fiberglass shower unit" is it? Need the brand and the model number. Quality varies!
22. What color are the switches and outlets?
23. Andersen is good, but there are no model numbers for windows here. Model numbers militate against misunderstanding.
24. "Whole-house fan"? Whose? Quality varies greatly, from something you could mount on an airplane to the purest garbage. And who repairs the roof after it has vents cut through it?
25. Need R-value of insulation.
26. "Oak flooring"? This varies in grade. What is being used here? Clear, Select, Common?
27. What kind of slate? How thick? Color? Where's it from? Quality varies.
28. Whose stainless steel sink? Elkay? Kohler? American Standard? Brand X? What's the model number? Quality varies!

    " 'Moen' single-lever faucet with spray"? Is this their top-of-the-line model? What's its number?

    What are the model numbers of cabinets?

    "Rear entry door with insulating glass door"? Whose door? Just saying it's "metal type with urethane core" doesn't say much. Quality varies.
29. "Oak flooring"? What grade? "Sheetrock and insulate as per code"? What's "code"?
30. Don't understand what "sheet goods" are.

In sum, this contract could lead to a lot of misunderstanding because the homeowner may imagine one kind of quality while the contractor gives him or her another—and saves thousands in the process, and maybe starts a war.

Or, everything could work—for a while. But when it starts to deteriorate or fall apart the war would begin.

CHAPTER 9

Be There If You Can

As much as possible, you should try to be around when the job is being done at your home. It has a number of benefits.

For one thing, if problems or questions arise, you're there to give immediate input.

Also, when something is being done, you can see if it is what you anticipated. If it isn't, then you may want to change it. When you're there, you'll be able to do this sooner rather than later.

Being there on certain jobs where it is easy to get ripped off—those where it is virtually impossible to see the final product—will help militate against this happening.

Following are some typical jobs:

Concrete driveway. If you're not there, then you won't know how deep the contractor poured the concrete. Is it the four inches you contracted for, or three?

Asphalt driveway. How thick was the mix? You have to be there to see.

Wall insulation. Here I mean the kind that's blown into walls. To do this job properly, shingles have to be removed, holes drilled through the sheathing, and the insulation pumped in. You can't know this is being done unless you're there.

Paint job. If you've contracted for two coats, how can you know you're getting two? One heavy coat may cover the existing coat—and you'll never know (but your house will).

Roof jobs. If repairs are required on the roof, how will you know they've been done unless you're there?

Windows. If you've contracted to have insulation put in around those new windows, how will you know it's been done when all the trim is back in place?

And there are other jobs.

All this does not mean that you have to climb into a tree with binoculars and put a contractor under surveillance, or become what one contractor called "a total pain in the ass." No one likes to have someone breathing down his or her neck, but being there at critical points is important.

It can't hurt, but the happy fact, despite what has been said above, is that even if you aren't there or can't be there, you'll likely be fine. Because the guy swinging the paintbrush or the hammer or whatever won't be just anyone, but a carefully selected individual. *Carefully selected by you.* And it is times like these that you'll be happy you did all that hard work to find him; endured a little pain to avoid a lot!

SUMMING IT UP

Following are the main points in finding, hiring, and dealing with a contractor. Give yourself plenty of time to do it all.

- Learn as much as you can about the job.

- Decide how much you can afford. Research where to borrow the money.

- Get the names of 8 to 10 contractors, preferably all from friends, relatives, and neighbors—people you trust.

- Check them all at a local consumer agency and BBB for complaints and for registration or licensing.

- Call the contractors who remain and invite their bids on the job.

- Take multiple bids (five or six) on the job, making sure all contractors are bidding on the same job. Keep careful notes on what each says.

- Check contractor you like in a very detailed way
- Visit his place of business.
- Ask the supplier about him. Does he pay his bills?
- Check out a couple of jobs he's done (from a large list he has provided) including one in progress. Ask his customers about him.

- Write a *detailed* contract. Use a lawyer if the job has many components, such as a room addition—but get a *remodeling* lawyer. Make sure you thoroughly understand the lien law in your state; and protect yourself against it. *Write the contract so that the contractor never gets ahead of you on the payments.*

- Be on the job whenever possible.

PART 2

BUYER'S GUIDE TO HOME IMPROVEMENTS

As suggested, you should learn as much as you can about the job you are contemplating before calling in any contractor. That's the goal of this section: to give you as detailed advice as possible on particular jobs and to help you evaluate the kind of job you want and can afford—and help you not to get victimized.

Here both improvement and maintenance jobs have been lumped under the category of home improvement, though the distinction is sometimes not so clear. As mentioned, what the work is called can have an important bearing in terms of new taxes being assessed on the improvement. Maintenance and repairs aren't taxed; improvements are.

Topics appearing in **boldface** can be found in more detail in other sections of part 2.

Each of the improvements is cast in the following form:

IMPROVEMENT: NAME OF THE JOB

Products/Materials

What is commonly used on a job; what's quality, what isn't.

How the Job Is Done

How the improvement or maintenance job is commonly done.

Workmanship

Signs of good—and bad—workmanship.

Possible Rip-offs

Special things to be wary of if the job has a history of rip-offs.

Do-It-Yourself

Evaluation of a job in terms of whether it can be done by the novice do-it-yourselfer. Sometimes great savings are possible.

Cost

This part of the form gives a sampling of job costs. It is by no means comprehensive or complete and is only intended to give you a sense of what to expect. A number of things make it impracticable to be definitive here. For one thing, costs of jobs vary greatly all over America, mainly because of labor charges. For example, in Charleston, South Carolina, a carpenter will charge $10 an hour plus fringes; in San Francisco the same carpenter gets *$23 plus fringes.* According to Walt Stoeppelwerth, who conducts business seminars for contractors nationwide, job costs vary 35 to 40 percent. The charts provided, which come courtesy of *Remodeling* magazine, provide common costs for jobs nationwide and show costs for labor, materials, and "markup"—overhead plus profit.

NATIONWIDE JOB COSTS

Prices for contracting jobs can vary widely from region to region. The following charts will give you the average price for the nation, east, south, midwest, and west for several projects, as well as a detailed project description. While these prices aren't set in stone, they will be useful when you do your initial budgeting.

Source: *Remodeling* magazine, October 1995. Copyright © Hanley-Wood, Inc.

TWO-STORY ADDITION
Project Description:

Over a crawlspace, add a 24 by 16-foot two-story wing with a first-floor family room and a second-floor bedroom with full bath. Addition features a prefabricated fireplace in the family room, 11 windows, and an atrium-style exterior door. Floors are carpeted and walls are painted drywall. The 5 by 8-foot bathroom has a fiberglass bath/shower, standard-grade toilet, wood vanity with ceramic sink top, ceramic tile flooring, and mirrored medicine cabinet with light strip above; bathroom walls are wallpapered. Add new heating and cooling system to handle the addition.

National Average: $50,415
East Average: $54,374
South Average: $44,121
Midwest Average: $49,514
West Average: $53,649

MINOR KITCHEN REMODEL
Project Description:

In a functional but dated 200-square-foot kitchen with 30 lineal feet of cabinetry and countertops, refinish existing cabinets, install new energy-efficient wall oven and cooktop, new laminate countertops, and new mid-priced sink and faucet, wall covering and resilient flooring, and repaint. Job includes new raised-panel wood doors on cabinets.

National Average: $8,014
East Average: $8,619
South Average: $7,035
Midwest Average: $7,898
West Average: $8,506

MAJOR KITCHEN REMODEL
Project Description:

Update an out-moded, 200-square-foot kitchen with design and installation of new cabinets, laminate countertops, mid-priced sink and faucet, energy-efficient wall oven, cooktop, and ventilation system, built-in microwave, dishwasher, disposer, and custom lighting. Add new resilient floor. Finish with painted woodwork and ceiling. Include 30 lineal feet of semi-custom-grade wood cabinets and counter space, including a 3 by 5-foot center island.

National Average: $23,243
East Average: $24,787
South Average: $20,692
Midwest Average: $22,958
West Average: $24,534

BATHROOM ADDITION
Project Description:

Add a second full bath to a house with one or one-and-a-half baths. The 6 by 8-foot bath should be within the existing floor plan in an inconspicuous spot convenient to the bedrooms. Include cultured marble vanity top, molded sink, standard bathtub with shower, low-profile toilet, lighting, mirrored medicine cabinet, linen storage, vinyl wallpaper, and ceramic tile floor and walls in tub area.

National Average: $11,639
East Average: $12,702
South Average: $9,973
Midwest Average: $11,436
West Average: $12,445

BATHROOM REMODEL
Project Description:

Update an existing 5 by 9-foot bathroom that is at least 25 years old with new standard-size tub, toilet, and solid surface vanity counter with integral double sink. Install new lighting, faucet, mirrored medicine cabinet, and ceramic tile floor and walls in tub/shower area (vinyl wallpaper elsewhere).

National Average: $8,365
East Average: $9,116
South Average: $7,210
Midwest Average: $8,234
West Average: $8,901

MASTER SUITE
Project Description:

On a house with two or three bedrooms, add over a crawlspace a 24 by 16-foot master bedroom with a walk-in closet. Master bath includes dressing area, whirlpool tub, separate ceramic tile shower, and a double-bowl vanity. Bedroom floor is carpeted; floor in bath is ceramic tile.

National Average: $35,560
East Average: $38,644
South Average: $30,673
Midwest Average: $35,075
West Average: $37,850

FAMILY-ROOM ADDITION
Project Description:

In a style and location appropriate to the existing house, add a 16 by 25-foot, light-filled room on a new crawlspace foundation with wood joist floor framing, matching wood siding on exterior walls, and matching existing fiberglass roof. Include drywall interior with batt insulation; 180 square feet of glass, including atrium-style exterior (doors, windows, and two operable skylights); and hardwood tongue-and-groove floor. Tie into existing heating and cooling.

National Average: $32,024
East Average: $34,583
South Average: $27,681
Midwest Average: $31,700
West Average: $34,131

HOME OFFICE ADDITION
Project Description:

Convert an existing 12 by 12-foot room into a home office. Install custom cabinets configured for desk, computer workstation, and overhead storage, and 20 feet of plastic laminate desktop. Rewire room for computer, fax machine, and other electronic equipment as well as cable and telephone lines. Include drywall interior and commercial-grade, level-loop carpeting.

National Average: $7,709
East Average: $8,282
South Average: $6,838
Midwest Average: $7,583
West Average: $8,132

ATTIC BEDROOM
Project Description:

In a house with two or three bedrooms, convert unfinished attic with rafters to 15 by 15-foot bedroom and 5 by 7-foot shower/bath. Add four new windows and a 15-foot shed dormer. Insulate and finish ceiling and walls. Carpet unfinished floor. Extend existing heating and central air-conditioning to new space. Retain existing stairs.

National Average: $21,795
East Average: $23,646
South Average: $18,848
Midwest Average: $21,425
West Average: $23,262

REPLACE SIDING
Project Description:

Replace 1,250 square feet of existing siding with new vinyl or aluminum siding, including trim.
Option: Use painted wood siding and trim instead of aluminum or vinyl.

National Average: $5,211
East Average: $5,555
South Average: $4,513
Midwest Average: $5,133
West Average: $5,643

REPLACE WINDOWS
Project Description:

Replace 10 existing 3 by 5-foot windows with aluminum-clad windows, including new trim. Replace sashes, frames, and casings.
Option: Replace sashes only.

National Average: $5,488
East Average: $5,840
South Average: $4,855
Midwest Average: $5,453
West Average: $5,805

DECK ADDITION
Project Description:

Add a 16 by 20-foot deck of pressure-treated pine supported by 4 x 4 posts set into concrete footings. Include a built-in bench, railings, and planter, also of pressure-treated pine.
Option: Same as above but use cedar or redwood.

National Average: $6,528
East Average: $7,107
South Average: $5,601
Midwest Average: $6,444
West Average: $6,960

The labor and materials charges for each job outlined in Pt. 2 (unless otherwise noted) are based on average charges in the Baltimore–Washington area. If you want a complete, detailed guide, I suggest you get *Home Tech Remodeling and Renovation Cost Estimator*. They have an 800 number. Or check your library. You can find area-specific prices that focus very closely, narrowing down costs according to the zip code one lives in. However, based on the idea of getting multiple estimates, I don't think such specifics are needed.

In some cases the grade of material is specified. In others it is not. When the grade is not mentioned, assume it is "builder's grade," the lowest grade available.

Also, costs outlined in Pt. 2 (unless noted) do not include markup. The costs listed here are for *labor and materials only*. Markup for overhead could range from 20 to 70 percent (usually bigger firms), and more if someone is very greedy (or desperate). Stoeppelwerth thinks a contractor should charge 50 percent markup to survive. In other words, if labor and materials cost $1,000, the job should be marked up to $1,500. So don't be surprised or dismayed if the job costs are a lot higher. Our goal here again is only to give you a sense of the range of prices.

Only information relevant to the particular improvement has been included in each entry. If a job is clearly not for the do-it-yourselfer, for example, that portion of the entry has not been included. If workmanship is classically not a problem, this hasn't been included, and so on. The information for the jobs was derived from surveying consumer agencies in all fifty states plus Guam, the Virgin Islands, American Samoa, and Puerto Rico. (Tragically, I never heard from American Samoa.)

Finally, before going to the specific improvement you plan, it is suggested that you read the three sections that follow on how a house is built and how plumbing and electrical systems work. It is good to have a context within which to think, and when it comes to home improvements, the context is the home.

DO IT YOURSELF—WITH CARE

If you embark on a do-it-yourself project, do make sure you do it right. Some people get involved in doing their own tilework or Sheetrocking or flooring—and the results are less than professional-looking.

The problem is that other people will be able to detect amateurish efforts easily, and if these happen to be home buyers, says John Heyn, of the American Society of Home Inspectors, "it will lower the value of the house."

Do it yourself—but only if you can end up with a professional-looking job.

How a House Is Built

Everything is built—from the Brooklyn Bridge to your house—starting the same way: on a solid foundation. The earth itself is usually too soft to withstand a lot of weight without shifting.

First the ground is staked out with string and batter boards—nailed-together boards used as markers—and the area excavated and the soil made firm.

The footings—flat, thick strips of masonry a couple of feet wide—are installed; they define the perimeter of the house. Then the foundation is installed.

There are three kinds. One kind, popular in Florida and other warm areas, is the slab, a deck of concrete at ground level.

Another, the full foundation, is basically a slab but with high walls, made of masonry or block, around it. This type of foundation forms the basement walls of the homes it is installed in.

The third kind of foundation is the crawl-space type. Here there are footings and short walls, but no slab. Inside the short foundation walls is the ground.

Footings for all foundations go below the frost line, below

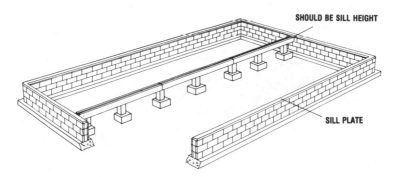

SHOULD BE SILL HEIGHT

SILL PLATE

11. Footings, foundation, and girder. The sill has also been placed, ready for framing. This is a crawl-space foundation. (American Plywood Association)

which the earth does not freeze. If they didn't, when the earth froze and expanded, it could shift the foundation.

Once the foundation is in, the house framing goes in.

On a full and crawl-space foundation the sill goes on first. This is double boards—2 by 8s—laid flat and bolted to the top of foundation walls. A termite shield, which is a section of bent-over metal—sheet aluminum works well—is sandwiched between the boards and the foundation. To install the sill, holes are drilled into it to align with the bolts that have been set in the concrete while it was wet.

In a slab foundation a shoe is substituted for a sill. You might think of the shoe as the bottom of the walls. This is composed of doubled-up 2 by 4s, laid flat and bolted to the slab.

Joists are installed next on the full or crawl-space foundation. First, 2 by 6 or 2 by 8 perimeter or so-called rim joists are installed to form three edges of a box on top of the foundation; the fourth side of the box is the house itself.

Then other joists are set on edge and span the box, one end of each joist resting on the sill and the other on the ledger strip fastened to the house. The joists are placed 16 inches apart and are nailed to the sill, and ledger strip and nails are also driven through the perimeter joists into the ends of the other joists.

Normally joists are laid across the shortest house dimen-

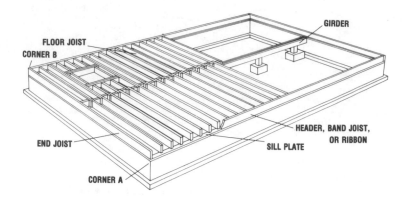

12. House with some of floor joists in place. Joists are given different names—lap joists, ribbon joists, and so forth—based on their use, but they are all really just joists. Corners A and B show views of joists looking straight down. (American Plywood Association)

sion. If the joist span is more than 16 feet, then girders are used as additional support. These are simply sandwiches of 2 by 6s nailed together or a metal I beam (in profile it looks like the letter I) that are set on Lally columns, round metal posts, or concrete posts. Joists are also reinforced by metal or wood bridging—short crisscross pieces—which tie the members together.

No joists are necessary for a slab foundation. The slab forms the basic floor. The 2-by-4 shoe forms the bottommost member of the wall.

On a full or crawl-space foundation the subflooring, or deck, goes in next. This may be individual boards but is usually 4-by-8 sheets of plywood nailed tightly to the joists.

Once the deck is in, the walls are installed.

First a shoe is nailed around the edge of the deck with openings cut in it where the doors will be.

Then stud walls are erected on the deck. Each wall consists of 2-by-4 vertical members (but in some localities 2 by 6s to allow for more insulation); doubled-up corner studs; and, to provide a recess for wall material and plates, members across the tops of the studs.

The common method of making walls is to mark the ends of stud locations on the shoe. Using these marks as a guide,

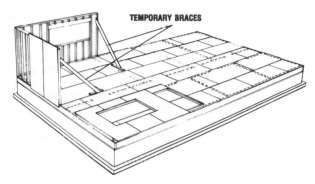

13. The plywood deck is almost entirely installed, as are a pair of walls and two sheathing panels on the walls. (American Plywood Association)

the top or cross-members of the walls, the plates, are correspondingly marked. Normally these marks are 16 inches on center, or OC—16 inches apart from one to the other.

The studs or vertical wall members are nailed to the plate following the marks, then lifted up and placed on the shoe following the marks. Then they are toenailed to the shoe. Headers—beefy horizontal cross-members—will also be installed and openings allowed where the windows and doors will be.

With walls up, window and door framing is completed. The openings left for doors and windows are known as rough openings.

In a two-or-more-story house, joists are laid across the tops of the plates, another deck laid, more walls, and so on. If just one story, then 2 by 4s—called ceiling beams because of this use—are installed.

The final framing members are the rafters. These are cut with ends notched to fit against the tops of the plates, with the other ends angled to lean against a central board called a ridge board. To make life easier, the ends of the rafters on the plate will be directly above the studs. If you look at the house, you will see studs and rafters in alignment.

Next sheathing boards, or plywood sheathing, is nailed to the outside of the house and then building paper or a house wrap such as Tyvek, is secured to the sheathing. First, though, all fixtures will be brought inside the structure—

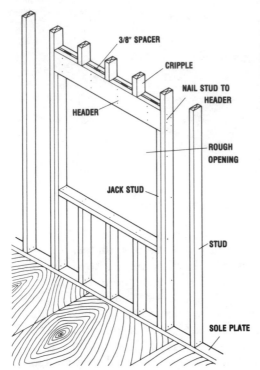

3/8" SPACER

CRIPPLE

NAIL STUD TO HEADER

HEADER

ROUGH OPENING

JACK STUD

STUD

SOLE PLATE

14. Close-up of a window's rough opening. It contains doubled-up boards, a header at the top, and double studs—jack studs on the side. Rough openings for doors are done the same way. Windows and doors are nailed directly into these openings, and extra-beefy framing is required to support them.

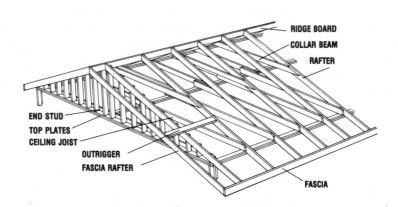

RIDGE BOARD

COLLAR BEAM

RAFTER

END STUD

TOP PLATES

CEILING JOIST

OUTRIGGER

FASCIA RAFTER

FASCIA

15. Completed roof framing. (American Plywood Association)

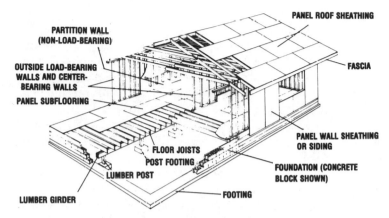

16. How a complete house is framed. Note the load-bearing and partition walls. Partition walls divide the space; load-bearing ones divide and support the house weight. (American Plywood Association)

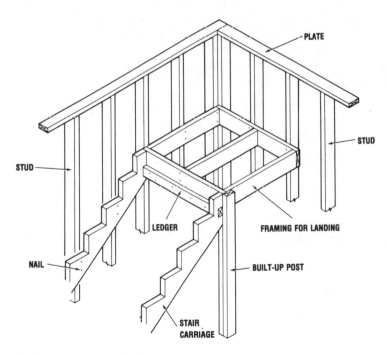

17. How stairs are typically framed.

the builder wants to make sure he can get them in before closing the house up.

With the sheathing in, the siding and roofing are applied and the windows and doors installed. When the house is thus completed—and is watertight—it is called the shell.

Meanwhile, as the shell is being done, the plumbing, electrical, and heating systems are being installed.

When they are in, insulation is installed between the wall studs; then flooring, Sheetrock wall, and ceiling materials are installed.

The last carpenter in is the trim carpenter. He installs the molding and trim and gives the house its finished appearance. He is followed by the painters and others, who add the final cosmetic touches.

18. The house is covered with building paper, or a house wrap, such as Tyvek.

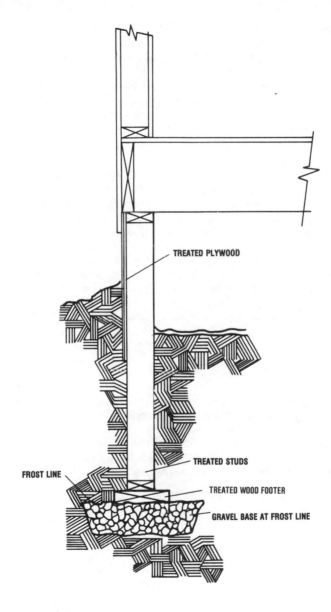

19. Side view of crawl-space foundation, this one made with a treated wood foundation instead of block or concrete.

WHICH WOOD IS BEST?

Just as with other products, the basic lumber used for building comes in grades. There are a number of grading systems in the country, and things tend to get complicated. Rather than delve into these, what follow are the recommendations of the Small Homes Council of the University of Illinois at Champaign–Urbana on what's good to use on particular jobs. Not all wood will be available in all areas, but the contractor should be able to get at least within each use category, and of course what is used should be specified in the contract. The grade will be stamped on the boards.

(Plywood is another much-used wood product that also has a fairly complicated grading system, and there are a number of other products as well. Individual sections contain our recommendations depending on the particular use, such as roof decking, wall sheathing, floor underlayment, and so on.)

Sill. Use Standard or No. 2 cedar, cypress, or redwood for the best job. Douglas fir, western larch, and southern yellow pine may also be used—in the same grades—but are not as good.

Joists/rafters: Douglas fir, western larch, and southern yellow pine are the best woods to use. Second-best are cypress, eastern and western hemlock, redwood, and yellow poplar. Use grade No. 2.

Studs. Use Stud-grade cypress, Douglas fir, western larch, southern yellow pine. Second-best are white fir, hemlock, white pine, and sugar pine in the same grades.

Plates: Use Standard or No. 2 Douglas fir, western larch, southern yellow pine. Second-best would be cypress, white fir, hemlock, and redwood in the same grades.

How a Plumbing
System Works

Typically water starts its journey to a home from a reservoir, where it is passed through a water-purifying plant, then proceeds—thanks to pressure applied at the water plant—along main pipes to end-use places.

It enters a house via a main pipe, which is tapped off the one coming from the water plant.

When a faucet or other water-using device is activated, the water flows. It passes through a main meter, which records its use, then branches out into hot-and-cold-water supply pipes, usually ½ inch in diameter.

These pipes travel side by side throughout the house, except that the hot-water pipe also routes the water through the heating plant before continuing its side-by-side journey.

The pipes end their run at the fixtures, the end users.

At various points in the system there are valves that control flow: the main house valve, which controls flow to the entire house, and individual valves, which control flow along the pipes. There are also valves under sinks, lavatories, and toilets so that you can turn them off at specific spots. It is good to learn where these valves are so that you can turn off the water in the event of an emergency, such

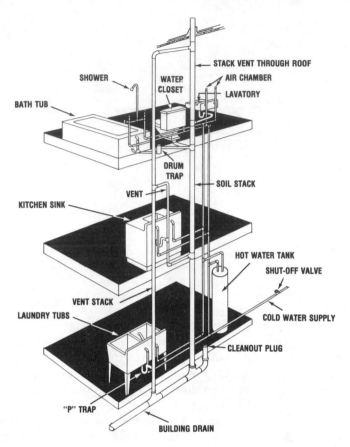

20. Typical plumbing system.

as a burst pipe. Of course if you know where the main is, you can just turn that off.

The other part of the plumbing system is the DWV, or drain-waste-vent system. This system eliminates waste and water from the house and at the same time vents it.

The core or spine of the DWV system is the stack, a central pipe—usually 4 inches in diameter—which runs vertically through the house, and to which all drain lines (those connected to sinks and lavatories) and waste lines (those connected to toilets) are connected by smaller pipes.

The DMV system operates by gravity only, with all the

pipes in it sloped to spill waste into the stack pipes, or stack. (The old joke is that a plumber only needs to know two things: Payday is Friday and shit runs downhill.) The waste passes through the stack and to a building drain, which is also sloped and which passes the waste to a sewer, cesspool, or septic system.

Gases build up within the waste system. To prevent these from backing up into the toilets, lavatories and sinks have traps. In sinks or lavatories these are simply curved sections of pipe, which trap water in the curved section, providing a seal of water against the gases backing up. Toilets are designed with a trap inside to similarly trap water and seal the gases off.

There is also a big trap—a curved section of pipe—at the bottom of the stack, which gives access to the stack itself and to the pipe running to the sewer. This trap (and others) allows lines to be probed if they need clearing.

The stack pipe serves two functions: While it routes all waste and water to the sewer, it also vents the gases and allows outside air pressure to act on water, pushing it downward once a toilet is flushed or a sink stopper lifted.

Plumbers are licensed for one main reason: Experience is required to ensure that pipes are set up so that water and waste systems never meet. That can cause sickness, even death.

How an Electrical System Works

An electrical system works like a plumbing system. The electricity enters the house by means of one main line, which feeds off high-power lines, which run from pole to pole (the highest lines carry current; the lines below this are telephone lines). The current begins its run from the electric-power plant.

The electricity feeds into the house and is divided up at the fuse or circuit-breaker box, which is usually in the basement and feeds various circuits: separate wires that snake through the walls and ceilings of the house and that terminate in switches and outlets.

Electricity is always on, that is, power is always being fed to the outlet. When something is plugged into an outlet, it becomes part of the process; the electricity courses through the wire in the device, or lamp, and powers it, then returns to the power plant, where it begins its instantaneous journey back again.

Switches control the power through a particular circuit. Turn one on and the power flows; turn it off and power doesn't reach the device.

Power is measured in terms of amperes, or amps, and voltage. Voltage is the push or pressure exerted on the current, while amps is the amount. Amps times volts gives wattage. Most homes have 110 volts and 60 amps, but many people increase that by installing new wiring to accommodate the increased power needs of today's modern living. In other words, there are more devices available today for use, but you do need the power to operate them.

The fuse box or circuit-breaker box is a safety feature. Fuses and circuit breakers—which are essentially switches—are part of every circuit, and if something goes wrong on the circuit—say, too much power is going through a line—then the fuse blows or the circuit breaker trips, thereby preventing the line from heating up and possibly starting a fire. Individual fuses and circuit breakers control individual lines.

Most devices can work on 110 volts of power. But some have heavier power needs: up to double that. These devices are on separate double circuits, which furnish 220 volts of power. But the principles remain the same. Power in, bounce back to the power station, then back to the device—all in much less than the wink of an eye.

More Space

IMPROVEMENT: ATTIC CONVERSION

Products/Materials

The main materials used in converting an attic to a living area are framing lumber and **Sheetrock**.

Framing **lumber** will be required for walls, ceilings, and perhaps floors to beef up the floor framing. For walls and ceilings so-called Stud-grade 2 by 4s are good. If larger lumber members are required, then No. 2 Construction grade is recommended.

Sheetrock is commonly used to form wall and ceiling material. The ½-inch thickness is the minimum.

A staircase is also usually required for access. This can be either custom-built at great expense or prebuilt. A **circular staircase** works very well and occupies very little space. The attic may have pull-down stairs, but this is essentially a ladder and is inconvenient and unsafe for heavy use.

Subflooring is also required. This may be sheathing-grade **plywood;** 1-by-4 boards; or 1-by-6 tongue-and-groove (T&G) boards. The latter have lips or tongues, which are slipped into grooves of adjacent boards as the material is nailed fast. The boards are good when access to the attic is too small to allow 4-by-8 plywood panels in.

A variety of cosmetic materials—ceiling, floor, and wall coverings—will be used. The kinds and grades of materials that can be used are discussed in other sections of the book.

Plumbing, heating, and electrical materials will vary from installation to installation. Tips on the various products and materials are also detailed in other sections.

How the Job Is Done

A prime concern of the contractor in doing an attic remodeling is the joists, or floor-framing members in the attic. These must be strong enough to support the weight of the products, materials, and furniture that will be going into the attic, as well as of the people who will be living there.

The joists are normally 2 by 8s on 16-inch centers.

If the 2 by 8s extend more than 14 feet long, they must be buttressed. One way the contractor may do this is by nailing another 2 by 8 of the same length to every other joist.

If the joists are 2 by 6s, the contractor will have to buttress them using other methods.

Once the joists are ready, the subflooring is nailed to them, then the walls are erected, as in building a house.

An attic converted to living area commonly contains knee, gable-end, and partition walls. Kneewalls are short walls installed along the long sides of the house, as opposed to tall gable-end walls at the short, or gable ends, of the house; partition walls are what are used to segment the various living areas.

The kneewalls are usually made first; they are commonly made 4 feet high so that 4-by-8 drywall panels can be cut in half and nailed on with no waste.

There are a few ways to build the kneewalls. Commonly contractors will nail a 2-by-4 board, or shoe flat, onto the floor, then toenail 2-by-4 studs to the shoe and to 2-by-4 plates, just as when building a house. The plates are usually nailed to the rafters. This process takes any sags out of the roof, but may make the ceiling nails below pop a bit, a malady that is easily corrected.

Next, ceiling beams are nailed between the rafters. Placement of these beams dictates the height of the ceiling. The ceiling should be a minimum of 7 feet and a maximum of 8 feet.

Once the beams are in, the partition walls are installed. Also, as in a house, these are composed of 2 by 4s on 16-inch centers and are nailed to beams and plates. Door openings are cut and framed out of these walls.

With framing completed, any windows are installed and the other systems put in.

Ventilation-wise, contractors usually install gable-end louvers (slatted windows) at both ends of the attic so that rising heat passes out of them.

A fan with a thermostat is also often used. This is armed to go on when the heat builds up, sucking hot air out and pulling air in through louvers.

Many attics are supplied with heat by simply extending the heating system in the house. Or sometimes a separate baseboard heater with its own thermostat is installed; if the attic is used as a guest room, the heater can be turned on as needed, saving money.

Another money-saving idea is to have individual thermostats in each of the rooms; these are turned on as needed.

Plumbing, if any, is usually planned so that the fixtures are close to plumbing water and waste lines; the further away they are, the more they cost to install.

The electrical system is normally tied in to the existing one.

The insulation is then installed. Batts (15½-inch wide sections) are usually used. The R-value of the insulation used will depend on the climate of the particular area.

Sheetrock is installed after the other systems are in, and then the cosmetic aspects of the job—flooring and wall and ceiling coverings—are installed.

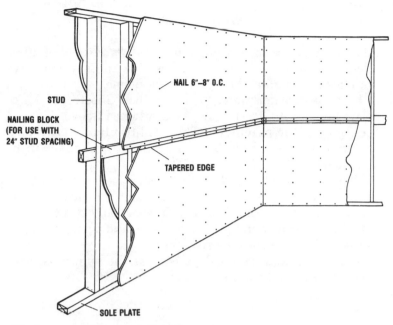

STUD

NAILING BLOCK
(FOR USE WITH
24″ STUD SPACING)

NAIL 6″–8″ O.C.

TAPERED EDGE

SOLE PLATE

21. A common way of installing Sheetrock.

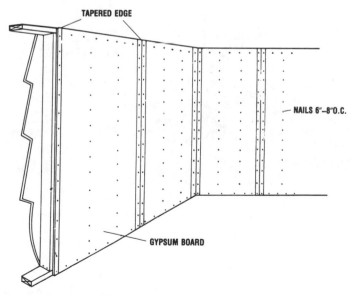

TAPERED EDGE

NAILS 6″–8″O.C.

GYPSUM BOARD

22. Sheetrock can also be applied vertically.

Workmanship

Some contractors may want to use 2 by 3s instead of 2 by 4s for wall-framing members (studs), but these are simply not strong enough and can lead to problems.

If the contractor wants to use ⅜-inch Sheetrock, don't allow him to; it's too flimsy. As mentioned above, ½-inch Sheetrock is the minimum. (There is little if any price difference between ½-inch and ⅜-inch Sheetrock, but ½-inch weighs more.)

When the Sheetrock is in, it's taped, sometimes by a person who installed the Sheetrock, but usually by a specialist known as a spackler. Some spacklers use only two coats of "mud" (joint compound), but three—two and a polish coat— is best simply because it's smoother.

Taping will take a few days because the mud must dry completely between coats.

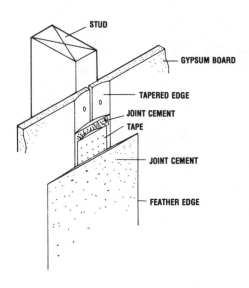

23. Sealing a joint with tape and mud.

Do-It-Yourself

Framing out an attic requires experience and precise cutting of framing members and should be left to the professionals.

Sheetrocking is also a job for the pros (it's too difficult for an inexperienced person to get the mud smooth the first time out).

Systems such as electrical and plumbing should also be done by pros; indeed, the building code may require this, and having electrical work done by an unlicensed electrician may void your fire insurance.

Applying paint, some wallcoverings (some are very difficult), and floor tile are within the capability of the novice do-it-yourselfer.

Cost

$30 per square foot.

IMPROVEMENT: FINISHING A BASEMENT

Products/Materials

The main materials used in a basement refinishing are furring strips, framing members, wall paneling, ceiling tile, and flooring. Enhancing the plumbing or electrical systems may also be required, including new fixtures if a bath is being installed.

Furring strips are 1-by-2 boards used to level walls in preparation for paneling; framing members may be 2 by 3s or 2 by 4s, depending on whether they are used to provide a level wall surface or partition walls.

Paneling comes in a wide variety of colors, styles, and quality.

Ceiling tiles are usually the acoustical type, but other things may be used.

Flooring is usually **sheet vinyl,** but may be anything you wish, as long as it is rated for installation in a basement.

24. The best way to get a level surface for paneling in the basement is to install 2 by 4s.

How the Job Is Done

The first thing a contractor will usually consider is whether or not the basement has a water or moisture problem. In some cases a bad water problem—such as a high water table that creates constant leaks—will make the job unfeasible. In most cases, however, waterproofing a basement is simple and a do-it-yourself job. It amounts to applying a thick water-proofing paint. It is a good idea to waterproof before finishing even if there is no sign of leakage. A leak could develop, and if this occurs it could cause damage that won't be seen for a while.

Framing out for the paneling will be done first. On masonry walls, paneling can be secured to furring, which is itself secured to the walls by masonry nails or to 2-by-3 walls built next to the masonry walls.

When the wall framing is complete, partition walls are made from 2 by 4s. Paneling is installed next, followed by wall and ceiling materials.

Ceiling in a basement is usually the suspended type to hide all the pipes and wire and framing members (see page 270).

Workmanship

Using 2 by 3s instead of 2 by 4s for partition walls can create problems: The 2 by 3s are simply not strong enough to support the paneling. Depending on its strength, paneling may be secured directly to the framing members, or these will be Sheetrocked first.

Securing paneling to furring strips on masonry walls is not as good as installing the panels on separate 2-by-3 walls. For one thing the masonry nails can chip the walls, and unless the furring strips are carefully leveled and trued up,

25. Remodeled attic. Kneewalls meet the slope of the roof. (Courtesy of Kentile Floors Inc.)

the paneling will not be as true as on a separate 2-by-3 wall that can be built true and level.

Do-It-Yourself

Framing is too precise a job for the novice to do. Paneling is definitely within the scope of the careful beginner. Flooring and ceiling materials may also be do-it-yourself jobs, depending on the type of material selected. For example, installing floor tiles is a do-it-yourself job, whereas installing sheet flooring is not, because cutting it to fit precisely around the edges of the room is very difficult.

Cost

$18 per square foot.

Dormers

Dormers raise the roof to some extent, allowing new headroom for walking, which translates into new space.

Two kinds of dormers are common: gable and shed, so described because of their shapes. (A gable dormer is also known as a doghouse type.)

Dormers are generally the least expensive type of improvement to do that involves modifying house framing.

IMPROVEMENT: GABLE DORMER

Products/Materials

The same kinds of products and materials, except fewer, are used in building a dormer as are used in building a house, namely, framing **lumber**, **sheathing**, **building paper**,

Sheetrock, window(s), flashings, and trim. And as usual one should strive to use the same quality materials as you would in any of the other projects. For example, you'd want to use **Stud-grade** studs in the wall framing and **No. 2-grade lumber** for the rafters. Because part of the roof and the interior surfaces are destroyed in the building, new materials must also be used here.

To determine quality, see "Room Additions," page 157.

How the Job Is Done

First the roof is opened up. This is usually done with a circular saw, cutting a rectangular opening through the roof between the rafters where the dormer is to go. Above all, the contractor will not want to cut any rafters he doesn't have to cut.

The inside of this opening is then beefed up by nailing new rafters to the insides of the existing one and then building the walls and roof of the dormer up from this.

The dormer is then finished like a minihouse. The window—or windows—are installed, then building paper, wall and roof sheathing, trim, and then siding and roofing.

Workmanship

The sign of a good dormer (or any addition, for that matter) is that it doesn't look added. It should blend, as much as possible, into the rest of the house.

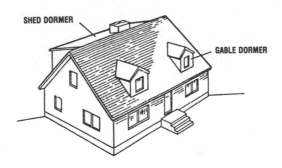

26. Two kinds of dormers.

Cost

$2,060 base price, plus $18 per square foot for good-quality materials and labor.

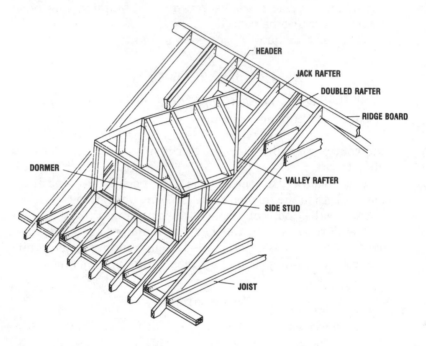

27. Dormer framing.

IMPROVEMENT: SHED DORMER

Products/Materials

The same materials that are used for the gable dormer are used for the shed dormer, except even more of them, since it involves a larger area.

How the Job Is Done

Again, the job is done the same way a gable dormer is. The roof is opened up, a framework built, **windows** installed, wall and roof sheathing installed, and siding and roofing put on.

Cost

$2,060 base price plus $11 per square foot for good-quality materials and labor.

Room Additions

Adding a room or rooms to a home is one of the more complex improvements that can be done, but it's not something that should elude understanding, even by the average person. Essentially it is like adding another house to the existing house using the same products, materials, and construction methods, but on a much smaller scale. I suggest that you read the section on how a house is built to get a better grasp of what is involved.

IMPROVEMENT: ROOM ADDITIONS

Products/Materials

As mentioned, the same kinds of materials are used in an addition as for a house, plus used materials; that is, materials such as siding and roofing are carefully removed from the house and reused on the addition in order to help it blend in better. **Sheetrock**, framing **lumber**, **roofing**, **siding**, and other materials are all used.

How the Job Is Done

As with a house, the first step is to stake out the addition on the ground, then draw strings between the stakes to mark it.

The area is then excavated beneath the frost line, and masonry **footings** and **foundation** are installed. Normally the top of the addition foundation will be level with the house foundation, and everything will be added with a view toward making the new floor level with the existing floor.

Sill plates and **joists** go in next. Joists are usually installed on 16-inch centers, with one end of each resting on a perimeter joist (one that is parallel to the house) and the other secured to a ledger strip attached to the house. Siding will have been removed to the sheathing, where the ledger strip is located. Later, removed shingles can be used to fill in around the perimeter of the new addition.

The **subflooring**, either plywood or boards, is installed on top of the joists, and **underlayment**, which will be the material directly beneath the **finished flooring**, is installed on it. This is known, as mentioned elsewhere in this book, as the deck.

For convenience the walls—which consist of studs nailed between sole and plates—are pushed up and braced in place. As usual, corner studs are specially constructed for strength and to allow a lip for installing siding.

Tip: Make sure all plumbing or other **fixtures** are brought inside the house while the house is open enough to do so; some fixtures are too big to fit through windows and doors.

The rafters are then secured to the top of the walls and tied to the house with other members.

Windows and any doors are installed. The sheathing is

nailed to the wall and the roof. Building paper is stapled to the sheathing; laths help hold it tightly to the wall. Or else Tyvek, a material that cuts down on air infiltration, is stapled on.

Sheathing and roofing materials are applied.

Inside, with the framing still open, wiring and plumbing pipes and fixtures are installed.

Next, walls and ceilings are Sheetrocked, trim is installed, and flooring laid. Finally, finish materials are applied.

Workmanship

See other sections: **roofing**, **Sheetrock**, **siding**, and so forth.

Possible Rip-offs

See other sections.

Do-It-Yourself

See other sections.

Cost

$90 per square foot. (For example, a 12-by-16-foot addition would cost $17,210.)

IMPROVEMENT: UPPER-STORY ADDITION

Products/Materials

Here again, the products and materials and construction methods used are more or less the same as for building a house or adding a room. It is just that the contractor will be building up rather than out.

How the Job Is Done

First the roof is opened up, that is, shingles are removed and an opening is made in the roof to the wall-framing members. Then the contractor will start to build up, on top of the wall plates, and frame out the addition. The attic floor becomes the floor for the new level.

Then construction proceeds as it normally would. Even on rainy days it can continue, because the contractor can

28. This house had its entire roof taken off and a new story added.

use an immense tarpaulin to protect himself and any workers—as well as the interior of the house—as he works.

Workmanship

See other sections.

Possible Rip-offs

See other sections.

Do-It-Yourself

Anyone can do the strictly cosmetic aspects of the job.

Cost

$90 per square foot.

Garages

IMPROVEMENT: ATTACHED GARAGE

Products/Materials

The materials for building an attached garage are just about the same as for a **room addition**. For example, it requires a **concrete floor**, walls, **siding**, **roofing**, and so on. It does not necessarily require **insulation, windows, Sheetrock,** or a ceiling. It would require a door from the house, and of course it will require some sort of **driveway**.

It should be noted that for longevity and possible conversion at some future date to a living area the products and materials used in building the garage should be as good as you would expect for a room addition. It is suggested that you check various sections throughout the book to determine what's available as well as its quality. Some people like to use ⅝-inch Sheetrock for garage walls because of its fire rating, which is better than ½-inch materials. It is also known as Type X.

For a single garage an 8-foot **garage door** is common— and is the minimum—but a 9-foot door will be well worth the extra expense. On a double garage a 16-foot door is the minimum, but an 18-foot door is desirable and is required if the approach to the garage is curved. Door heights range from 6 feet 4 inches to 7 feet and must be in harmony, design-wise, with the rest of the house. The top of the garage door should align with the tops of adjacent windows.

How the Job Is Done

The garage is built just like a room addition. The ground is staked out and the area of the garage excavated. Masonry footings and foundations are installed, and then wall and roof framing are erected. Wall and roof sheathing is applied, then siding and roofing. There will also be a doorway cut between the house and garage, or this may already be in place. Wiring will also have to be run to provide electricity for light fixtures.

To help light it better, and possibly make it easier to convert in the future, one or more windows may be installed.

Of course there will also have to be a garage door installed, and a driveway.

Workmanship

A main consideration with a garage, as with a room addition, is that it looks like it is part of the house rather than tacked on. One way of doing this effectively is to re-side and reroof the house, blending the garage in at the same time, but this is not essential. A good contractor can make it fit.

The concrete floor is of particular concern. It should be finished by the mason so that it is nonskid, rather than slick. Water or oil could make a slick masonry surface treacherous underfoot. The garage floor should be at least 4 inches thick with a 4-inch base of sand or stone to prevent cracking.

Cost: $90 per square foot. A 10-by-10-foot garage would cost $9,000, plus the cost of the driveway.

IMPROVEMENT: DETACHED GARAGE

Products/Materials

Here, again, building a detached garage is like building a small house, except that there will be fewer windows and no interior finishing, unless the garage doubles as a workshop or similar area. Then provision must be made for heat as well as light.

How the Job Is Done

Construction starts with a masonry foundation and works up. See the various sections—roofing, lumber, siding, et cetera—for details on products, materials, and building techniques employed. For heating you would probably use a portable heating system.

Workmanship

Though isolated from the house, the detached garage should be designed so that it looks like it belongs on the property.

Cost

$90 per square foot.

Kitchen Remodeling

IMPROVEMENT: NEW CABINETS

Products/Materials

Kitchen cabinets are either the base type, meaning that they rest on the floor, or hanging, that is, they are secured to walls.

Cabinets come in stock sizes, a graduated series of set sizes, or custom, meaning they are built to fit the space available. Usually custom is the best course to take because all available space is used. Stock sizes don't add up to a number that fills all the space. For example, if you had 8 feet 6 inches of space to fill and the closest stock sizes you could get filled 8 feet 2 inches, you'd lose 4 inches, a space that would have to be covered by filler boards.

Stock hangers and base cabinets are commonly available in 6-inch-width increments (12 inches, 18 inches, 24 inches, etc.) up to 48 inches. Hangers are normally 12 inches deep, base cabinets 24 inches. Base cabinets are 34½ inches to 35 inches high. Hangers that fill most of the wall will be 30 to 34 inches high, but there are shorter ones to fit over the

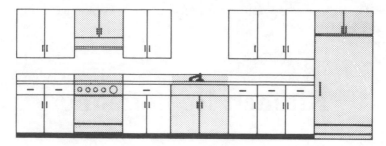

29. Kitchen cabinets may be hangers or base types. (Small Homes Council)

30. Wood cabinets. Like most other products and materials, quality varies. (Haas Cabinet Co., Inc.)

refrigerator and stove: these are 15 inches, 18 inches, 20 inches, and 24 inches high. These heights are the same as for custom cabinets—in other words, only the width differs. The overall height of cabinets from the floor up is 7 feet.

Cabinets are made either of wood, plastic-laminate-covered, or metal. Wood and plastic-laminate-covered cabinets are available in both stock and custom sizes, but metal only in stock sizes.

Solid-wood cabinets are generally the best cabinets you can buy, but there are quality differences to note.

Wood cabinets may be made of solid-wood stock or plywood or a combination, except for the back, which will probably be hardboard.

One key to detecting quality is to examine the way the parts are assembled. The front frame—and you can ask the salesman or cabinetmaker how it's done if you can't see the joints—should be either mortise-and-tenon joints (the joint looks like fingers joined together) or doweled (pins of wood fit into edges of frame parts) or rabbeted (edges are cut to fit together). Such joinery indicates care—in other words, quality construction.

Also check the bottoms of hangers. They should be substantial—not just ¼-inch-thick hardboard—so that you can screw things into and hang things from the bottom.

On base cabinets check to see if 5-foot-wide base cabinets

31. The hallmark of a well-made wood cabinet is mortise-and-tenon joints. Inside clips holding cabinet sections together is hallmark of poor quality. A sign of poor quality on plastic-laminate cabinets is parts that have been made piecemeal, then assembled with visible joints. A sign of good quality are no seams (except in the corners). Here, the cabinet has been made, then covered with laminate.

or extra-wide hangers are braced to prevent sagging. Base cabinets should also have extra-heavy bottoms to hold pots and the like, or else they should be reinforced.

The sides of base cabinets should be ½-inch plywood—not boards, which can split. Hangers more than 12 inches deep should also have ½-inch plywood sides.

Some cabinets have backs and some don't; backs are not structurally important, but they will keep dirt out of the cabinet.

Cabinet doors may be made of boards or plywood. Woods used vary a lot. The more exotic the wood, the more you'll pay, though exoticness doesn't make a cabinet better made.

Cabinets usually have a clear lacquer finish or something else—it's hard to tell what. But it should have something. If it's just stained, it's an invitation to disaster, because stain itself won't protect the wood, it only colors it.

The way plastic-laminate-covered cabinets are made also indicates quality. Particleboard is cut up into cabinet sections, covered with laminate, and then assembled. This is a poor way to build a cabinet.

Here look for clips holding the parts together inside the cabinet or on the back, as well as visible joints where parts are joined on the front and sides of the cabinet.

Good-quality cabinets are made of particleboard, except for the front, which should be solid wood, and *then* are covered with laminate. The only joints are at the corners.

Sometimes it's hard to determine if a cabinet is made of solid wood or particleboard. Look at the bottom of the cabinet. You'll be able to see the division between laminate and whatever the material is.

There is limited availability of metal cabinets. They are finished with spray enamel, but if chipped, the mar is obvious. Metal cabinets are not recommended.

Good cabinets should also have good hardware. Drawer hardware should be metal slides with ball bearings. Bread boxes should be stainless steel.

One key point: Don't tear out the old cabinets until the new are guaranteed for delivery. Horror stories abound of people who have waited forever for cabinets, with the old cabinets long gone into the dumpster.

How the Job Is Done

Base cabinets usually go in first. The installer will want to make sure, first, that they are level and true, and he will use some sort of shim under them to get them that way.

Once they are level and true, he will mark where their back edges fall against the wall, then remove them temporarily and secure a nailing board so that its top edge is level with the line.

The cabinets will then be moved back into position and nailed or screwed to the nailer and to each other. They become one solid, homogeneous mass.

Hangers go in next. If there is no countertop to rest them on, the installer will likely secure a nailer to the wall on which to rest them as he works.

Hangers are secured to the studs. As each is positioned, it is plumbed, then screwed or nailed to the studs and through the edges, or stiles, to each other. To ensure that they are plumb, the edges of cabinets will likely have to be trimmed.

With the cabinets in, the fascia above the cabinets is installed. This is a facing piece of Sheetrock between the tops of the cabinet and the ceiling. The fascia will be finished to harmonize with the cabinets.

Workmanship

A good installer will strive to get the cabinets level and plumb. If they're not, drawers and doors won't work properly. Also, while nails are faster, screws are more secure and some carpenters declare they are essential—nails are no good.

Do-It-Yourself

Cabinet installation is a job for a pro, but tearing out the old cabinets can be done by the do-it-yourselfer. All that is needed is a pry bar, though sometimes they have to be demolished in place.

Possible Rip-offs

Just make sure that the cabinets you get are the ones you ordered. Some contractors may try to switch them to a bargain-basement variety.

Costs

Premium base cabinet, per linear foot:
Materials: $61
Labor: $15
Total: $76
Premium hanging cabinet, 30 inches high, with 1 or 2 doors, per linear foot:
Materials: $36
Labor: $16
Total: $52

IMPROVEMENT:
PLASTIC-LAMINATE COUNTERTOP

Products/Materials

Countertops must be custom-built to the space available, and the standard material used in kitchens is plastic laminate, a thin, hard material that comes 2 to 5 feet wide and in varying lengths all the way up to 16 feet. It also comes in a large variety of colors and textures. Most of the material has a color facing and a brownish core. The newest material has the color all the way through—at three times the price.

Plastic laminate is available in various thicknesses. Standard is .050 and is meant for countertops, but there is .042 material, which is meant for applying to vertical surfaces such as the sides of kitchen cabinets. This is inadequate for countertop use, because it can't take punishment.

Also inadequate is roll laminate, which is thin, flexible, and stains easily. Don't mistake this for the real thing. Two brand names of quality laminate are Micarta and, the grandaddy of them all, Formica.

Countertops may be the edge-glued or the post-formed type.

If a post-formed type, a base is covered with the laminate at the factory and is delivered ready for installation—screwing to the tops of base cabinets. In other words, edges, back splash, and counter are covered with the laminate and there are no seams.

If edge-glued, it is built on the site. The carpenter will first cut the base, then cover it with laminate applied with a contact cement—it grabs instantly.

Then the excess on the edges will be trimmed with a router and edge material glued on and trimmed. Here, of course, there are seams: brown if regular laminate is used, but the same color as the laminate if the material with the color clear through is used.

Two other quality pointers: Standard laminate is harder than post-formed, which is also not available in as many colors. And you can't make a countertop longer than 12 feet if post-formed.

On the positive side the post-formed type ordinarily has higher back splashes than the edge-glued variety and, as mentioned, no seams.

How the Job Is Done

Explained above.

Workmanship

If using laminate with color all the way through, you can't use a **plywood base** if using Formica brand. The company will not guarantee it because of a difference in "drying coefficients," which tends to make the laminate crack. Formica recommends a ¾-inch base of industrial-grade particleboard.

Possible Rip-offs

The contractor could give you thinner material than you ordered.

Cost

Formica on a ¾-inch particleboard base, counter with 4-inch back splash, per foot:
Materials: $ 7.37
Labor: $26.00
Total: $33.37
Post-formed: same as above.

IMPROVEMENT:
REFINISHING WOOD CABINETS

Products/Materials

One way many people try to save money is to spruce up wood kitchen cabinets with various and sundry finishing materials. Paint works well, but taking off an existing finish can be problematic unless one is willing to expend a lot of effort. Many people opt for a professional job.

How the Job Is Done

It's usually a two-phase operation. The refinisher will take the doors and drawers to his shop and refinish them there, but leave the cabinet bodies in place and do them on the site.

Either way, first the wood is stripped to bare wood, then sanded and resanded and a sealer applied to seal the wood pores. When the sealer is thoroughly dry, the finish is sprayed on using a lacquer-based finish that dries very quickly so that additional coats may be applied quickly, to reduce the chance of dust getting on the wet surface. The refinisher will also supply new hardware, and the net result can be astonishingly good.

Workmanship

A spray gun *must* be used to achieve a smooth finish on this job, and the fact is that this plus the knowledge of color and wood takes years of experience to gather; it is simply not a job for a beginner.

Cost

Many refinishers charge by the number of drawers and doors. In New York you can get this job done for $35 per drawer or door. So, for example, if there were ten doors and five drawers, the total job would cost $475.

IMPROVEMENT: REFINISHING A REFRIGERATOR

Products/Materials

Instead of lacquer, most refinishers will use auto enamel for this job. It takes longer to dry than colored lacquer, but it is a very tough, high-quality **paint**.

How the Job Is Done

The refrigerator is cleaned thoroughly, then successive coats of the color are sprayed on. The sides are done first and the top last because, as refinishers explain, it's the top that is most susceptible to dust gathering during the hour or so it takes for the enamel to dry. If dust does get on the refrigerator, the refinisher will wait until it's dry, sand it off, and spot-finish.

Workmanship

This exercise, too, requires a spray gun and great crafts-manship.

Cost

$140 for a straight refrigerator, $165 for a side-by-side.

Bath Remodeling:
Fixtures and Faucets

Toilets, tubs, and lavatories—the name given to bathroom sinks—are called **fixtures**. The operating mechanism for **toilets** comes with the toilet, but the faucets for **lavatory**, **tub**, and shower come separately and have to be installed in factory-drilled holes, and then connected to the rough plumbing, which, as mentioned in the section on how a house is built, are points in the house where water and drain pipes emerge from walls and floors.

Faucets are bought according to their center-to-center measurements—or centers, the distance between the center of the cold-water handle and the center of the hot-water handle, that is, the holes in the fixtures. The centers of faucets that are deck-mounted, that is, mounted on the back of a lavatory, are usually 4 inches apart, but may be 8 inches. Those that are mounted in the wall are usually 4½ inches apart, but may be 8 inches. Tub faucets may have two or three handles, one each for hot and cold water and a middle one for diverting water back and forth from the shower to the tub. Centers on tub faucets are commonly 8 inches, but 6-inch and 11-inch centers are also used. Old-style clawfoot tubs use 3½-inch centers.

IMPROVEMENT: TUBS

Products/Materials

Tubs are commonly made of three kinds of material—enameled cast iron, steel, and fiberglass—and come in four different shapes—standard, corner, platform, and clawfoot.

Cast iron is the most durable material, the Cadillac of tubs. It comes in a variety of colors, resists chips and scratches, and holds heat well. It is very heavy, around 500 pounds, and costs more than other tubs.

Enameled steel is the least costly tub. It is available mostly in white, but can be ordered in color. It's lighter than

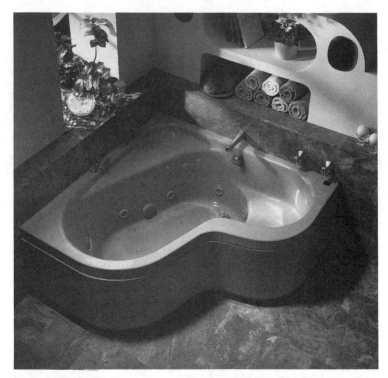

32. Tubs are available in all kinds of shapes. This one fits into a corner . . . (Kohler)

cast iron and is available in more shapes, but it will dent and chip more easily and it is noisy when impacted.

Many different shapes and a tremendous variety of colors are available in fiberglass. However, these can be scratched and need to be cleaned with a special cleaner.

Shape-wise, standard tubs are squarish and rectangular and usually only have the front finished. The tub is designed to be slid into a bath alcove so that only the front shows.

You can also get a standard tub with one finished end. And standard tubs come with other design features, including oval interiors and sloping sides.

Corner tubs have two straight sides designed to fit snugly into a corner; the front is a series of angles. Such tubs are usually made of cast iron.

Clawfoot is the old-fashioned-style tub with claw feet and exposed water-supply lines and is always made of cast iron. Such tubs are designed to fit into Victorian-style baths.

Molded-platform tubs, made of fiberglass, are available in a tremendous array of styles and colors and are designed to be installed with the top at floor level or in a platform.

Whirlpool tubs are also very much on the scene. These are essentially tubs with plumbing designed to make the water swirl.

The more stylish the tub, the more you'll pay. Or you can simply get a well-made tub (with little style). To insure quality buy within proven brands such as Eljer, Kohler, or American Standard.

How the Job Is Done

The first step is to turn off the water. Then the tub is removed, and this depends on what type it is. If a clawfoot, it's just a matter of loosening the exposed connections between the water pipes and the tub.

If the tub has hidden connections to pipes, the walls must be broken out with a sledgehammer or other tool to get at them. As you can imagine, it's a messy job.

The tub must also be disconnected from the drain line.

Getting the old tub out of the bathroom may also involve removing the door or vanity if either of them is in the way. Cast iron tubs can be broken up and removed piecemeal.

The new tub is then put in place, the connections made, and the walls **Sheetrocked** and **tiled**, or otherwise covered, and the gap between tub and wall sealed with a high-quality caulk.

Workmanship

The main thing the plumber has to be careful of is that the water connections inside the wall are watertight. If there's a leak, it means tearing out the walls again to fix it.

It should be noted that tear-out work should not begin until the new tub is available for installation. More than one job has waited for a tub that was late—or never arrived.

33. Whirlpools are getting to be very popular. Jets agitate the water. (Kohler)

Possible Rip-offs

One potential rip-off here is that the installer will use regular instead of water-resistant Sheetrock. If water gets to the Sheetrock, it can destroy it. Waterproof Sheetrock is blue or green (regular is gray or cream-colored); a tab on the end will identify it as being water resistant.

Better than Sheetrock is cement-based board—common brands are Wonderboard and Durock.

Do-It-Yourself

Installation of a tub is a job for a pro, but you may be able to contract for disconnecting and removing the old tub. As always, you should get your overall price and then ask what the discount would be to remove the tub. Do remember, however, that this can be very hard work—a cast iron tub, as mentioned, can weigh 500 pounds.

Cost

The following are prices for quality replacement fixtures. (These prices include $60 for the faucets and $75 for the drain assembly.)

Cast Iron:
Materials:	$385
Labor:	$475
Total:	$860

Fiberglass:
Materials:	$310
Labor:	$400
Total:	$710

Steel:
Materials:	$286
Labor:	$370
Total:	$656

IMPROVEMENT: LAVATORIES

Products/Materials

Like tubs, lavatories are available in a variety of materials, qualities, styles, and colors.

Lavatories may be wall-hung, which means mounted on the wall; pedestal, which means a one-piece unit with the basin mounted on a pedestal; self-rimming, which means it is dropped into a hole in a vanity; and rimless, when it is secured in a vanity by means of a mounting rim. A molded lav is one where basin and vanity are all one piece and fitted into the top of the vanity.

Shapes are usually round, oval, or rectangular, but special shapes to fit in corners and small spots are also available.

Lavatories range in size from around 12 inches by 12 inches to over 3 feet wide and 2 feet deep, good for washing hair and light clothing. (Indeed, you could bathe the baby in these.)

Lavs are made of various materials, as follows:

Enameled steel: Steel covered with baked enamel; steel is light, and low in price.

Vitreous china: This is a heavy material that is available in many different colors. It resists chipping and scratching.

Enameled cast iron: Also a very heavy material. It is scratch and chip resistant and is more durable than any other type of lav.

Cultured marble: This is actually plastic manufactured to look like marble.

Pottery: Comes in a variety of earth colors. It is not as resistant to chipping as other types.

China: A hard-glazed clay, the same stuff used to make all toilets.

Three manufacturers who make quality lavatories are Eljer, Kohler, and American Standard. Within a type—say steel or cast iron—you are going to get a quality lav—one that's durable—if you stick within name brands. Price dif-

34. Pedestal-style lavatory. (Kohler)

35. Self-rimming lavatory. (Kohler)

ferences—and they can be hundreds of dollars within brands—are based on style. The more stylish the lavatory—in the opinion of the manufacturer—the more you'll pay.

As with other fixtures, you'll pay around 20% less if you buy white rather than color. Sometimes to save money and retain design, people will use white fixtures but colorful accents such as tile.

How the Job Is Done

Installing a replacement lavatory essentially consists of turning off the water, disconnecting the old lavatory from the **water-supply** and **drain pipes**, dropping the new in place, and linking it up again with the water-supply and drain pipes.

If it is new work, the lavatory is simply hooked into the water-supply drain and pipes.

Cost

White wall-hung, cast iron lavatory, 20 inches by 18 inches:
    Materials: $180
    Labor: $160
    Total: $340

IMPROVEMENT: TOILETS

Products/Materials

Toilets come with three basic flushing actions, in various shapes and colors, and either floor or wall-mounted, but of only one material, vitreous china, which is a hard, durable material that can chip or crack if mishandled. Care has to be exercised during its installation.

Toilets come in one-piece or two-piece styles. The one-piece has the flushing tank and bowl in one, while the two-piece has a separate tank on top. The one piece bowl always

36. Two-piece toilet plus bidet. (Kohler)

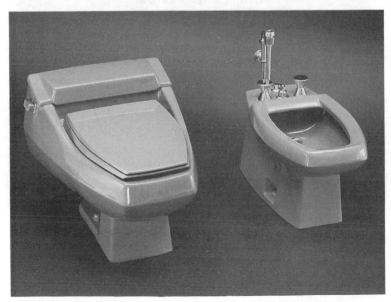

37. Siphon-jet toilet. The siphon jet one-piece toilet is usually the top of the line for manufacturers. (Kohler)

has a siphon-jet action. Today, by law, all toilets flush with 1.5 gallons to conserve water. The siphon-jet also provides the quietest flush of all flushing mechanisms.

Toilets are available in various colors, and you can save up to 20 percent on the price by buying white. (That goes for lavs too.)

Like other fixtures, toilets are available in a variety of styles, and like others, it is mostly style which makes a toilet cost more. While the flushing mechanism for siphon jet toilets costs more, it is the style which adds the most cost. You can get a good toilet for $100 and for $700, a good toilet but with greatly improved style.

The caveat is to stay within proven brand names, such as Kohler, American Standard and Eljer. Occasionally one of their toilets might have some problems because of manufacturing processes, but essentially all will be good. On the other hand, if you stray from brand names, you might run into problems.

How the Job Is Done

Installing a toilet is a simple job. If you are replacing a toilet, the old one is removed by removing nuts that hold it to the floor and lifting up, then inserting a new wax seal over the drain pipe and setting the new toilet in place.

If it is new work, the job is essentially the same, but there's no toilet to remove. If the plumber has not already done the rough plumbing—water and drain lines—it is a complicated and fairly expensive job.

Cost

One-piece toilet (white) plus rough plumbing:
    Materials: $ 376
    Labor: $ 800
    Total: $1,176*

Two-piece toilet (white) plus rough plumbing:
    Materials: $166

Labor: $700
Total: $911*

*Includes water-supply installation and toilet-seat price, $45 (one piece) and $56 (two pieces).

IMPROVEMENT: LAVATORY FAUCETS

Products/Materials

Today's faucets generally have good working parts; indeed, manufacturers can guarantee them for 10 or 15 years. The body of the faucet, though, can range in quality from poor to long-wearing. In general, the design of the faucet dictates price. The fancier the design and finish, the more it will cost.

Faucets come in a tremendous array of styles and colors to match any decor imaginable, but are made in one of five basic kinds of materials: pure plastic, chrome-plated plastic, chrome-covered pot metal, chrome-covered tubular brass, and cast brass.

Pot metal and plastic faucets are nicknamed builder's specials and are to be avoided—they will go bad fast. Tubular brass is better, but doesn't compare to cast brass, the best faucet material of all.

Spotting quality can be difficult because chrome makes even inferior materials look good. But do the weight test. Lift the various faucets. You'll be able to deterine the big difference of cast-brass faucets—they'll be much heavier—than those made from other metals.

Delta, Kohler, American Standard, and Moen all make good faucets, but here again you have to know what you're buying: American Standard, for example, makes a number of different lines of faucets. Look for their cast brass if you want good quality.

How the Job Is Done

Replacing a faucet or installing one is mechanically simple—just secure the new unit to two water supply sources.

Cost

Replacement faucet, good quality.
Materials: $ 90
Labor: $ 45
Total: $125

IMPROVEMENT: TUB FAUCETS

Products/Materials

Tub faucets are available made of the same materials as lavatory faucets but they only come with compression-style mechanisms. Cast-brass faucets are best. Good brands are Moen, Kohler, Delta, Symmons, and Powers, but do remember there are various grades. (Moen, for example, makes top-of-the-line faucets for plumbing-supply houses and what one insider called "garbage" for sale in home-improvement centers.)

How the Job Is Done

The job is done essentially like a lavatory faucet—just connected to the water supply—but there is an additional connection if a faucet spout is involved (this is secured to the water pipe). If it is new work, the **rough plumbing** will be exposed and the connections can be made simply. If faucets are being replaced, the wall will have to be broken out to gain access to the connections.

Cost

Open and close wall: $232, plus faucet installation.

IMPROVEMENT: SHOWERS

Products/Materials

Showers come as self-contained units made of either fiberglass-reinforced plastic, tin, or enameled steel. Tin is noisy and can rust, and enameled steel can chip.

The best is fiberglass; it's also the most expensive. It is available in a variety of bright colors, unlike tin and steel, which only come in white.

The shower may have a seat, molded floor, soap dish, and so on. You'll have to see what's available.

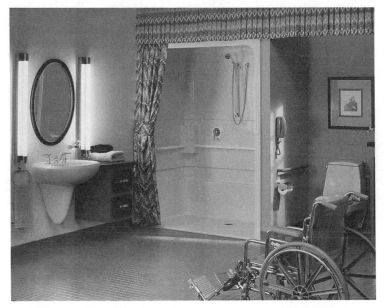

38. Showers come in various configurations and an extra-wide size for wheelchair users. (Kohler)

Cost

Glass with aluminum frame, 27 inches wide, 24-inch sides, 72 inches high:
Materials: $195
Labor: $ 47
Total: $242

IMPROVEMENT: EXHAUST FANS

Products/Materials

Exhaust fans are essential to keep humidity levels down in the bath. Left unchecked, water vapor can condense on inside walls and create mildew, ruin insulation, and attack **wallcoverings** and **paint finishes**.

Fans come in varying degrees of quality. All, according to federal guidelines, must be able to change the air inside a room at least eight times an hour. Fans are measured in terms of their ability to remove air a certain number of cubic feet per minute: 50 cfm is adequate for a small bath; 90 cfm or, better, 100 cfm for an 8-by-10-foot bath. You want a fan that will remove the air fast enough, but not so fast that it leaves the room chilly.

Exhaust fans (also called ventilating fans) make noise and this is measured in sones. One sone is about equal to the amount of noise a refrigerator makes. Fans with less than three sones at high speed are good.

Automatic controls should also be considered: The fan goes on when the light switch goes on and off when the light goes off. Otherwise people tend not to use the fan, or forget to turn it off long after its job is done.

An even more useful arrangement is to hook the fan up to a dehumidistat, which will turn the fan off automatically once the humidity reaches a certain level.

How the Job Is Done

To install an exhaust fan, a hole is made in the wall from inside to outside the bath. Depending on the location, ducting will or will not be required. The fan is also wired to a switch.

Workmanship

The key here is that any ducting should take as direct a route as possible to the outside and not first be routed through a ceiling or attic, where warmth on the ducting could cause the water to condense. To lessen noise, one can also mount the ducting or fan in suitable foam or other noise-reducing materials: the less vibration, the less noise.

Cost

$170 for fan plus installation.

Flooring

Flooring for most homes is usually one of three materials: hardwood, ceramic tile, or resilient (which includes such materials as vinyl that give when you step on them).

Flooring materials come in grades, but when a problem occurs it usually relates to inadequate preparation—no flooring, however outstanding, can perform well over an inferior base.

IMPROVEMENT: RESILIENT TILE
OR SHEET FLOORING

Products/Materials

Resilient tile is available in three forms: vinyl composition, pure vinyl, and (sometimes) asphalt. Asphalt tiles come in 9-by-9-inch size; the others are 12-inch square. Tiles also come in ⅟₁₆-inch, ³⁄₃₂-inch, and ⅛-inch thicknesses; the thicker the better. Thin tiles are notorious for wearing out; indeed, resilient tile itself is not highly durable. Buying brand names doesn't help. (Some famous companies make infamous flooring.)

One company I know, NAFCO, makes a vinyl tile that is 3 inches by 36 inches long and simulates wood flooring quite well. It is durable and easy to clean.

Of the different kinds of tile, pure vinyl is the best. Tiles come in dry-back form, meaning that they are applied with a separate adhesive. Or they can be self-adhesive; you peel off a paper and stick the tile in place.

Generally sheet flooring is more durable than tile—but not all sheet flooring. It comes in two forms.

Inlaid is one and this is best. It has pattern and color all the way through to the backing and a shiny no-wax finish. It comes in 6-foot and 12-foot widths in virtually endless rolls.

Its poor cousin is rotovinyl. This is made of vinyl but color and pattern are only on the surface, not all the way through, and there is a vinyl wear layer of various thicknesses. Sometimes the rotovinyl has a cushion backing. It may also have a urethane coating.

Rotovinyl comes in various thicknesses; the thinnest is very low-quality.

How the Job Is Done

As mentioned, the key is preparation. There are various ways of preparing a floor, but it all comes down to having a base that is clean, sound, and firm.

If the floor is in good condition, the tile or sheet goods can probably go right on top of it. If the floor is in such poor condition that it has to be removed down to the subflooring, then ½-inch plywood underlayment should be applied first.

If the flooring cannot be removed easily, then ⅛-inch untempered hardboard should be nailed on, rough side up. (The contractor shouldn't use tempered hardboard—the nails won't sink well.)

Like other flooring materials, the floor is first laid out for the tile with the idea of having more than half tiles at the perimeter.

If adhesive is used, the contractor will usually do a quarter of the floor at a time, applying first the adhesive, then the tile. Most contractors don't use self-adhesive tile.

If sheet flooring is to be installed, the entire piece is cut to cover the floor, or if necessary, it is cut in a couple of pieces—the goal is to minimize the seams. The piece is cut to fit when dry, then installed with adhesive.

Some rotovinyls are only cemented at the edges.

Workmanship

As one flooring contractor once said, "Preparation, preparation, preparation!" A good craftsman will hammer down loose nails, cut out high spots and patch them, and otherwise prepare the floor so that it is flat and sound, ready for the new material.

Do-It-Yourself

Self-stick tiles can be installed by the do-it-yourselfer.

Cost

Sheet vinyl, premium, per square foot:
    Materials: $3.74
    Labor: $ .50
    Total: $4.24
Vinyl tile (⅛-inch thick), per square foot:
    Materials: $3.00
    Labor: $ .56
    Total: $3.56
Composition Tile (⅛-inch thick), per square foot:
    Materials: $1.89
    Labor: $ .56
    Total: $2.45
Asphalt (top grade), per square foot:
    Materials: $1.18
    Labor: $ .66
    Total: $1.84

IMPROVEMENT: HARDWOOD FLOORING

Products/Materials

Hardwood flooring comes in oak, birch, maple, pecan, and in various forms or grades, but the grades relate to appearance rather than durability or any other characteristics.

Unfinished strip flooring goes together tongue-and-groove at the edge. It comes in various lengths and is 1 to 3 inches wide and $\frac{3}{8}$ to $\frac{25}{32}$-inch thick.

Plank flooring is tongue-and-groove at the ends. It comes 6 to 7 inches or so wide as well as in random widths down to 3 inches. Plank flooring is often screwed to the floor with plugs inserted at the ends to give a wood-peg effect.

Parquet flooring comes as squares, ranging from 9 to 36 inches; it also has tongue-and-groove edges.

Strip and plank flooring can come either unfinished or prefinished. Because factory processes are imperfect, the

39. Strip flooring can be installed with a nailing machine.

40. Plank flooring is screwed to the floor through drilled holes, then plugs are used to fill holes. (Oak Flooring Institute)

boards produced are fractionally different in thickness. Hence finished plank and strip flooring is made with slightly grooved edges so that the height differences are not noticeable when the floor is installed. If you dislike these grooves between boards, buy unfinished. Here the material can be sanded down and the boards made perfectly flat. All unfinished flooring, incidentally, must be sanded.

The different woods have slightly different grading systems, which add up to the same thing.

Oak, the most popular hardwood, has four basic grades: Clear, which has almost no imperfections, such as knots; Select, which is is almost all clear but has some knots and color imperfections; and Common 1 and No. 2, which have natural imperfections. Some people prefer those grades for that very look.

Other hardwoods are similarly graded, and as you move down or up the line you pay accordingly.

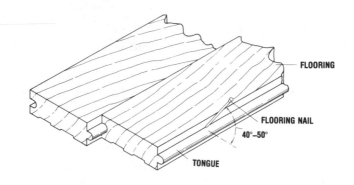

FLOORING

FLOORING NAIL

40°–50°

TONGUE

41. Close-up of how strip flooring is nailed.

How the Job Is Done

Strip and plank flooring are nailed in place as shown in the sketches; parquet flooring is usually installed with mastic (glue).

One to three weeks following installation the floor, if not prefinished, is sanded, and a clear finish applied. The idea is to enhance the beauty of the wood and let it show through; the finish is mainly to protect the flooring.

Cost

Parquet (Clear prefinished oak), installed with mastic, per square foot:
    Materials: $4.50
    Labor: $1.53
    Total: $6.03
Prefinished planks with screws and plugs, per square foot:
    Materials: $7.70
    Labor: $1.61
    Total: $9.31
Strip oak, Select, 25/32-by-2¼-inch, per square foot:
    Materials: $4.13
    Labor: $1.27
    Total: $5.40

IMPROVEMENT: CARPETING

Products/Materials

Though manufacturers may attach their own name to carpeting, it is basically made of five different materials: wool, or any of four synthetic fibers—nylon, polyester, acrylic, and polypropylene.

Wool is still considered the best material. It is soft, luxurious and can keep its look and feel for up to twenty-five years.

Nylon is also good and very popular; some 75 percent of all carpet is made with it. It is more stain resistant than wool (particularly if it has been given a stain-resistant coating), though most stains can be removed from wool if cleaned up immediately.

Acrylic and polyester are down the line of quality; these are not as resilient as wool or nylon and are more susceptible to staining.

Polypropylene is mainly used in indoor-outdoor carpeting.

In addition to fiber, one should check the thickness of the pile. To do this, bend the fiber backing in half—it's called grinning—to see how dense the fiber is. The less backing that shows, the denser the pile, the higher the quality of the carpet.

Manufacturers are skilled in making carpets seem more dense than they really are—particularly with nylon—so it's also good to find out what the pile weight is per square yard. The heavier it is, the better the carpet will wear. You can get such weights from the label, or ask the retailer.

Padding is also a good idea (it can make a carpet last up to 50 percent longer), but it must be neither too thick nor thin: both can have an adverse effect on the wearability of the carpet. Discuss what's best with your dealer based on the carpet you want to buy.

Carpet warranties vary and, like most, in order for the warranty to be honored, the carpet must be installed and maintained according to the manufacturer's instructions. Look for ones that guarantee against manufacturers' defects as well as wear. Most warranties are for five years, but some are for ten. Look for a warranty where you get full value, not one that is prorated down as time goes by.

How the Job Is Done

Installing carpeting is a job for a professional. The carpet is unrolled, cut to fit, then a device called a kicker used to draw the carpet taut; it is then tacked along the edges to the floor.

Possible Rip-offs

Carpeting is one area where retailers will gleefully rip you off, because a poor product can look good. Take care when buying.

Cost

Wool is $32–$105 per square yard; nylon, $42–$70; acrylic and polyester, $25–$30; and polypropylene, $17–$20.

These are averages. Starting prices may be much lower, with comparably less quality.

Doors

IMPROVEMENT: GARAGE DOORS

Products/Materials

Garage doors are available in five basic materials: pure wood, wood and hardboard, metal, solid vinyl, and fiberglass.

Wood doors are usually made of redwood or pine squares and have the design tooled in them. Such doors are designed to be painted or, more often, stained. Pure-wood doors are considered the Cadillacs of the field, and people like the beauty of the wood to show through.

Wood doors may also have hardboard panels set into a fir or redwood frame. The hardboard should be made of tempered hardboard; doors with untempered hardboard can deteriorate in two or three years. Doors come unpainted and must be given a prime and two coats of finish paint and touched up right away if the finish is damaged.

Metal doors may be either molded steel or framed. The molded types consist of metal panels that form a skin on both sides of a layer of insulation and have been bonded to

42. Hardboard panels in a frame of pine. This garage door must be painted.

it. Steel gauge varies, from very thin, low-quality material, to thicker, high quality. If there are active children around— the kind that throw baseballs or who would use a garage door as a hockey backstop—then steel is a bad idea because it is subject to denting.

Frame metal doors have rigid insulation set into the frames. Indeed the back side of the insulation board can be seen on the inside of the garage door. Steel doors are better insulated than wood doors, and this can be important in high ranch-style homes or others where pipes are exposed: They keep water from freezing in the pipes and facilitate warmer rooms above the garage.

Metal doors come in a variety of styles, but in only two colors, white and brown.

Vinyl doors are made of a very tough plastic—polyethelene, as opposed to the PVC used to make vinyl siding—and are made of pure vinyl. They come in a variety of designs

43. A panel from a frame metal door showing how insulation is part of the door.

but only two colors, brown or white (over 80 percent are white).

The pure-vinyl sections are set into a metal framework, so the big bugaboo of vinyl—expansion and contraction—is not a negative factor because room is left in the framework for movement.

Vinyl has tremendous impact resistance and would definitely be a good choice where kids are around. It also has good insulating qualities.

Fiberglass comes in a variety of colors but is very light; indeed the material is thin enough to allow light to penetrate into the garage. Installers do not like it.

The problem in selecting a garage door is that manufacturers can make poor-quality doors look good, somewhat the way fitting companies use chrome to make poor bath fittings look respectable. Hence it's safer to go with brand names that use thicker basic materials and better hardware. Three good brands are General Doors, Gadco, and Therma-Core.

Electric garage door openers are also of varying qualities. Price is one criterion. Some sell in the $100-plus range, while others can cost $200 plus. The $200-plus units are well worth it. However, a low-cost but good opener, praised by a number of contractors, is the Sears opener, which at this writing listed for around $170.

How the Job Is Done

Installing a garage door opener is a job for a professional, even someone who specializes rather than a carpenter; a specialist can do it in two hours, whereas a carpenter might take all day. A homeowner can take forever.

Essentially the job involves installing track in such a way that the garage doors, which have rollers on the sides (garage doors are made of panels that are assembled on the site), slide smoothly and fit well into the door opening. It is mechanically simple to do, but it takes a lot of experience to get the door to work and fit properly: Fractions of an inch make a big difference.

Cost*

Raised panel, pressed board, 8 by 7 feet:	$450–500
Metal, 8 by 7 feet:	$420–700
Wood and Hardboard:	$350–450
Vinyl:	$575–700
Redwood:	$735–850

*Here, costs are labor plus materials and markup. Costs provided by Freelance Garage Doors, Northport, N.Y. As costs go up, quality goes up.

IMPROVEMENT: PATIO DOORS

Products/Materials

There are five basic kinds of patio doors: solid vinyl; solid aluminum; vinyl-clad wood (on the outside of the frame only); aluminum-clad wood; and pure wood, no cladding. In essence you can consider patio doors from the same viewpoint as windows because that essentially is what they are: large horizontally sliding **windows**.

The clad doors are the Cadillacs of the field, and of course are more expensive. Solid vinyl tends to be of lesser quality than clad or wood doors. Some of the extrusions may be thin

44. A patio door. (Marvin Windows)

and subject to attack from the ultraviolet rays of the sun, which tend to warp them.

There are well-made good-quality solid-vinyl doors, but caution when buying is the byword.

One of the big bugaboos of any patio door is condensation, and it is here that solid-aluminum doors are particularly vulnerable. In chilly weather cold migrates through the metal, condenses on the warmish metal inside, and runs down the framework. Some manufacturers build in a thermal material to block the migration of cold, but it is only partially effective.

Wood, aside from its intrinsic beauty, is a good insulator, and any condensation problems would be minimal.

Clad, solid-vinyl doors and solid-aluminum doors do have the advantage over wood; they require little or no maintenance (except for cleaning), whereas wood requires periodic painting inside and out.

The standard size for a patio door is 6 feet 8 inches high (sorry, Kareem!), and they can be obtained anywhere from 5 to 8 feet wide. If you wish, you can also have sidelights—solid rectangles of glass installed on each side of the door, which will create a virtual wall of glass—just the thing if your home commands a particularly pretty view.

The classic style for a patio door is the plain framework: one panel of solid fixed glass and the other a sliding panel.

Also available, though, are "atrium" doors, French doors, sidelights, and special circletops, which give doors an elegant look.

French and atrium doors operate like standard doors—they swing in or out. Instead of a plain expanse of glass, French doors are segmented by muntins, or moldings. While some moldings are fixed, some—either plastic or wood—can be snapped out, a boon for cleaning.

The standard color of patio doors is white, but you can also get them in beige and brown. Wood doors are available in natural wood colors. Pella makes aluminum-clad doors in custom colors but they're very expensive.

Under the law all patio doors must be double-insulated glass—a sandwich of glass with dead air space between. The panes of glass may be a plain formulation, though, or a special low-E glass that helps cut down on energy costs.

Good patio doors have good hardware; their poorer cousins do not.

When selecting a patio door it's important that it blend, visually, with the style of the house.

Patio doors, like so much else, come in various degrees of quality. Examine the doors closely and ask to see the performance data on the door, as well as the warranty. If you want a clad door and stick to brand names as you would

45. Patio doors also come in French-style, swinging in and out like regular doors as opposed to sliding. (Photo courtesy of Andersen Windows, Inc.)

with windows—Andersen, Pella, Peachtree, Marvin, Morgan—you can't go wrong.

How the Job Is Done

First an opening is cut through the wall, and then the carpenter will concern himself with the header. He will want to make sure that it's strong enough to support the wall above. Then he will frame out the rest of the opening and simply put the door in, like a window, then caulk around it.

Cost

Good-quality wood (6 feet 8 inches by 8 feet):
    Materials: $ 956
    Labor: $ 90
    Total: $1056
Aluminum
    Materials: $ 402
    Labor: $ 88
    Total: $ 490

Standard Doors

Interior and exterior standard doors are available in wood, steel—for entry only—and fiberglass. Wood is still the most popular; wood doors are available in a much wider variety of designs than steel or fiberglass, though there are many handsome designs available.

Following is a consideration of all entry doors, plus wood closet doors, which mostly are a cut-down version of interior doors.

IMPROVEMENT: EXTERIOR OR INTERIOR WOOD DOORS

Products/Materials

Wood doors are basically divided into interior and exterior types. While some kinds within these types may be made the same way, or essentially the same way, the main difference is that parts of an exterior door are assembled using glue that is weatherproof. Exterior doors are also usually 1¾ inches thick, whereas interior doors are ⅜ inch less, or

1⅜ inches. Their thickness helps exterior doors resist warping.

Doors may be either the flush or the sash type.

Flush doors are covered on each side with a thin, smooth plywood panel. One type of flush door is the hollow-core type, which is hollow except for a solid block of wood where the lock is located. To lend rigidity, the rest of the door is filled with strips of wood, cardboard, or honeycombed paper.

The other type of flush door is solid, meaning that it has solid innards—blocks of lumber-core plywood. This type of door is far superior to the hollow-core type.

The skin, or veneer, on flush doors tends to be some pedestrian wood such as luan, but it is also available in birch, ash, and oak, though not as commonly. Hollow-core doors can also be obtained with a hardboard skin instead of plywood, which is even further down the quality scale.

The veneer on either door may be good-looking enough to stain, but in lumberyards and other outlets one usually only finds veneer that is suitable for painting. The only way to tell what's what is to visit the outlets and take a look.

The sash type of interior and exterior door is unlike the flush in that it is composed of parts instead of one smooth skin of plywood or hardboard. (The term *sash* comes from the fact that the door is constructed like a window.) Sash doors are made of solid sections of wood.

Like flush doors, sash doors come 1⅜ and 1¾ inches thick. In most cases they are used as exterior doors—entry doors, back doors, pantry doors, side doors to garages, and so on.

Sash doors are available in a great variety of styles, including panel, crossbuck, and so forth, and with or without windows—"lights," as they say in the trade. The more lights—and decorative the door is—the more you'll pay for it.

Doors are usually categorized in catalogs under such headings as "entrance doors," "sash doors," and "flush doors," sort of mixing everything together. All wood doors come unfinished.

For exterior use, 1¾-inch-thick doors are recommended; interior doors can be 1⅜ inches thick.

For large-size closets, it's best to use a door that's 1⅜

46. Sash doors are composed of parts. (Masonite Corporation)

inches thick. For regular or smaller closets, or dividers, you can get doors that are 1⅜ inches thick, and with blinds, slats, or louvers.

Doors come in standard sizes that graduate in 2-inch increments starting at 1 foot and going to 3 feet wide as well as 15 inches and 42 inches wide, and in heights of 6 feet 6 inches, 6 feet 8 inches, and 7 feet. (Narrow doors are hinged together to form bifold doors, such as for closets.)

Sizes normally required are the following:

For baths and bedrooms, 2 feet wide and 6 feet 8 inches high

For a backdoor to a house, the same height as for baths

and bedrooms, but either 2 feet 6 inches or 2 feet 8 inches wide. For a front-entry door, 3 feet wide and 6 feet 8 inches high on newer homes, and the same width but 7 feet high on older homes

Doors come without hinges and locks, which can vary greatly in quality and cost.

Doors come with a guarantee, but as mentioned earlier, the guarantee is only as good as the manufacturer behind it. And it pays to read it carefully: Some doors are guaranteed against warpage and delaminating (plies of plywood coming apart), but to make the guarantee good, you have to paint both the bottom and the top edges so that moisture doesn't get in; if you don't, the guarantee is void.

It's also good to check the door when it comes in. Many come with dings and mars on the edges, but this won't matter if the carpenter is going to be trimming the door to fit. However, if the problem is on the face of the door and won't be covered by finish, it should be rejected.

Wood doors are also available prehung, that is, the door is already mounted in its frame. You should look critically at these the same way you would doors that aren't prehung.

How the Job Is Done

The job of hanging a door is one of seemingly endless placing and replacing the door in the frame, gradually and carefully trimming it so that it fits into the frame with about ⅛-inch total clearance all around.

Once the door fits, the hinges are installed. This requires cutting mortises, or recesses in the door itself so that the leaves of the hinges can fit in neatly, and if the mortises in the frame are not in good condition or the screwholes are not in the right places, it involves cutting new mortises.

The saddle—the wood section across the doorway—may also be replaced. The carpenter will normally remove this prior to installing the door.

If the door is prehung and replacing another door, then both the existing door and the framework must first be removed.

Workmanship

A good carpenter will hang a door so that it works well and there is a slight space around it. One way to tell is to sight down the door on the knob side: You should see an even line of light.

Do-It-Yourself

Hanging a door is right up there as one of the most difficult—if not the most difficult thing—for a carpenter to do. One carpenter with twenty years' experience once told me that the prospect of doing it still made his stomach gurgle. However, a do-it-yourselfer can install a prehung door.

Cost

Flush, solid, exterior birch, 1¾ inches thick, two feet eight inches by six feet eight inches:
    Materials: $233
    Labor: $103
    Total: $336
Sash-type exterior, pine, three feet by six feet eight inches:
    Materials: $361
    Labor: $103
    Total: $464
Prehung exterior, birch, two feet six inches by six feet eight inches:
    Materials: $216
    Labor: $ 42
    Total: $258
Flush, hollow-core, interior, mahogany, two feet by six feet eight inches:
    Materials: $ 91
    Labor: $ 63
    Total: $154

IMPROVEMENT: STEEL ENTRY DOORS

Products/Materials

Steel doors come in far fewer styles than wood doors, but many handsome ones are available.

Steel doors are made like flat boxes, and there are various criteria by which to evaluate quality.

One is the gauge of steel used. Commonly this is either 22, 24, or 26; the lower the number, the heavier the steel. Good doors can be 24 gauge, but 22 is better.

Most steel-door manufacturers tout the energy-saving capacity of a steel door, and to that end will fill the door with insulation, either Styrofoam or polyurethane; polyurethane is better. Some poor-quality doors have no insulation.

47. Steel door has insulation core.

Manufacturers of quality doors like to tout R-values of over 15, but this can be misleading. They are measured "at the core," as they say, and do not figure in lights—windows—which will allow a lot of heat out and cold in and will considerably lower the R-value. If you wish, manufacturers will furnish performance data on their doors that will include R-values.

48. Metal and wood doors come prehung for dropping into the rough opening.

Weather stripping on these doors—in fact on any prehung door—is usually very good. Such doors are, as companies are fond of saying, "as tight as a refrigerator door."

Some steel doors come unfinished. Most come primed (one coat), and a few come prefinished. Some doors that are purportedly finished come with jambs and edges unpainted; check this out.

Almost all steel doors come prehung because you can't trim a steel door to fit into a frame as you can a wood one.

How the Job Is Done

Hanging the door involves removing the old door, then the interior trim and threshold, and then setting the new door and frame in place and ensuring that it's plumb. In most cases it will not be necessary to modify the door's rough-opening framework or interior or exterior wall materials. The door will normally be painted (with latex paint) before it is hung.

Possible Rip-offs

Some contractors will provide doors that are only primed and tell customers they are finish painted. The difference between the two jobs is discovered six months later when the door starts to rust.

Cost

22-gauge steel with polyurethane core (includes lock):
    Materials: $222
    Labor: $ 44
    Total: $266

IMPROVEMENT: FIBERGLASS ENTRY DOORS

Products/Materials

A number of manufacturers make fiberglass doors. Both entry and fire-rated doors are made.

The entry doors are designed to simulate fine wood. For example, a number of companies make doors that come in a light oak color and with grain simulating oak that can be stained or painted. Such doors are prehung in a steel frame and are installed like a steel door (see above). The doors are insulated like steel doors. Companies say such doors have an R-value of over 15. But here again, this is through the core; windows lower the average R-value considerably.

Fiberglass doors are not cheap, costing about what a good oak door would cost. Staining the door has to be done carefully. Practicing first on a piece of wood is recommended.

Do-It-Yourself

Since it's prehung, this could be a job for a do-it-yourselfer.

Cost:

Materials: $468 (quality door)
Labor: $ 50
Total: $518

Windows

Windows are high on the list of most-popular home improvements—and they top many lists of complaints. This is ordinarily a big investment, so one should go slowly.

Many people think of windows as composed of sills and various other trim sections, but this doesn't constitute the basic window. Actually what you get is a framework in which the sash or movable parts are mounted. The trim is added once the window is in place in the wall opening. When you buy a window installed, the job includes everything.

The most common window by far is the double-hung. Much of what is said about it applies to other windows as well.

IMPROVEMENT: DOUBLE-HUNG WINDOWS

Products/Materials

A double-hung window gets its name from the fact that two sashes ride up and down inside the framework. (If there

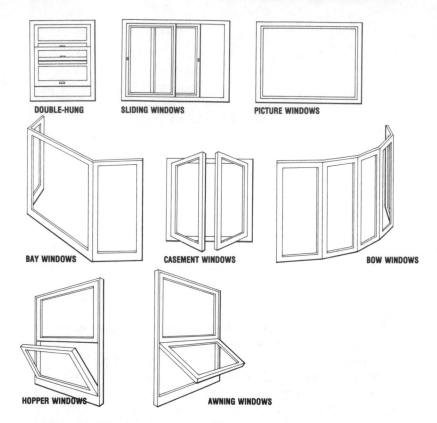

DOUBLE-HUNG   SLIDING WINDOWS   PICTURE WINDOWS

BAY WINDOWS   CASEMENT WINDOWS   BOW WINDOWS

HOPPER WINDOWS   AWNING WINDOWS

49. Various window styles. (Vinyl Window and Door Institute, division of the Society of the Plastics Industry)

were three sashes, it no doubt would be called triple-hung.)

A typical double-hung window is constructed as shown in the sketch. The rough opening is constructed of 2 by 4s, as described in the section on **building a house**. The window itself is composed of a sash with a framework around it and in which it rides.

For remodeling work where new windows are going to replace regular windows, there is a choice between so-called replacement windows and stock sizes, depending on the material the window is made of. Essentially replacement windows are custom-made to fit into the existing openings. Windows that come in stock sizes usually don't fit exactly.

They come in a range of sizes; the closest size to the rough opening available is picked and installed and any gaps around the window are filled in. For example if the window were 26 inches wide, the closest stock size might be 24 inches, so you'd have to install the window and fill in either side with filler boards. The same goes for the height.

There are five types of windows available: solid vinyl, wood, vinyl-clad wood, aluminum-clad wood, and aluminum. Vinyl commonly can be made into direct replacement sizes, and one manufacturer, Pella, makes vinyl-clad wood windows to exact sizes needed.

Following is a discussion of advantages and disadvantages:

Pure Vinyl Vinyl replacement windows are primarily replacement windows for a simple reason. They are very easy for manufacturers to make. The vinyl—PVC, or polyvinyl chloride—can be easily extruded into the components necessary to make the windows, so they are a high-profit item. It's much more difficult to make a wood or metal window.

Vinyl windows vary greatly in quality. Some fly-by-night companies buy the component vinyl parts and slap them together, calling them windows, but it's not too long before they start falling apart.

Other legitimate companies make good vinyl windows, typically ones with welded, mitered corners rather than with mechanical fasteners. Good vinyl windows are also thicker, with parts 2.33 millimeters compared with the 1.5 millimeters found in lesser windows.

Such vinyl windows are usually cheaper than wood or metal and are much easier to install than other types because all the trim on the inside and outside can stay intact. The sashes are removed; the stop molding on the insides of the framework, or jambs, is removed; and the new window, made to the exact size of the opening, is slipped into place, secured, and caulked. Or a window almost exactly the size needed is slipped into place and fillers are used around it.

This does mean, however, that the new window will be smaller than the old, simply because the window framework (jambs on the side and top and bottom piece) is staying in place. In essence, you are putting a new window inside an

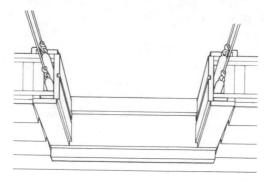

50. To use a replacement vinyl window for a wood window, the sash is re-moved by the frame is left in place. Hence, the new window is smaller. (Small Homes Council)

old framework. In a sense you are getting less window. The window is smaller and no trim is installed. Hence you can see why they're usually cheaper, particularly if they're low quality.

Replacing an aluminum window with a vinyl one is more problematic. The interior of the window framework, being metal, can't be easily cleaned out: The whole window has to be removed. Still, vinyl windows are cheaper than good-quality wood windows of any kind.

Despite ease of installation and cost savings, many con-tractors do not like vinyl windows—even good-quality ones—because a problem can occur down the road.

The problem, these contractors say, is that vinyl expands and contracts greatly, and the seal around the frame—made with caulk—ultimately breaks, allowing drafts and leakage.

Some contractors, however, like them.

Who's right? I don't know. Vinyl windows have not been around long enough to tell a story. Personally, though, plas-tic doesn't make my day, and I wouldn't buy it.

Solid Wood The classic wood window is pure wood inside and out and ranges in quality from builder's specials (bad) to good quality. (The heavier the wood members, the higher the window quality.) They are available in a wide range of sizes that graduate in 2-inch increments. (Some few com-

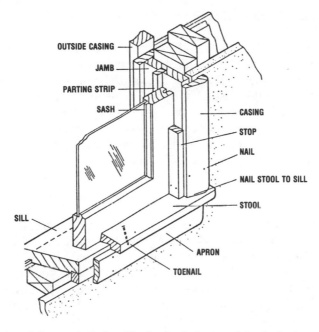

OUTSIDE CASING

JAMB

PARTING STRIP

SASH

CASING

STOP

NAIL

NAIL STOOL TO SILL

STOOL

SILL

APRON

TOENAIL

51. Anatomy of a wood window. The basic window consists of a jamb and a sash.

panies also make replacement windows.) Some people just love wood and will have them installed no matter what.

Installation varies in complexity, depending on siding and the size of the window being installed. To clean out the old window, however, some siding will have to be removed because it will, in some fashion, overlap the edges of the window and will have to be taken out in order to get the window out. The normal procedure is to remove the siding carefully, then reinstall it once the new window is in.

Aluminum siding is particularly problematic. It has to be cut extensively to take the old window out.

Of course if you are installing a smaller window, a framework can easily be built for it.

Any kind of wood siding, such as clapboard or shakes, does not represent a problem, nor does asbestos; though, to be sure, the siding will be damaged during the removal.

Masonry also presents something of a problem because it

is a solid material that has to be cut. The job will cost more.

Wood Clad with Vinyl   Another type is wood clad with either vinyl or aluminum. Vinyl-clad windows usually come only in brown and white, but aluminum comes in a wide variety of colors. Such windows never have to be painted on the outside, so people have the best of two worlds: no maintenance outside and the beauty of wood inside.

One manufacturer, Pella, makes vinyl-clad windows in a variety of colors. Vinyl-clad wood windows are also made in stock sizes. Most manufacturers do not make them to fit exactly, though at least two—Marvin and Crestline—do.

Solid Aluminum   Solid-aluminum windows are also available in a range of stock sizes, but they are widely disliked because they conduct cold and this creates condensation. That means water, and the result is pitting, corrosion, and all the other maladies to which metal is heir when it marries water. Some aluminum windows have thermal break material in them to prevent this, but the results are not that good. (Aluminum-clad windows don't have the same problems because the core of these windows is wood, not metal.)

Aluminum comes with an anodyne finish and in assorted colors.

All windows also come with or without insulated glass— both double- and triple-glazed, an energy-saving feature. Double glazing means there is usually dead air space between the two panels, which resists cold-and-hot air migration. Glass itself is a poor insulating material, so double glazing is a good idea. Triple glazing is said not to be cost efficient except in the coldest climates.

Instead of a sandwich of glass with dead air between, some manufacturers inject argon, a harmless gas, which supposedly does a better insulating job than dead air.

Glass also comes with or without low-E. The *E* stands for emissivity. Such glass contains a nearly invisible material that helps cut down on energy loss and reduces ultraviolet rays, the rays that make colors fade. In a few years, as predicted in another context, all glass used for windows will be low-E.

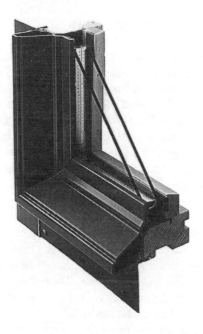

52. Double insulated window glazing. (Photo courtesy of Andersen Windows, Inc.)

The consensus, among contractors at least, is to get either aluminum-clad or vinyl-clad wood—and stick to brand names such as Andersen, Pella, Marvin, Peachtree, and Morgan. These companies don't have a range of qualities. They make good windows, period.

All windows have a track for screening. If you buy single-pane glass, the window will have track for a storm screen.

How the Job Is Done

The method for installing vinyl replacement windows was touched on above—simple if replacing a wood window, more difficult if the window is metal.

Workmanship

The biggest complaint about window workmanship is that drafts come in around the frame of the window. This is either because the window has not been tightly installed or because insulation has not been used. Good contractors will always use foam or fiberglass insulation to plug the gaps around the window frame and keep drafts out. Correcting the problem means removing and then reinstalling the window.

If a double-hung window with a sash cord is being replaced (no new windows work by this method anymore), then the cavities where the weights ride should be insulated, and sometimes they aren't.

Another complaint is that the windows "cloud up." When this occurs, it means that the dead-air seal has been broken. Cold and warm air are meeting on the inside of the exterior glass and condensation is occurring. This should be covered by the warranty on the window, but the window will also have to be taken out and reinstalled.

Another problem people have is the look of a window. To cite an extreme example, white vinyl replacement windows would look much out of place in a stately old Victorian. (An example of this was given in chapter 1.) Most look fine— almost as if new work had not been done—but the job must be planned and done carefully.

Do-It-Yourself

Installing windows is a job only experienced people should do. In fact if a do-it-yourselfer does the job, it may void the warranty, which runs one to ten years (the length also tells you something about what the manufacturer thinks of the window). Follow the manufacturer's instructions when installing the product to preserve the warranty.

Possible Rip-offs

The one big complaint is that people don't get the windows they think they're going to get. A contractor will show them a small sample window, which is the one they think they are going to get. Meanwhile they sign a contract for a different model, and when they complain, the contractor can say, "This is the window you contracted for. Check the contract."

Cost

Wood, double-glazed, 2 feet 4 inches by 2 feet 10 inches, builder grade:
    Materials: $139
    Labor: $ 59
    Total: $198
Wood clad with vinyl, premium quality:
    Materials: $187
    Labor: $ 59
    Total: $246
Aluminum, single hung, double-glazed, 2 feet 8 inches by 3 feet:
    Materials: $ 68
    Labor: $ 34
    Total: $ 97
Vinyl, double hung, replacement, 72-inch width plus height:
    Materials: $192
    Labor: $ 62
    Total: $254

IMPROVEMENT: CASEMENT WINDOWS

Products/Materials

Unlike a double-hung window, which has two panels that slide up and down, a casement window has one panel that swings out off the jamb by the action of a crank handle. These are available in a variety of stock sizes in wood, aluminum- and vinyl-clad wood, and aluminum. They are also available in vinyl-replacement-window form.

Workmanship

The same criteria for good workmanship apply here as for double-hung. Windows should be well-insulated around the frame to prevent drafts.

Possible Rip-offs

Again, make sure you are getting the window you think you're getting. Don't let the contractor show you one good window and sign you up for another of lesser quality.

Cost

Premium-quality vinyl-clad wood, insulated glass, 1 foot 11 inches by 2 feet 6 inches:
    Materials: $177
    Labor: $ 53
    Total: $230

IMPROVEMENT: FIXED WINDOWS

Products/Materials

Once, windows had very plain, rectangular designs. Then, as the energy crisis of the 1970s came along, windows got some hard scrutiny because they were such energy wasters. As an outgrowth of this attention to energy conservation, windows also received attention in design, and one of the big results was the fixed window. It has no operating parts and comes in a wide variety of designs—trapezoid, half circle, circular, triangular—you name it.

These windows were created to increase natural light inside the house but also provide design interest. They are often—and are intended to be—combined with other operable windows to create stunning designs.

Like other kinds of windows the fixed kind come double-

53. A group of separate windows, such as pictured here, can make a stunning design. (Photo courtesy of Andersen Windows, Inc.)

and triple-glazed, with low-E glass and in vinyl or aluminum cladding and wood and vinyl.

Cost

As one contractor said, the more curves a thing has, the more expensive it is to install; the straighter the line, the cheaper. For casement-shaped wood window:

Materials: $195
Labor: $ 53
Total: $248

IMPROVEMENT: SLIDING WINDOWS

Products/Materials

Sliding windows, or sliders, are just that: One or both window panels slide horizontally in the frame. Many people replace these if they're small because, among other things, they can be a fire hazard—difficult to get through quickly.

How the Job Is Done

They are installed the same way other windows are.

Cost

Wood, 3 feet by 3 feet, builder grade, insulated glass:
   Materials: $202
   Labor: $ 42
   Total: $244
Vinyl, replacement, up to 9 square feet:
   Materials: $170
   Labor: $ 64
   Total: $234
Vinyl-clad, premium, 3 feet by 3 feet:
   Materials: $274
   Labor: $ 42
   Total: $316

IMPROVEMENT: JALOUSIE WINDOWS

Products/Materials

These are composed of a series of overlapping glass panels 3 to 8 inches wide. The slats can be opened using a crank handle.

The problem with these windows is poor energy conservation. Even with a storm sash much heat escapes. They should not be used in colder climates.

IMPROVEMENT: AWNING WINDOWS

Products/Materials

These windows have a single glass panel hinged at the top. They can also be obtained stacked—several windows running vertically. The window has a push bar or crank operator, which allows it to be operated without removing the screen or storm sash. The hinges should be the kind that allow space for one's arm between sash and frame so that the window may be cleaned.

Awning windows can be left open during light rain. They are good over a kitchen sink because the operator makes them easy to open without straining.

Cost

Wood, premium, 2 feet 8 inches by 1 foot 8 inches:
    Materials: $157
    Labor: $ 37
    Total: $194

IMPROVEMENT: HOPPER WINDOWS

Products/Materials

Also known as bottom-hinged windows, these are popular for basement use. These windows swing down and in, allowing for good ventilation and easy cleaning. They are often used to replace the old metal basement windows.

How the Job Is Done

These are installed like other windows, but those that are set in masonry are difficult to make bigger without a lot of work.

IMPROVEMENT: TOP-HINGED WINDOWS

Products/Materials

These windows are similar to the awning type in that they are hinged at the top, but they swing in rather than out. These windows are much used in the basement.

How the Job Is Done

Like other windows.

IMPROVEMENT: BAY OR BOW WINDOWS

Products/Materials

Bay windows and bow windows are similar. Bay windows have one straight and two angled sides, while bow windows are curved, just like a bow.

54. Bow windows give much more interior space. (Marvin Windows)

A bow or bay window increases floor space because it is in effect like building a mini-extension onto the side of the house. New **flooring**, **roofing**, and **framing** material will be required.

The same quality considerations apply for bay and bow windows, and they are commonly available in the same materials. Best bet, as with any window, is to stick to a quality manufacturer.

Cost

A wood-clad bow window with two venting sashes 2 feet by 5 feet 6 inches, with insulating glass would cost (roofing material and all trim included) around $2,300.

Electrical
Improvements

A number of electrical improvements around the house, such as new light fixtures, are small and can be done by the do-it-yourselfer. However, before doing so, you should check your local electrical code to be sure that you are permitted to do it. You might be capable of doing it but then may be required to have it inspected.

If you use an electrician for anything, make sure he has an electrician's license. It is separate from a home-improvement license, and all towns require it.

IMPROVEMENT: REPLACING A SWITCH

Products/Materials

Switches are available in standard and what is known as specification, or "spec," grade—a high-quality switch primarily used for commercial buildings. For the home, standard switches are fine.

The louder the switch on-off mechanism, the cheaper the switch is; the quieter—mercury is the quietest—the more expensive. The more elaborate the design, the greater the cost. (Switches are cheaper when bought loose rather than packaged.)

How the Job Is Done

After turning off the electricity the cover plate of the switch is removed (one screw holds it on), and then the screws holding the switch to the electrical box inside the wall are removed and the switch wires and switch pulled out. The switch is unhooked from the wires, and then it's just a matter of connecting the wires to the screws on the new switch, following a certain color code.

Do-It-Yourself

This is well within the abilities of even the beginner.

Cost

For the do-it-yourselfer, the cost of a switch is a dollar or two. To hire an electrician (labor and material): $31.

IMPROVEMENT: REPLACING A STANDARD SWITCH WITH A DIMMER

Products/Materials

Dimmer switches allow you to raise or lower the level of light as you see fit. They cost a dollar or two more than standard switches. Like standard switches, the more elaborate the design, the more they cost.

Do-It-Yourself

This is well within the province of the do-it-yourselfer.

Cost

To hire an electrician (labor and material): $38.

IMPROVEMENT: INSTALLING A RECEPTACLE

Products/Materials

Receptacles, also called outlets, are what plugs are plugged into. They are made of plastic, usually brown or ivory colored, and have slots for accepting the plug—two slots or three (two straight and one round for a grounding plug). In the latter case, if any of the current goes awry, it will go into the ground rather than through the user.

Like switches, receptacles come in spec and standard grade. Standard is good for around the house. If you have a lot of receptacles to install, you can buy them by the box, like switches.

Do-It-Yourself

Yes.

Cost

$35.

IMPROVEMENT: INSTALLING A GROUND FAULT CIRCUIT INTERRUPTER

Products/Materials

Ground fault circuit interrupters, or GFCIs, are relatively

new devices that look like receptacles but are wired to detect minute electrical leakages in a line and instantly shut down the circuit.

GFCIs are available in three different forms: One kind is wired to the circuit breaker box, another serves as the outlet, and the third is portable and gets plugged into a grounded outlet.

GFCIs are used wherever electrical hazards are more severe than other places, such as the bath, kitchen, or swimming pool—wherever water is present.

How the Job Is Done

It is installed just like a receptacle, except at the circuit breaker box, where wiring is more elaborate.

Do-It-Yourself

Installing a GFCI in a **circuit breaker box** is a job for a pro. Installing one as an outlet could be done by the do-it-yourselfer.

Cost

To hire an electrician for installation as an outlet where wires are accessible (labor and material): $50.

IMPROVEMENT: INSTALLING A CEILING LIGHT FIXTURE

Products/Materials

Light fixtures are available in a vast array of colors and styles. They come prewired, ready for installation. The quality of the fixture can vary greatly, from cheap to elegant and expensive, but the wiring is always good, because that's the law.

How the Job Is Done

The job is essentially one of connecting the wires on the fixture to the wiring sprouting from the wall or ceiling and finding the combination of hardware devices to attach the fixture to hardware within the wall or ceiling.

Cost

For an electrician (labor and material): $74.

IMPROVEMENT: UPGRADING ELECTRICAL SERVICE TO 150 AMPS

Products/Materials

The main ingredient here is wire, which refers to either Bx or Romex. The former encases the wire—actually insulated wires—in a flexible metal conduit. Romex is covered with a tough insulation. Which will be used will depend on what your town building code allows.

Electrical wire is characterized by gauge from 000 to 42; as the numbers get higher, the wire gets thinner. A No. 2 wire would be the diameter of a pencil, while a No. 38 would be about the diameter of a hair. Around the home the most common sizes used are Nos. 12 and 14.

As you might expect, there is no quality difference in wire: It's all good.

How the Job Is Done

To do this job, the electrician has to be part carpenter. Starting from the circuit breaker box, or fuse box, the wire is run through walls and ceilings and terminates in outlets. Cutting holes for the wire and fishing it through takes experience.

Cost

Materials and labor: $536.

Walls

IMPROVEMENT: SHEETROCK WALLS
OR CEILING

Products/Materials

Years ago so-called wet wall, plaster, was the normal material for walls and ceilings. But today drywall, also known as plasterboard and the brand name Sheetrock, is the way most contractors go because it's cheaper and faster to install than plaster. Also, finding craftsmen who can do wet wall is not that simple.

All drywall comes 4 feet wide but in various lengths—6, 7, 8, 10, 12, and 16 feet—and in ⅜-, ½-, and ⅝-inch thicknesses. Normally the 4 by 8 panel is used and the ⅜- or ½-inch thickness. The ⅝-inch thickness, which is very heavy, is used for fireproofing. It's commonly known as Type X.

Plasterboard has straight and tapered edges that are designed to be butted, that is, meet to form a joint. Then the seams are covered with a combination of tape and joint compound, known in the trade as mud.

No matter who the manufacturer is, plasterboard is uniform in quality. There are no hidden defects; either it's visibly damaged or it isn't.

How the Job Is Done

Following is how Sheetrock would normally be installed on walls and ceilings in a typical room.

The ceiling is Sheetrocked first. The Sheetrocker will start in a corner and usually lay the panel at right angles to the joists. Then he will secure it with 1⅜-inch blued nails or screws driven through the Sheetrock into the joists and about 7 to 8 inches apart. The Sheetrock will be cut so that the ends and sides of panels meet on the joists, but the placement will be staggered. If the ends fall on one joist, it makes taping difficult. Also, it is likely that some pieces at the edge of the room will have to be trimmed to fit since no room is perfectly square.

Sheetrock is heavy, so two people will be needed to install it on a ceiling. Once the ceiling is done, the walls are "rocked," as they say.

Contrary to popular belief, the panels are usually installed horizontally rather than vertically because this minimizes the number of joints that must be taped.

The panels are nailed or screwed to the studs (screws are more secure). The sheetrocker will try to use panels in such a way that he minimizes joints—the more joints, the more taping. As he goes, he will cut openings for receptacles and the like.

When all the panels are in, the taping is done. This is a job for a specialist, and the same person who installed the Sheetrock will usually not do the taping.

Two and three coat jobs are done—two if the wall is going to be covered with wallcovering, three if it will be painted (the more coats, the smoother). On a curved wall a fourth coat of mud could be used.

First a broad knife is used to apply a coat of mud. The tape—thin, 2-inch-wide perforated tape—is embedded and smoothed into the compound.

When the mud is dry (next day), more compound is applied and the edges feathered out even wider.

If a third coat is applied, it is applied the following day, and the edges are feathered out so that the mud width is a total of 18 inches.

Nailheads or screwheads will also be covered with two coats of mud.

Workmanship

A good Sheetrocker will not have to sand the joints, but if this is required, he will take care not to sand the Sheetrock because the paper can get fuzzy.

Using ⅜-inch Sheetrock is not advised: It is too flimsy. Also, make sure that a painted surface gets three coats of mud. (They call it two coats and a polish coat in the trade.)

Do-It-Yourself

There is some disagreement on this, but I do not believe that this is a do-it-yourself job. It's just too difficult to get the joint compound really smooth. It takes a certain touch, which only experience can teach.

Cost

Per square foot, ½-inch, Sheetrock:
   Materials: $.19
   Labor: $.35

Wallcoverings

IMPROVEMENT: WALLPAPER

Products/Materials

Years ago one could speak of wallpaper, because that was
the main material, and sometimes the only material, used
to cover walls. But today *wallcovering* is the term commonly
used because there are many different kinds of materials
available, including vinyl, grasscloth, and burlap.

Wallcoverings normally contain 36 square feet per roll
but come in different widths—usually 20½, 27, 36, and 54
inches. Some coverings come from overseas and are metri-
cally measured, yielding 28 square feet per roll. You can get
one-, two-, or three-roll bolts.

Some wallcoverings must be adhered with paste, some
are prepasted (but the paste must be wet). Some are dry-
strippable, meaning that they can be peeled off rather than
having to be steamed off like pure paper.

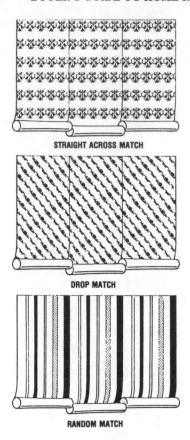

STRAIGHT ACROSS MATCH

DROP MATCH

RANDOM MATCH

55. Wallcovering patterns. Drop is the most difficult to match when hanging and therefore the most expensive. (Wallcovering Bureau)

While paper is paper, vinyl varies. It may be paper with a thin coating of vinyl, cloth with a vinyl coating (such as Sanitas) or very thick, covered with a vinyl coating and simulating different materials such as grass, suede, and wood. Such heavier materials are difficult to clean and very expensive but they have a certain look.

General wallcoverings come in three different pattern groups, with the patterns determining the difficulty of hanging.

Most difficult is the drop match, followed by the straight-across match. The random match is simplest. Hence the more difficult the paper is to hang, the more it will cost. The narrower the roll, by the way, the easier it is to hang; 54-inch-wide material is the most difficult.

How the Job Is Done

Most wallcoverings are installed in one of two ways. Either paste is applied to the paper and then the strips adhered or the covering is the prepasted kind. It is thoroughly wet in a water box and is then secured to the wall. If the wall is rough, the paperhanger will first apply lining paper to the wall to provide a smooth, level surface.

Do-It-Yourself

Only the meticulous person should try to hang wallpaper. It is more difficult than painting, and it's not that easy to get a good job without care and patience. Some coverings, such as grasscloth, require special care and should only be done by a professional. Still, it is estimated by experts within the wallcoverings industry that around 70 percent of the jobs are done by do-it-yourselfers.

Cost

Medium vinyl, per square foot:
  Materials: $ .72
  Labor: $ .40
  Total: $1.12
Grasscloth (premium):
  Materials: $1.55
  Labor: $ .87
  Total: $2.42

IMPROVEMENT: PANELING

Products/Materials

Paneling comes in two basic sizes: panel size or plank size. Panel size is 4 feet by 8 feet, while plank size can be various thicknesses, widths, and lengths, as detailed below.

Paneling may be made of exotic plywoods, which raises the price greatly, but not necessarily the quality.

Another type of 4-by-8 paneling is made of hardboard. Here, the designs are imprinted on the surface and come in a wide variety of colors and styles, many of which imitate wood.

Plywood paneling may be covered with vinyl on which is imprinted a simulated wood grain or else have real wood veneer with a high-quality finish. Such wood may have a hardwood core, which will make it difficult to cut, or a softwood core, which will make it easy.

One relatively new kind of 4-by-8 paneling is the fabric type, which is a panel covered with fabric, including the edges. Installed, it looks like wallpaper.

Plywood paneling may be ⅛ or ¼ inch thick. The ¼-inch material is much better.

Planks may be 3 to 12 inches wide and in lengths of 8, 10, 12, and 14 feet and in thicknesses from ½ to 1 inch, nominal size. They are tongue-and-groove (the boards fit into each other).

Planks are basically divided into clear and knotty grades. The clearer the material, the more you will pay. Thickness will also add to the cost. Knotty grades for paneling run from 1 Common (the clearest) to 3 Common. The clear grades run from Superior Pine (the clearest) to D Select.

How the Job Is Done

Paneling or planks are applied directly to the wall material or to furring or framing strips; it depends on the condition of the wall and the thickness of the material. I recommend ¼-inch material for direct application to walls.

56. One advantage of stud walls in the basement is that insulation can be applied before the panels are secured.

Cost

Per square foot:
   Materials: $2.50
   Labor: $1.50
   Total: $4.00

Painting

Painting is the one big area where even the most inexperienced do-it-yourselfer can shine—and save a lot of money. While the product-labor costs for most home-improvement and maintenance jobs run one-third to two-thirds, paint has a disproportionately low product cost—perhaps 15 percent of the average interior or exterior job.

The key to a good job, aside from careful preparation, is to use good-quality paint and good painting tools. Cheap paint and cheap tools lead, ultimately, to expensive problems.

IMPROVEMENT: INTERIOR PAINTING

Products/Materials

As suggested above, paint is not an item to skimp on. It is available in a wide variety of grades—even from the same manufacturer—and it pays to get the top or near-top grade. It covers better, looks better, lasts longer, and goes on more easily. Of course if you're just sprucing up a place for sale, you might want to go with lower-priced paint.

Paint is one of those products that is always on sale, and if you shop around, you can find big bargains.

For the inside of the house, the main paints used are flat, satin flat, semigloss enamel, and high-gloss enamel. Flat gets its name from the fact that it has a flat sheen; satin flat has an "eggshell" sheen; semigloss has a slightly shiny sheen; high-gloss has a wet look.

Most people favor the looks of flat or satin flat on the walls and semigloss on the woodwork; semigloss is also favored for all areas—walls and woodwork—in the bath and kitchen because it is easier to clean than flat. High-gloss is also easy to clean, but it can seem too shiny.

Interior paint is available latex and solvent-based. Latex is the way to go: it thins and cleans up with water, much more convenient than solvent-thinned paints.

Every now and then *Consumer Reports* does a ratings report on paint. Check your local library.

How the Job Is Done

As suggested, one key to a good job is preparation: patching all areas and cleaning any greasy areas before the paint is applied.

These days most paint jobs are done with a roller and brush. Rollers are used on the walls and brushes on the trim. One of the main differences one notices between the way a pro and a novice does the job is the amount of paint used. Many neophyte painters use too little; a pro will always use plenty—he lets the paint do the work.

Possible Rip-offs

Occasionally a painter will try to use paint not contracted for by bringing bargain-basement paint onto the job in quality paint cans. I suggest that you check to make sure that the contractor works from mostly sealed cans. As mentioned, quality paint is the only way to go.

Cost

For one prime and one finish coat with quality paint, figure the following:

Per double-hung window (casement, awning, picture):
Materials: $ 1.80
Labor: $16.60
Total: $18.40
Per paneled door:
Materials: $ 2.50
Labor: $24.50
Total: $27.00
Walls, per square foot:
Materials: $.15
Labor: $.17
Total: $.32
Ceilings, per square foot:
Materials: $.15
Labor: $.17
Total: $.32
Molding, per running foot:
Materials: $.07
Labor: $.42
Total: $.49

IMPROVEMENT: EXTERIOR PAINTING

Products/Materials

Like paint for the interior, exterior paint comes in various sheens, from flat to high-gloss.

As with interior paint, the key is using a quality paint. Here again you can check the library for the *Consumer Reports* issue that rates house paints.

Rollers and brushes may be used. A particularly good accessory is an aluminum tube that comes in various lengths—up to 15 feet—which accepts a roller and allows much of the siding to be done from ground level. (There is also an accessory that can be attached to the tube and then a brush attached.)

Anyone attempting to paint a house, by the way, should take care when using a ladder. It's a prime place for an accident.

Workmanship

As with interior painting, the test of a good paint job is how well surfaces are prepared. Blistering, alligatoring, peeling, whatever, must be handled before the job is done.

Before the painting starts, one should know why the problem that is to be remedied occurred. For example, excess moisture is the cause of most paint problems, so it's important to eliminate that excess—so that the problem doesn't recur.

Do-It-Yourself

Painting the outside of a house is physically more strenuous than painting the inside, and if the house is high, there is some danger, but it still is within the capabilities of the beginning do-it-yourselfer.

Possible Rip-offs

The painter may use low-quality paint instead of the high-quality paint contracted for.

Cost

For siding, using a prime and a finish coat, per square foot:
Siding:
    Materials: $.11
    Labor: $.47
    Total: $.58

Fascia, per running foot:
   Materials: $.08
   Labor: $.60
   Total: $.68
Soffit, per running foot:
   Materials: $.11
   Labor: $.74
   Total: $.85
Sash (paneled) door:
   Materials: $ 2.50
   Labor: $24.50
   Total: $27.00
Window:
   Materials: $ 1.80
   Labor: $16.60
   Total: $18.40

Ceramic Tile

Ceramic tile, which is basically made from clay that has been fired at high temperatures, is a very durable, water-resistant, easy-to-maintain material. For years it was mostly used on bath walls and floors, but today the larger sizes of the tile have found their way into foyers, living rooms, sunrooms, and elsewhere. No other flooring product, in fact, can equal the growth rate of ceramic tile. Since 1975 sales have doubled nationwide, though the United States still trails a number of foreign countries—Italy is the leader—by wide margins.

Like almost all other products and materials, it comes in a variety of colors, styles, and grades, and care must be exercised in selecting the right product for the right job—and so that you get your money's worth.

Ceramic tile can be expensive, but once down it will last for years—the life of the house, if you wish. Indeed its overall cost, when you consider how long it lasts, makes it one of the cheapest materials available.

IMPROVEMENT: NEW WALL/FLOOR

Products/Materials

Ceramic wall and floor tiles come in various sizes ranging from an inch to a foot square. Colors vary from pale neutrals to bold primary colors. Textures include tiles that simulate shiny sand, leather, and wood, and patterns range from octagons to French to Art Deco—you name it.

Grout, the material that fills the spaces between the tile, is available in dozens of colors; one manufacturer says they have forty-three shades.

Ceramic tile comes in three grades, as follows: Standard is the top grade. Seconds is beneath standard and refers to tiles that have some imperfections, such as slight surface discoloration. Thin decorative tile refers to very thin tile that is usually white and is designed only for use on walls.

The grading should be stamped on the box of tile, and the box should be sealed with a colored label: blue on standard boxes, yellow on seconds, and orange on thin decorative tile.

Following is a lineup of the kinds of tiles commonly available:

Mosaic: This is composed of 1- or 2-inch-square tiles that are ¼ inch thick. They are secured to a mesh that forms a one-foot-square piece of material. Tiles may be glazed or unglazed (shiny or flat), and they may be either the same color or different colors. These are mostly used on floors.

Quarry Tiles. These usually come in a dull finish and are red and in larger sizes up to a foot square. The surface may be smooth or textured and the shape square or fancily curved. Thicknesses vary. Many people use them outdoors.

Pavers. These are rectangular tiles and come in various thicknesses and have a rough surface. They are unglazed and are commonly used on floors.

Patio Tiles. These are thick and irregular in shape and are used outside, but usually only in warm climates because they absorb water and have other drawbacks.

Sculptured Tiles. These have a decorative design of high and low areas molded into the face.

Standard Tiles. These are wall tiles 4¼ inches square and come in a wide variety of colors. For years this material and mosaic tile were all that was available.

Pregrouted Tiles. These arc standard tiles that are joined by an elastosmeric (flexible) material that simulates grout and allows the tile to be installed in large sections.

How the Job Is Done

Tile is installed with either the thick-set or the thin-set method. Thick-set uses more than ½ inch of cement to set the tile in, while thin set sets the tile in ¼ inch or less of mortar or adhesive. The thick set, also called a mud job, is by far the better job, and much more expensive.

Either way the job starts with ensuring that the material the tile is going on is good.

For bath walls, water-resistant **Sheetrock** is good, but **cement board** (in both cases ½-inch) is better.

Tile is laid out so that border tiles will be more than a half tile in size.

Laying the tile is a straightforward operation. It is placed in the cement or adhesive and twisted and settled into place so it sets well. As each tile goes in, spacers are used to make sure the gaps are even. (Some tiles have lugs that make them self-spacing).

Various pieces of trim, such as cove and bullnose, are used to close gaps at the corners and elsewhere.

Once the tile is in place, the grout is swabbed on, then wiped down, and the joints tooled a bit to make them look good.

Workmanship

The key to a good tile job is preparation: The floor or wall the tile is going on must be tight and solid. Floors need to be solid, not springy. Springiness can move tiles and make them crack. To guard against this, a solid base of exterior-grade plywood at least ⅜ inch thick is advised. It should be nailed or screwed down securely (screws are better).

Cost

Mud job, per square foot (includes trim):
    Materials: $ 3.15
    Labor: $ 9.00
    Total: $12.15
Thin set:
    Materials: $2.10
    Labor: $5.60
    Total: $7.70

Insulation

Insulation is one of the most important energy savers a house can have. It is also an area where the do-it-yourselfer can get very much involved: Most insulation is applied to framing members that are accessible, and it does not take great skill to apply the materials available, so labor costs could be saved.

Insulation works by reducing what engineers call heat transfer. In the winter, heat passes through openings, through house walls and through the roof and migrates to the cooler air outside. In the summer the reverse is true: Heat migrates into the house.

Insulation is a barrier to this migration, and its ability to accomplish this is measured by its "R," or heat-resistance factor. By law, all insulation has its R-value stamped on it. The higher the R, the more effective the insulation will be.

Just how much insulation, what R-value is needed, will depend on local climate; you will certainly need more in Broken Rifle, Colorado, than in Palm Beach, California. Local utility companies can help you to determine what R-value is sufficient in your area; in fact some utilities have energy specialists who would be good to talk with to answer any energy questions you might have.

Insulation is cheap, but if you are operating on a tight budget and want to get the most energy savings for your dollar, insulate the attic first. More heat rises up out of the house than from any other area.

IMPROVEMENT: BATTS OR BLANKET INSULATION

Products/Materials

Both batts and blankets consist of insulation, the filler of which may be fiberglass or rock wool, covered on one side with a foil or paper moisture barrier (it's this side that faces the inside of the house when installed—it prevents heat-laden moisture from making the insulation filler wet) or no foil barrier. Batts and blankets are generally available from R-11 to R-38. They come 16 to 24 inches wide to fit between house framing members (most framing members are 16 inches apart, but older homes are 24 inches). Thickness will depend on the R-value—the higher the R, the thicker the insulation. Also, blankets are made just long enough to fit wall height, while batts come in long rolls with pieces cut off to the lengths needed.

Insulation is like **drywall** in terms of quality—consistently good. It is either visibly good or damaged.

How the Job Is Done

Installing batts or blankets is normally done with a staple gun. The insulation is laid loosely between the framing members and the flaps, or flanges, on it stapled to the wood. Cutting, where needed, is done with a utility or razor knife.

57. Batt insulation will have an R-value clearly marked on the face.

Workmanship

Insulation should not be compressed when installed. It's the fluffiness of the material that maintains its ability to impede warm air flow.

Do-It-Yourself

As mentioned, this is very much a do-it-yourself project, but one should wear protective gear—safety glasses, a mask, gloves, long sleeves, and pants—to protect against insulation fibers.

Possible Rip-offs

It is unlikely that rip-offs can occur here. The R-value will be self-evident on the insulation, and the installed material is exposed to view, so none of the work is hidden.

Cost

For an R-11 insulation for walls you would pay around $.58 per square foot for labor and materials but save the cost of overhead and labor ($.21 per square foot) by doing it yourself.

IMPROVEMENT: RIGID INSULATION ON BASEMENT WALL

Products/Materials

Rigid insulation comes in a variety of materials and in various R-values. Depending on the material chosen, the panels may be 2 feet by 8 feet or 4 feet by 8 feet.

The big advantage of board insulation is that it has high R-values, relatively speaking, based on its thickness. Exactly what this is will depend on the material, but it ranges from around R-3.5 to R-8 and is ½ to 1 inch thick.

Generally, rigid board is used to line interior and exterior foundation walls, over cathedral ceilings, or as sheathing; it can also be used between studs.

In general, too, when it burns, it can emit poisonous fumes. So, depending on the material, it must be installed in combination with materials such as **Sheetrock**, which will impede its burning until people are safely out of the building.

How the Job Is Done

Rigid-board insulation can be cut with a sharp knife and is secured directly to the surface with beads of adhesive.

Do-It-Yourself

It's simple to install, a good job for a do-it-yourselfer.

Cost

½-inch board would cost around $.41 cents per square foot to install yourself.

IMPROVEMENT: LOOSE-FILL INSULATION

Products/Materials

Loose-fill insulation comes in large bags and in various forms, including cellulose, perlite, vermiculite, and fiberglass. It may be poured or blown in place by machine. The most common use for loose fill is to pour it between an attic's floor framing members.

The R-value and recommended coverages are on the bag. Typically, around 6 inches of loose fill would equal an R-11.

How the Job Is Done

In an unfinished attic loose-fill insulation may simply be poured from the bag between the joists, then raked smooth to the depth desired.

Do-It-Yourself

A simple do-it-yourself job.

Cost

For a depth of R-19, around $.43 per square foot to have done professionally.

IMPROVEMENT: BLOWN-IN INSULATION

Products/Materials

Loose-fill materials such as fiberglass and macerated cellulose (shredded newspaper treated with chemicals) are used for the job.

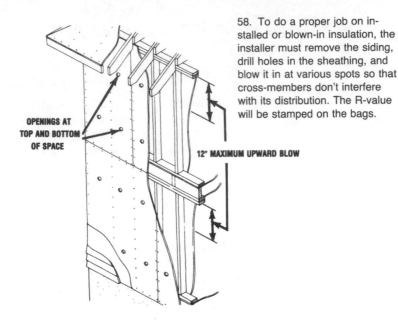

OPENINGS AT TOP AND BOTTOM OF SPACE

12" MAXIMUM UPWARD BLOW

58. To do a proper job on installed or blown-in insulation, the installer must remove the siding, drill holes in the sheathing, and blow it in at various spots so that cross-members don't interfere with its distribution. The R-value will be stamped on the bags.

How the Job Is Done

The **shingles** are removed and then holes are drilled in the sheathing into the wall cavities between the studs. Sometimes the shingles are partially lifted to drill the holes, or the holes are drilled into the siding. A hose is inserted in the holes and insulation pumped in. When the cavities are filled, the holes are plugged and the shingles replaced.

Possible Rip-offs

One must take care here to contract for a certain R-value within the walls. This R-value will be achieved once a certain number of bags of loose-fill insulation has been used, and the contractor should use them; some may try to use less. You should contract for a specific number of bags and then count the empties at the end of the job to make sure all the material was used.

A good job usually requires that two holes per cavity be

drilled, one at the top and one at the bottom. Otherwise material pumped in at the top may not filter down because a cross-framing member (called a cat) blocks it.

Cost

For blowing insulation behind shingles or **aluminum**, it costs around $1.11 per square foot and probably 10 to 15 percent more if going through brick or other masonry, which requires extra effort.

Stairs

IMPROVEMENT: PREFAB FOLD-UP STAIRWAY

Products/Materials

Prefab stairways are designed to create access to an attic when it is used for storage. Though models vary, essentially prefab stairways are a fold-up or accordion-fold ladder and not intended for use when the attic is used as a living area. It pulls down for use and folds up into the attic; a painted panel on the bottom serves as a ceiling section, which covers the opening.

The stairway comes complete, ready for installation. Some are made of wood, some metal; some have a safety rail included, while others do not—this has to be installed separately.

How the Job Is Done

This is essentially a job of preparing the opening and then building a framework in the ceiling opening so that it is strong enough to support the staircase. This will vary from installation to installation, but it may mean cutting into joists; if so, the contractor will have to beef these up so that the attic-floor structure is not weakened.

Cost

About $207 for a wood stairway, plus $295 or so for the contractor to install it.

IMPROVEMENT: CIRCULAR STAIRCASE

Products/Materials

Circular staircases are for when space is at a premium and you want new stairs between two floors. Such staircases are circular and only occupy an area 5 feet in diameter or less on each floor. The stairs come in prefabricated sections, including triangular stair treads. The stairs may have a center post of aluminum or iron and stair treads made of wood or metal.

Other materials will be required for framing out the ceiling and floor that the staircase penetrates, and the floor and ceiling must be finished with trim, flooring, or other materials as needed.

How the Job Is Done

First the contractor will cut through the ceiling where the stairs are to go, then through the floor above.

The stairs are assembled and mounted in the opening, and then the opening is beefed up and trimmed out as required.

Do-It-Yourself

There is too much sophisticated carpentry involved here to make this a do-it-yourself project, but the stairs assembly is something the novice could do and perhaps get a discount from the carpenter.

Cost

Oak treads, a metal spiral staircase with, say, fourteen steps and a platform plus rails would cost around $2,500, plus about that to do the carpentry to penetrate the floors.

IMPROVEMENT: SIMPLE WOOD STEPS

Products/Materials

Standard treads for simple stairs are made of 1⅛-inch yellow pine. No. 2 Common pine is good for the risers. The side-enclosing pieces can be ¾-inch exterior plywood. The steps also require a footing, which can be made of cement blocks and assorted nailers, nails, and plastic resin glue.

How the Job Is Done

The first step is to dig a small trench for the footing, then the cement blocks are inserted on end. Then the side pieces are cut out and nailers secured to the top edges. The side pieces are set in place—nailed to the house—and then risers and treads are glued and nailed in place and holes drilled in the treads for water drainage.

Workmanship

The key consideration in making steps properly is the relationship of height tread to riser; if they're not correct, the stairs can be difficult to walk on. Riser height should fall between 6½ and 8½ inches, with treads 2 inches longer than whatever the risers are.

Do-It-Yourself

A careful beginner could do this job.

Cost

4 feet wide, 2-by-10-inch tread with 2-by-12-foot stringers (side pieces). When made of pressure-treated lumber, $19 per step; with construction-grade redwood, $32.

IMPROVEMENT: CUSTOM WOOD STEPS

Products/Materials

These may be stairs that are made to order on the site by the carpenter, or actually bought in almost kit form. There are companies who will work with the homeowner to create a plan for the stairs, then ship the components to the site for assembly and finishing there.

Quality varies, so before ordering anything make sure that you understand what you are getting.

Cost

One manufacturer quoted us a price of $300 per oak stair, which would include stair and rail section; eight steps, which would include a landing at the top, would be $2,400.

Skylights

IMPROVEMENT: FIXED OR MOTORIZED SKYLIGHTS

Products/Materials

Skylights come in two basic kinds: glass and plastic. Glass skylights are flat, while plastic have a raised or bubblelike configuration.

Skylights are also available with a variety of features, including being fixed (the glass or plastic may not be opened) or movable (the skylight may be opened by a pole or remotely by motor). Movable skylights are also known as roof windows.

Shades are also available, and the glass may be plain or low-E (low emissivity), in which case the glass is impregnated with a virtually invisible material that lowers energy costs. Predictions are that within a few years all glass will be low-E.

59. Glass skylight. Glass skylights are flat, plastic ones are formed (Photo courtesy of Andersen Windows, Inc.)

Skylights come in a wide variety of sizes and may also be custom-made. Sticking with brand names is a good way to get a quality skylight. Three are: Venterama, InsulaDome, and Wasco Industries.

How the Job Is Done

In most cases the installation of a skylight involves making a hole in the roof between the rafters, carefully removing the shingles for reuse, then framing the opening, dropping the skylight into place, caulking, replacing the roof shingles, and finishing the interior as required.

In some cases people want the benefits of a skylight in a room where the roof is on an upper floor. In this case the skylight is installed as usual, but a shaftway is built between the roof and the room ceiling. Much more elaborate carpentry is involved.

60. Roof shingles are first carefully removed when installing a skylight.

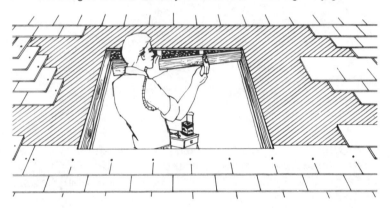

61. An opening is cut in the roof between the rafters, and the inside of the opening is framed out.

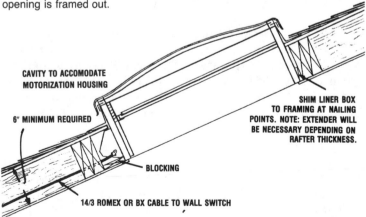

CAVITY TO ACCOMODATE
MOTORIZATION HOUSING

6" MINIMUM REQUIRED

SHIM LINER BOX
TO FRAMING AT NAILING
POINTS. NOTE: EXTENDER WILL
BE NECESSARY DEPENDING ON
RAFTER THICKNESS.

BLOCKING

14/3 ROMEX OR BX CABLE TO WALL SWITCH

62. A motorized skylight in place.

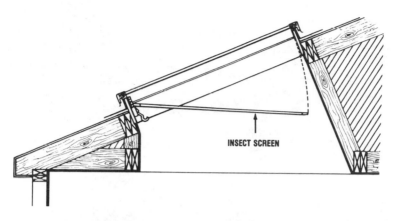

INSECT SCREEN

63. A light shaft is built when installing a skylight where roof and ceiling are not close together. (Drawings courtesy of Ventarama)

Workmanship

The main problem with skylight installation is leakage. It is all too easy for them to leak either right away upon installation or later, such as when leaves pile up on the roof and become dams for water, which can back up and find its way under the skylight. This is a particularly potent example of why it is important to check a contractor's previous jobs: See if his skylights have leaked in the past.

Cost

A wood-framed 30-by-22-inch skylight with tempered, insulated glass (including patching the ceiling) would cost $260. A rod control would add $42, a motorized control $220. A light shaft 2 feet deep would add another $236; one 6 to 8 feet around $490. Costs are based on a roof with asphalt shingles.

Ceilings

IMPROVEMENT: ACOUSTICAL CEILING TILE

Products/Materials

Standard 12-by-12-inch ceiling tile is made of a blend of cellulose, clay, starch, and vermiculite. It comes in a variety of earth colors and surfaces (pebbled, fissured, striated, etc.) and comes washable and nonwashable.

Acoustical tile gets its name from the fact that it absorbs sound. While it would seem that it would prevent sound from entering or exiting a room, it does not. It just deadens sound within a room. The only thing to cut down on sound escaping or exiting a room are walls and ceilings specially constructed to do that.

One problem recently discovered with acoustical tile is the starch in it. If this gets wet, a fungus can form in it that causes health problems for some people. As long as they are dry, however, there is no problem.

64. 12-by-12-inch fiber tile secured to furring strips.

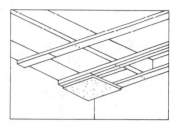

How the Job Is Done

The ceiling contractor will prepare the ceiling in a variety of ways depending on what's there. If the ceiling is wood, no further preparation will be necessary—the tiles can be secured directly to the wood with adhesive or staples. If Sheetrock (drywall), one has an option either to use furring strips (1-by-2-inch boards nailed at intervals) or not. If there is no ceiling material, furring strips will also be used. If the ceiling is plaster, furring will also be used.

He will then lay out the ceiling—with marks, or in his mind—so that when installed all cut border tiles are more or less the same size, with none less than one half tile wide.

Workmanship

Border tiles are the key to good looks. They should be at least a half a tile wide all around.

Do-It-Yourself

It is not that simple getting tiles to run square or to measure them, but cutting is easy, and tiles are an easy material to work with. It is a job for only an adventurous do-it-yourselfer.

Cost

12-inch tiles, per square foot, on furring strips:
  Materials: $.38
  Labor: $.50
  Total: $.88

IMPROVEMENT: SUSPENDED CEILING

Products/Materials

A suspended ceiling consists of a metal gridwork, wires to secure it to the ceiling, molding, and the panels that are laid into the gridwork. It is commonly used in the basement, where it hides pipes, wires, and exposed floor joists.

A number of different materials are used for a suspended ceiling, but the most common are 2-by-2- and 2-by-4-foot panels made of insulation board and plastic panels below where light fixtures are located. Light fixtures are installed separately; the grid doesn't support them.

Acoustic panels come in a wide variety of textured surfaces. Some panels are made of Styrofoam, but these are said to be very light, with a tendency to blow out of the grid. Acoustic ceiling panels have fairly consistent quality. Celotex, the inventor of the suspended ceiling seventy years ago, is one of the best brands.

Plastic materials—egg-crate design, flat, pebbled, and so forth—come in the same sizes as solid panels, but they have no sound-absorbing quality.

Grids for a suspended ceiling are sold separately. When buying them make sure that the color of the acoustic panel or plastic harmonizes with the color of the grid.

How the Job Is Done

First the contractor will snap a level line around the walls of the basement near the ceiling but low enough so that the gridwork, which is installed following the line, will clear

65. Panel being installed in a suspended-ceiling grid. (The Celotex Corporation)

anything hanging down from the ceiling. Following a predetermined plan, the contractor will lay out the locations of the main runners, which are 12-foot lengths of metal, and cross-tees, which look like the letter T in profile and are 4-foot and 2-foot strips that fit into the slots in the main runners.

Then he will mount the runners, using wire and nails to secure them to the ceilings or joists, and lay the cross-tees in place, forming the gridwork. Last he will lay the panels in place on the lipped portions of the runners and tees. As with a tile ceiling, his goal will be to make the border panels as even as possible and at least half a panel wide.

Cost

Per 2-by-4-foot panel plus grid section:

Materials: $1.20
Labor: $1.18
Total: $2.43 per 8 square feet.

Fireplaces

Many people think that a fireplace is an energy-saving device. In fact it is not and should not be purchased for that reason. It must stand on its own merits, as it were, these being to provide light and to lend a certain coziness (and perhaps just a bit of warmth) to a room.

There are two basic kinds: freestanding and built into the wall. The latter may be prefab metal or masonry. In any case, installing a fireplace is one improvement that must be carefully checked with the local building department to ensure that all building codes are being followed.

IMPROVEMENT: FREESTANDING FIREPLACE

Products/Materials

A freestanding fireplace is just that—there is free space all around it. Though masonry units can be built, what is meant here is a prefabricated metal type.

These come in numerous styles and colors, but all are

composed of three basic elements: the firebox itself, a hearth of fireproof materials it's set on, and a flue pipe that carries off the heat and smoke.

The parts of such a fireplace may be essentially assembled, or else they must be put together.

How the Job Is Done

A suitable spot must be found in the room and must be selected in part so that the flue pipe that penetrates the **ceiling** and **roof** (or two floors and the roof) passes between framing members without the necessity of cutting them.

Installation is relatively simple: A hole is cut into the ceiling (or ceilings) above the fireplace location and then is framed out and finished with appropriate materials. The portion of the flue that passes through floor and roof is insulated (zero clearance) so that there is no danger of fire; the other parts of the flue may not be, so they can give off a small amount of heat.

Workmanship

The main consideration is that the flue be straight, and fire codes be adhered to. If a flue is crooked, it can lead to the release of sparks and possibly a fire.

Do-It-Yourself

The assembling of the fireplace is a do-it-yourself job, but running the flue through a floor plus roof is a job for a professional. He has to ensure that it is watertight.

Cost

Professional installation, 30-by-30-inch fireplace with flue pipe 50 inches from base to chimney:

Materials:　$525
Labor:　　　$226
Total:　　　$751

IMPROVEMENT: BUILT-IN FIREPLACE

Products/Materials

The heart of this improvement is a prefabricated metal fire-box that comes complete, ready to be installed and, like the freestanding type, accept a flue pipe. Happily the box is not very heavy, so it can be manipulated into place without great difficulty.

Such a unit can be built into the corner of a room, or midway down a wall, or in the wall, extending to the outside. The materials that front it can be anything one wishes: **brick, ceramic,** stone, whatever one likes, as long as it is fireproof.

Framing around the unit will be required. Standard 2 by 4s are used.

How the Job Is Done

The job will vary according to the location selected for the fireplace but will involve framing work, including the use of **fire-resistant Sheetrock**. The unit will be moved into place, then the holes for the flue made and framed out in the ceiling and roof. Framing work around the firebox will be made, then finish materials—stone, brick, or whatever—will be installed. A hearth of appropriately fireproof materials will also have to be constructed.

Cost

Same as freestanding plus cost of framing and finishing opening in wall.

IMPROVEMENT: BRICK FIREPLACE

Products/Materials

Many people prefer a brick fireplace. It has a charm all its own, and is virtually indestructible. It's expensive, however, and must be done by someone who is experienced not only with masonry construction but with fireplace function as well. It must also be determined that the area that the fireplace is going in is strong enough to withstand the weight of it.

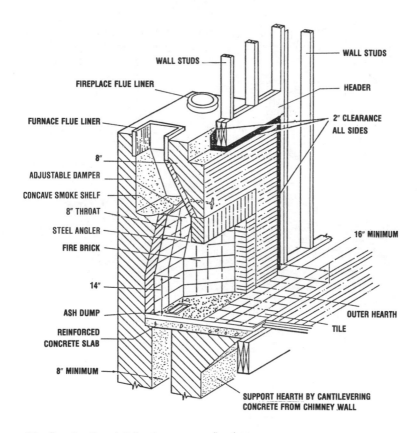

66. Construction details of a masonry fireplace.

Ordinary bricks can be used to build the fireplace, but firebricks, which can withstand intense heat, are used in the firebox.

How the Job Is Done

Building a brick fireplace goes like any other project involving the use of brick. It is built brick by brick, with mortar gluing the bricks together and also serving as a decorative element.

Cost

36 inches wide by 29 inches by 16 inches deep, lined with firebrick, including damper and cleanout, and brick, slate, or tile hearth:

Materials: $ 642
Labor: $1,786
Total: $2,428

Roofing

IMPROVEMENT: ASPHALT OR FIBERGLASS SHINGLE ROOF

Products/Materials

Over 80 percent of the roofing market is the asphalt shingle, which today really refers to asphalt and fiberglass. Whichever, the material is relatively light, works easily, and provides good protection.

Shingles are made using a base of an organic felt or a fiberglass mat. This material is saturated with asphalt, and then the surfaces coated with ceramic mineral particles, which help protect the base.

Shingles come in a variety of sizes and shapes as well as colors—white, black, brown, green, red.

So-called strip shingles are rectangular, measuring approximately 12 inches long by 36 inches wide, and may have as many as five cutouts along the long dimension; the resulting "flaps" are called tabs. It is these tabs that are exposed to the weather when the shingles are overlapped. Installed, strip shingles look like they are composed of individual shingles. If you wish, you can get shingles without cutouts.

Most shingles come with dabs of adhesive on the underside so that they stick better and resist lifting by the wind.

Shingles come in various fire ratings—A, B, and C—which indicate their resistance to fire.

Asphalt shingles were once sold by weight. Fiberglass shingles came along, and though they were considerably lighter in weight than asphalt, they could perform equally as well. Hence, weight considerations became meaningless, and manufacturers now sell shingles by the length of the warranty.

Manufacturers warranty the shingles for twenty or twenty-five years, but there is debate as to which is better.

Some installers think the 25 year warranty is a gimmick, because no one is going to have the same roof for twenty-five years. The warranty, in their opinion, becomes meaningless.

On the other side, however, shingles with a 25 year warranty are also viewed positively. Says Ed Lindstadt, the Northport, Long Island owner of Lindstadt Seamless Gutter, who has installed thousands of roofs, "the 25 year one is worth it, because it lies flatter and looks better and the cost per square [around $3 more on Long Island] is well worth it."

Whichever warranty you choose, make sure that the roof is shingled following the manufacturer's directions. If not, the warranty could be voided.

An alternative way of selecting shingles is to buy them according to the tests they've passed. Hence if you get a fiberglass shingle that has an ASTM (American Society of Testing and Materials) designation of D3462, you'll get a good shingle, no matter what brand you buy. Such specs come with product literature.

For asphalt, a Class C with an ASTM D225 is good.

There are pros and cons about asphalt and fiberglass shingles. Both have good and bad points, but both types are basically good. Fiberglass is newer, but that doesn't make it better: asphalt shingles have been protecting roofs for decades.

The consensus is to choose fiberglass shingles if you live

in a hot-weather climate and asphalt if you live in snow country (that is, it starts getting cold in October). Reason: Asphalt cooks in hot weather, whereas fiberglass doesn't, but fiberglass gets brittle in cold weather, whereas asphalt does not.

The shingles discussed here are standard types. Manufacturers make many other kinds, however, including ones that create a shadow effect and other looks.

How the Job Is Done

Before installing any shingles, the roofer will have to determine a couple of things: whether he can apply the new roofing over the existing roofing, and whether the **deck**— the board underlayment the roofing goes on—needs repair or replacement.

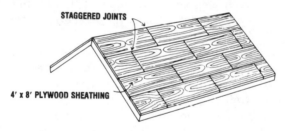

67. A properly installed roof "deck."

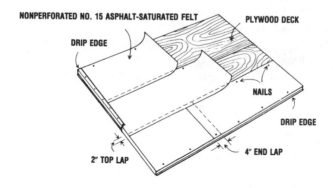

68. Building paper is then installed on the deck, followed by shingles

Most communities have building codes that will allow no more than three "roofs"—an original and two reroofs—because the framing would not be strong enough to support it. If there are too many roofs, the roofer will have to tear one off before installing the new one.

House framing is another thing the roofer will check: Is it strong enough to support the weight of the new roof, whatever that is? This is rarely a problem.

Certain types of roofing must also usually be removed before new roofing can be installed. Normally roofs covered with asphalt shingles, wood shingles, roll roofing, or built-up asphalt roofing (see below) can remain. Slate, cedar shakes, and concrete/ceramic tile must be removed because they have irregular, raised surfaces and are difficult to nail through. More, the irregular surface would show through the new roofing.

The roofer will also check **gutter** condition and alignment; adjacent wood, such as fascia board, for rotting; and the condition of the flashing, which may need repair or replacement.

In the unlikely event that the existing roof needs to be removed, the roofer will do it with a tool such as a flat shovel. As he goes, all protruding nails will be taken out or hammered down, as well.

If the roof must be removed to the deck, the roofer will remove all roofing as well as building paper—15-pound felt (15 pounds of paper covers one "square")—and then inspect for damage (rot, resinous areas, cracks) and patch as required. It is usually possible to patch this with sheet metal, so no extensive carpentry is required.

If the previous roofing is to remain, then the roofer will inspect it to make sure that whatever needs to be repaired, such as warped or broken shingles, will be. The goal is a flat, sound base for the new material.

If the roof is just old and the shingles are curled, it doesn't mean that it has to come off. Clipping off the curls and replacing very bad shingles can be sufficient to get the roof ready for the new material.

On a new roof, building paper is used beneath the shingles. If the former roofing is going to stay in place, this serves

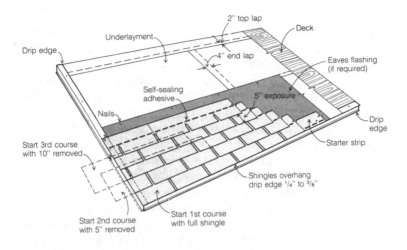

69. Installation details for the most popular roofing of all, asphalt shingles.

as the underlayment. Some building codes, however, will require that 30-pound felt be used over old wood shingles.

Once the roof is prepared, the shingling begins. The so-called starter or first course (line of shingles) is laid along the bottom edge of the roof, and the roofer works his way up the roof, nailing the shingles in place so that just so much of them is exposed to the weather, and trimming the ones at the edge of the roof. He will roof all the way up to the ridge, or peak.

Then he will go up the other side starting from the other edge of the house, work his way up in the same way until he reaches the ridge, and then will finish the job by capping the ridge with overlapping partial shingles.

Workmanship

The most important thing here is that the roofer follow the manufacturer's instructions for installation. If he doesn't, the warranty can be voided.

Possible Rip-offs

The area of most concern here is just how much work has to be done in preparing the roof for new roofing. Roofers may be all too willing to do a "tear-off" quickly, at greatly increased cost. Or some will say that the decking needs to be replaced.

The facts are these: In the vast majority of cases new roofing can be installed with only a minimal amount of work being required to prepare it. As rare as tear-offs are, the need for a new deck is even rarer. Bill Baessler, director of licensing of Suffolk County and a former contractor, says, "Only one in a thousand roofs will need a new deck."

If it's a new roof, then the decking needs to be of high enough quality. The contractor should use ¾-inch plywood or comparable oriented strand board (see glossary) as decking.

Cost

For 235-pound asphalt or fiberglass shingles, per square foot:
    Materials: $.37
    Labor: $.34
    Total: $.71

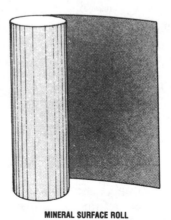

MINERAL SURFACE ROLL

70. Mineral surface roll roofing.

IMPROVEMENT: ROLL ROOFING

Products/Materials

Roll roofing consists of the same kind of material as asphalt shingles but comes in rolls that range from 36 to 38 feet long and varies in weight from 40 to 90 pounds per roll. The heavier the material, the better.

It can be bought smooth-surfaced or with a granule-covered surface and in a variety of colors. Roll roofing may also be used as a flashing.

How the Job Is Done

To make it more manageable and to prevent cracking, roll roofing should be installed when warm; either the weather should be warm or the material should be heated before installation.

Strips are then cut and applied as shown in the drawing. They are nailed, and lap cement, a soft black cement, is used to secure them at the edges.

Cost

90-pound roll roofing, per square foot:
    Materials: $.20
    Labor: $.23
    Total: $.43

IMPROVEMENT: CLAY TILE

Products/Materials

Clay tile is made from slate and tile that is fired at high temperatures. Shapes are various (see sketch), and the tiles

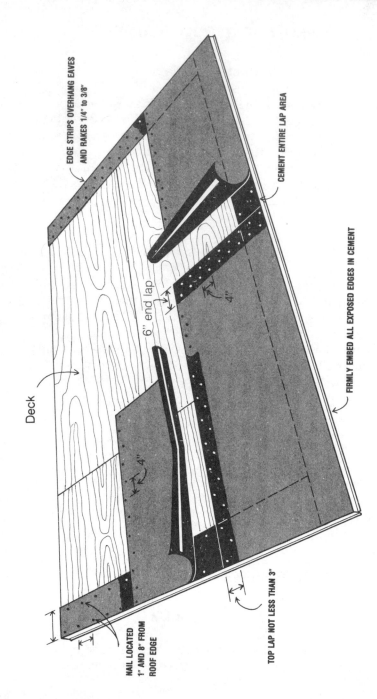

EDGE STRIPS OVERHANG EAVES
AND RAKES 1/4" to 3/8"

CEMENT ENTIRE LAP AREA

6" end lap

4"

FIRMLY EMBED ALL EXPOSED EDGES IN CEMENT

Deck

4"

NAIL LOCATED
1" AND 8" FROM
ROOF EDGE

TOP LAP NOT LESS THAN 3"

71. Proper installation method for roll roofing.

are made to interlock or lie flat. Colors are usually earth tones, but bright blues, reds, and other colors are available but very expensive. They also come glazed. Tiles are very heavy.

How the Job Is Done

Clay tiles have holes punched in them and are secured to the roof with any of a variety of corrosion-proof nails. Tiles may interlock or lie flat, and installation is similar to any other roofing. The tiles are installed starting from the eaves and working up toward the ridge.

Workmanship

A skilled craftsman must install tile and must be particularly careful to install roof flashings correctly.

72. High-profile concrete roof tile.

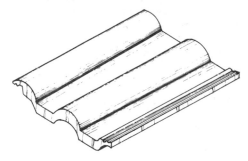

73. Low-profile concrete roof tile.

Cost

Spanish tile, per square foot:
Materials: $3.81
Labor: $2.03
Total: $5.84

IMPROVEMENT: CONCRETE TILE

Products/Materials

Concrete tiles are formed from concrete. They are very close in appearance to clay tile (see sketch) and come in a variety of colors and shapes. But they are cheaper than clay tile. All concrete tile comes unglazed.

How the Job Is Done

Concrete tile has holes punched in it and is installed like clay tile.

Workmanship

As with clay tile, the flashings are important.

Cost

11-by-17-by-1¼-inch flat tiles plus two layers of 30-pound roof felt and various lath nailers, per square foot:
Materials: $1.25
Labor: $1.13
Total: $2.38

IMPROVEMENT: CEDAR SHINGLES

Products/Materials

Cedar shingles are flat, machine-cut units that range in length from 16 to 24 inches. They are naturally tan, highly resistant to decay, and will weather to a gray color.

Shingles are wood and, as such, present a fire hazard. If they are treated with a fire-retardant compound, they can get a Class-C fire rating, still not so wonderful. Using them could mean an increase in insurance rates. Some building codes prohibit their use.

Like most roofing, cedar shingles range in quality. Top is No. 1 Blue Label, which are 100 percent heartwood and 100 percent clear—no blemishes.

Next down the line, and the grade favored by most people, is No. 2 Red Label, which is mostly clear and looks good, though it does not contain all heartwood by any means. In addition, there are three or four grades below this.

Of all common roofing, cedar has the shortest life span— eleven years on the average.

How the Job Is Done

Shingles are applied one at a time in courses, starting at the bottom of the house. Hot-dipped galvanized nails are used to secure them.

Cost

16-inch long shingles plus 15-pound felt paper and nails, per square foot:

Materials: $2.39
Labor: $1.06
Total: $3.45

IMPROVEMENT: CEDAR SHAKES

Products/Materials

Unlike cedar shingles, cedar shakes are largely cut by hand with a tool called a froe. They come in various lengths and thicknesses and, depending on grain and size, enjoy various characteristics. Long, thin shakes are less likely to warp than wide ones, for example. Also, shakes of heartwood will stand up better to decay than other woods.

The appearance of shakes is rough and textured as opposed to the smooth, uniform appearance of shingles.

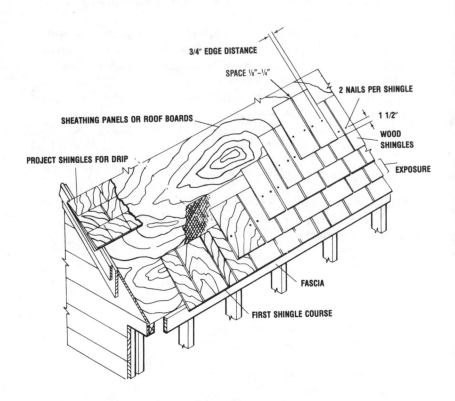

74. Application of wooden shingles.

How the Job Is Done

These are installed like shingles using hot-dipped galvanized nails.

Cost

Handsplit, 24-inch long, ½- to ¾-inch thicknesses, including 15-pound felt and rust-resistant nails, per square foot:
Materials: $1.93
Labor: $1.18
Total: $3.11

IMPROVEMENT: SLATE

Products/Materials

Slate is probably the most expensive roofing material one can use.

It comes in a variety of grades and colors. The colors—gray, maroon, green, black—depend on which quarry the slate comes from. Slate mostly comes from states in the Northeast; that from Vermont and Maine is considered the best.

There is a quality range going from material with a very straight grain across its length and an even, strong color to material that is coarse-grained and may be streaked with errant colors. The better the slate, the less susceptible it is to fading.

How the Job Is Done

Slate is secured to the roof with nails that go in holes punched in each of the slates near the bottom, and it is cut with a power saw.

Workmanship

There are many different quality aspects to installing a slate roof, and anyone who is hired to do the job must be very experienced. It's no job for a nonspecialist.

Cost

Vermont slate, per square foot:
    Materials: $4.50
    Labor: $1.76
    Total: $5.95

Siding

Siding refers to the exterior covering of a house, and today there are a number of different kinds available. Perhaps twenty years ago vinyl siding was not that popular, but today it leads the pack, probably because people like its characteristics; remodelers push it because it is a high-profit item.

Vinyl siding, like other sidings, is available in various grades of quality. One can't just say, for example, as I've emphasized throughout this book, "I'd like CertainTeed vinyl siding," and leave it at that—the grade has to be specified.

All siding is sold, like **roofing**, by the "square," meaning a 100 square feet of siding. The average house has twenty to twenty-five squares, or 2,000 to 2,500 square feet.

There are a couple of points to pay particular attention to.

First, in most cases, the siding that's on the house *can remain* and the new siding be applied over it. In fact, the old siding acts as additional insulation. As long as it's in good condition or a few minor repairs can spruce it up as a base, it will be fine.

In some cases thin strips of wood can be attached to the

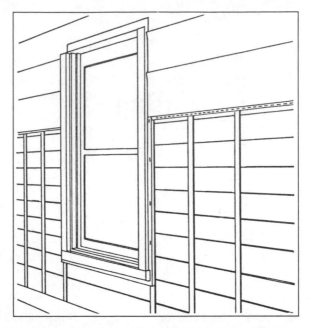

75. If the siding is flat, not wavy, it doesn't need to come off when re-siding with vinyl. If a level surface is needed, furring strips can be applied as shown. (Vinyl Siding Institute)

house to provide a perfect level base. Or a thin, rigid plastic sheeting called **backer board** can be used.

Some installers like to say that removing it will make for a better job, but there is no reason for this in most cases. And there's a good case for leaving it: It will save hundreds, even thousands of dollars.

Second, some installers will champion plastic **board insulation** under new siding, acting as if it's going to solve your energy problems. Don't believe it. Exterior rigid board insulation *may* be good if installed on a new addition, but in remodeling work the cost of putting it in hardly ever justifies it over the long run. (I could see it on an igloo.) The R—or heat-resistance factor—ranges from around 4 or 5, or less, which is minuscule, comparatively speaking.

More than this, though, many contractors now have a strong suspicion that plastic insulation traps water vapor and can damage not only existing siding but the new stuff. As of this writing, a study was being conducted by a large western firm that is concerned that insulation-trapped water vapor is making its cedar siding warp.

Backer board, which is ordinarily used behind some aluminum siding, is also championed. It does exactly nothing insulation-wise and is merely a stiffener for too-thin siding.

If it is finally decided that it's best to remove the existing material, you may be able to do it yourself and thus achieve the good savings. Removing siding does not require great skill, just a little know-how to determine how it is secured. Once you know, you might be surprised at how fast it comes off. (You will have to hire a dumpster to have it hauled away.)

If the existing siding has a problem such as peeling, which is probably due to moisture, this should be solved before the new siding is applied. New siding won't solve old problems, but old problems can create new ones for new siding.

Some siding installers will include new gutters for the job, but this should be determined before the job begins. You don't want to assume you're getting gutters and then be disappointed.

IMPROVEMENT: VINYL SIDING

Products/Materials

Vinyl siding comes in lengths of around 12 feet and in various thicknesses or gauges, colors, and textures. It is generally about 8 inches wide and simulates clapboard; it also comes in forms that can be installed vertically. If you live in a house that has been declared historic, local law may not allow you to install vinyl siding.

Matching trim pieces are available for all kinds of trim, including windows, doors, and soffits. In sum, the entire house can be covered with vinyl.

Vinyl doesn't chip, dent, or scratch that easily. If it does, it hardly matters because the color goes clear through. In very cold weather it can become brittle and susceptible to

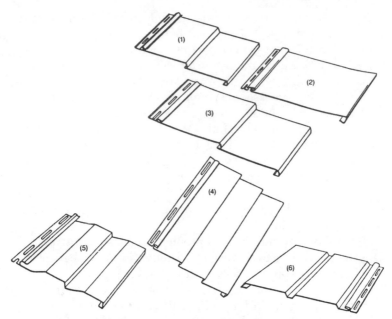

76. Various types of vinyl siding: (1) double 4"; (2) single 8"; (3) double 5"; (4) triple 3"; (5) Dutch lap; (6) vertical siding, which is also available in various sizes. (Vinyl Siding Institute)

breaking if hit with a hard object. Repair is relatively easy: The offending panel is simply replaced. Vinyl also has shallower textures than aluminum and will fade more easily.

Maintenance is minimal. Hosing it down once a year does it.

There is no specific grading system, but, rather, the siding is divided into three groups and the characteristics define the grade. These characteristics are: color, gauge, profile (shapes), texture, and sheen.

The lowest-quality group, the so-called builder's grade, is available in a limited number of colors, chiefly white, gray, cream, and clay, a gauge or thickness of around .040 inch, and one or two styles or profiles. Generally such builder's grade has a high-gloss finish.

In the midrange of quality products is a group that is available in a broader range of colors (seven to twelve), has a richer, thicker gauge (.042 to .044 inch), and comes in a

77. This house shown was redone with vinyl siding. Trim is an important consideration to maintain the finished look of a house. Many installers skip the area around windows and doors (because it takes a long time to install the vinyl in those places), and it shows. (Vinyl Window and Door Institute)

broader selection of profiles. These also have a lower gloss than builder's grade. Most people will select from this range.

The premium vinyl siding line is thicker, comes in a wide variety of colors, and can have special designs and textures. It has a low sheen.

Gauge matters. In the thinner gauges the vinyl, which is flexible, will reflect the siding or house "bumps" and so forth beneath it, so it is all too easy for the new siding to have a wavy look. Even the heaviest gauges may not do the job. As mentioned above, if a house is uneven with ridges and bumps, the installer will either use backer board or will nail on thin vertical wood strips to assure a level surface.

How the Job Is Done

Vinyl siding is really hung rather than nailed to the house. The vinyl panels have slots in the top through which nails are driven, but not so tight that the vinyl can't move—that is, expand and contract. If it can't move, it can buckle.

The job is started at the bottom of the house, and as the panels are nailed in place, the one above hooks onto the one below. The ends of the panels are slipped into various types of formed molding. Cutting of vinyl is usually done with a circular saw equipped with a bit designed to cut plastic.

Workmanship

The key consideration in installing vinyl siding is that the sections be installed loosely enough so that the siding, while hanging securely in place, is not so tight that it can't expand and contract. Such expansion can lead to parts pressing against one another and buckling.

The installer should also strive to have the siding joints occur over doorways and windows to make them less obvious.

78. Vinyl is hung loosely rather than nailed tight.

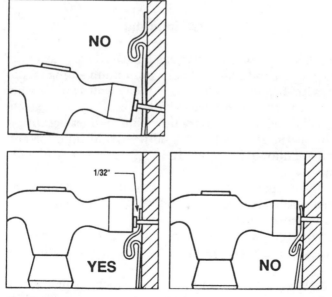

79. The proper way to nail vinyl siding—loosely—is shown at the lower left.

Possible Rip-offs

The biggest rip-off here is someone telling you you have to take the existing siding off when you don't need to, and charging you thousands for the privilege.

Make sure, also, that when getting bids on a job you know whether trim is included. Some installers leave this aspect vague, and you may think it's included in the price when it isn't. In some cases very limited trim is required, and this can be, as mentioned, an important cost consideration.

Cost

Per square foot, not including trim:
Materials (mid-quality): $1.30
Labor: $ .97
Total: $2.27

IMPROVEMENT: ALUMINUM SIDING

Products/Materials

Aluminum siding comes in various lengths and a variety of styles, textures, and colors. Classic aluminum siding is aluminum with baked-on colors, but today you can also get aluminum covered with a fluorocarbon coating, such as Du Pont's Tedlar, which is a more desirable product because it sheds dirt better and helps the siding retain its color better than regular aluminum. It is, of course, much more expensive.

The big bugaboo of aluminum is that it can be dented and scratched. Otherwise, it's a good product and has better colors and deeper textures than vinyl.

Like vinyl it will fade with time, but repainting is possible, though this would defeat its low-maintenance feature.

Gauge differs. Much aluminum is .019 inches thick, which makes it necessary to use **backer board** behind it. Thicker,

.024-inch gauge does not require backer board. The thicker gauge is the better material.

You'll also pay more or less for aluminum depending on surface texture. The more work the manufacturer puts into the product, the more you pay.

How the Job Is Done

Aluminum siding is installed like vinyl. The job starts with a starter strip at the bottom and then proceeds up, the panels interlocking and nailed in place through perforated tabs in the tops.

The ends of siding sections fit into various kinds of channels, and there is material for building out windows.

If existing siding is particularly wavy or ridged, vertical or horizontal furring strips can be applied to achieve a level surface.

Cost

Per square foot:
  Materials (thickest gauge): $1.75
  Labor: $ .97
  Total: $2.72
(includes accessories)

IMPROVEMENT: STEEL SIDING

Products/Materials

Steel siding is available in roughly the same sizes as aluminum but is sturdier than both aluminum and vinyl. It comes in a wide variety of colors and simulates wood siding.

Two drawbacks of steel: If scratched, it must be touched up or it will rust; and it can't be used in ocean areas.

How the Job Is Done

Steel is installed like aluminum: a starter strip is installed at the bottom, and then lengths of panel are secured to the wall with nails driven through perforations at the top; subsequent panels overlap and hook onto previously installed panels.

Like aluminum, trim is available for finishing windows and the like.

Cost

For 8-inch smooth steel siding, per square foot:
    Materials: $1.45
    Labor: $1.00
    Total: $2.45

IMPROVEMENT: PLYWOOD SIDING

Products/Materials

These are 4-by-8-foot plywood panels that come in a variety of facings or veneers—redwood, cedar, Douglas fir, southern pine, and so on—and with various finishes from rough-sawn to textures and with vari-spaced grooves. Thickness as well as facing defines the grade. Thickness can range from thin to thick—$^{11}/_{32}$, $^3/_8$, $^1/_2$, $^{15}/_{32}$, and $^3/_4$ inch—though the latter must be special-ordered. Take care not to order a panel that is too thin—it can reflect any waviness in the wall beneath, even when installed over good **sheathing**.

Depending on the veneer, the plywood will be either stained or, if a lesser quality, painted.

The American Plywood Association (APA) puts its stamp on the panels it makes, and all will use exterior glue. Some foreign manufacturers do not use exterior glue, and this can lead to delamination of the panels. To be safe, look for the APA grading stamp.

APA	APA	APA
RATED SIDING	RATED SIDING	RATED SIDING
24 OC 19/32 INCH	303-18-S/W	LAP
SIZED FOR SPACING	16 OC 11/32 INCH GROUP 1	16 OC 7/16 INCH
EXTERIOR	SIZED FOR SPACING	EXTERIOR
000	EXTERIOR	000
NER-QA397 PRP-108	000	NER-QA397 PRP-108
	PS 1-83 FHA-UM-64	
	NER-QA397 PRP-108	

80. Buying APA-rated siding is the safe way to buy. Information is stamped on the panels as shown. (American Plywood Association)

How the Job Is Done

Plywood panels can be used over any existing siding. Sometimes the siding will be removed and the panels nailed side by side to the studs. If it is new work, sheathing is applied and the panels are also nailed to the studs. In cases where there is an existing rough siding, such as masonry, furring strips may be applied to level the surface for the panels as they are nailed on.

Windows can usually stay as is, or aluminum trim is used over them. The panels can either be painted or stained.

Cost

Texture 1-11 cedar panels, ⅝ inch thick, per square foot:
   Materials: $1.69
   Labor: $ .63
   Total: $2.32

IMPROVEMENT: BOARD SIDING

Products/Materials

Today a number of products, such as aluminum and vinyl, do a good job of simulating wood siding, but the real thing is most certainly still available. It comes in various thicknesses of ½ to ¾ inch; in widths of 4 to 12 inches; and in random lengths. Some sidings have a rough-sawn side and

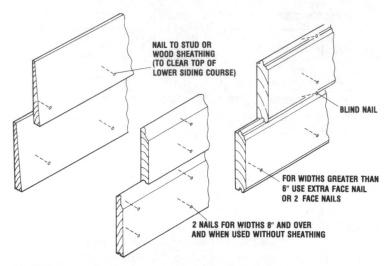

NAIL TO STUD OR
WOOD SHEATHING
(TO CLEAR TOP OF
LOWER SIDING COURSE)

BLIND NAIL

FOR WIDTHS GREATER THAN
6″ USE EXTRA FACE NAIL
OR 2 FACE NAILS

2 NAILS FOR WIDTHS 8″ AND OVER
AND WHEN USED WITHOUT SHEATHING

81. Various wood siding, also showing installation details. The top left is bevel siding; the lower left is drop pattern, the upper right is paneling pattern. They come in various woods and thicknesses.

a smooth side; the former is for staining, the latter for painting. Profiles vary. The classic is bevel siding, which is basically a tapered board, and drop siding, which is an even thickness. Many people who buy wood siding prefer to stain it. Most wood is beautiful, but expensive. Why hide the beauty with paint?

Also available is lap siding, which is basically ⅜-inch-thick plywood pieces 8 to 16 inches wide that hang and overlap each other.

Cost of board siding varies greatly according to the kind of wood used, style, and thickness.

How the Job Is Done

Some board siding, such as drop siding, can be nailed directly to the studs, but it is usually nailed to the sheathing.

Installation varies to some degree, but it normally starts at the bottom of the house and works upward.

Cost

1-by-8-inch redwood drop siding, per square foot:
Materials: $2.42
Labor: $1.00
Total: $3.42

IMPROVEMENT: CEDAR SHAKES OR SHINGLES

Products/Materials

Cedar shingles are cut by machine and have a striated face. They are 18 inches long and are ⅜ or ½ inch thick at the butt, or bottom. They are parallel on the sides, and the butt ends are more or less square. They come in three common grades: Perfections No. 1, No. 2 and "undercourse," with No. 1 the best.

There are also sawn shingles, but these come 18 to 24 inches long.

So-called handsplit—made by hand—shakes are rough-hewn, neither parallel at the butts nor at the sides, and range in thickness at the butt from ⅜ to 1¼ inches. (They are actually sorted into three groups by thickness: ⅜ to about ½ inch, ½ to ¾ inch, and ¾ to 1¼ inches, but thicknesses can go all the way to 2 inches.) They are also available in 18- or 24-inch lengths.

How the Job Is Done

Cedar shingles are installed with or without an undercourse (lesser quality shingles), which tends to push the bottom of the shingle out and give a shadow effect. The first course is nailed to the bottom of the wall and the installation proceeds upward.

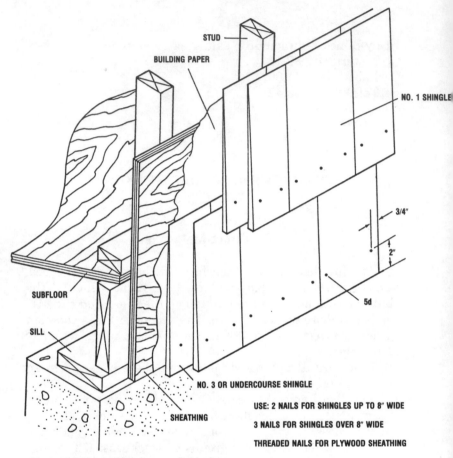

82. Installation details for wood shingles.

Cost

No. 1 Perfections shingles, 18-inches fire retardant, per square foot installed:
   Materials: $1.17
   Labor: $1.16
   Total: $2.33
Shakes 24 inches:
   Materials: $1.21
   Labor: $1.46
   Total: $2.67

IMPROVEMENT: HARDBOARD SIDING

Products/Materials

Hardboard siding comes in large-panel or board forms. It is available in a variety of textures and qualities. An indication here is the warranty; some manufacturers offer five-year warranties, some fifteen, but to put it in effect, the siding must be **painted** within a certain period of time—thirty, sixty, or ninety days, depending on the make and maker. Unfinished hardboard can deteriorate.

The cost of hardboard, like other sidings, will depend on its texture and just how fancy it is.

How the Job Is Done

Hardboard is applied with nails, which go into either studs or sheathing. Then it is painted just like any wood or wood-composition product.

Workmanship

The key to a quality hardboard-siding job is that it be painted with quality paint following manufacturer's directions. Some contractors use cheap paint, which doesn't last and shortens the life of the material.

Also, if the surface is dented or broken while nailing, it is imperative that the dent be patched with caulking so that no water can possibly penetrate.

Cost

12-inch-wide cedar-finish panels, primed, per square foot:
Materials: $ .90
Labor: $ .67
Total: $1.57

Gutters

IMPROVEMENT: GUTTERS

Products/Materials

Gutter comes in a variety of materials: aluminum, wood, copper, plastic, and galvanized steel.

The most popular gutter is aluminum, and this comes either standard-cut or seamless. Standard-cut is usually of 10-foot lengths and .027 gauge, which is so thin that it will bend when you lean a ladder against it. Aluminum comes 4 or 5 inches wide; water-carrying capacity is much greater with 5-inch material.

The best is .032 gauge seamless, which can be gotten in 32-foot lengths at shops that specialize in gutter but is most commonly extruded on the job to the exact lengths needed by the contractor. This is always .032 gauge. If you buy standard-cut, it's usually only available in white; seamless material may be white, green gold, brown, or black.

Wood gutter is available at lumberyards in lengths up to 50 feet. It is usually made of fir and weighs up to six times what aluminum does.

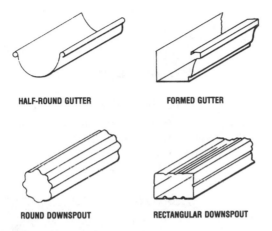

HALF-ROUND GUTTER   FORMED GUTTER

ROUND DOWNSPOUT   RECTANGULAR DOWNSPOUT

83. These are the forms that gutter and downspout come in.

Copper is a very expensive material and it comes in standard 10-foot lengths; the joints need to be soldered together.

Galvanized steel comes in standard 10-foot lengths and various baked-enamel finishes. It can also be found in 20-foot lengths and comes in various profiles, including half-round and fluted.

Vinyl gutter comes in various lengths from 10 to 32 feet but only in 5-inch widths and in either white or brown.

Various accessories come with gutter, such as leaders (vertical portions of the gutter system), tubs, and grids for catching leaves. Professionals call gutter rainware, which presumably sounds more elegant than gutter.

How the Job Is Done

Gutter is hung with three different types of hangers depending on house design: one is to drive spikes through the edges of the gutter, another utilizes straps, and a third has hangers attached to brackets. In any case a level line is first snapped across the house fascia. Then this is used as a guide for snapping a slanted or pitched line. The gutter is installed with its top edge even with this so that the water will run out of it. The gutter is attached with various hangers. Attachment of end pieces and the like and the joining of sections is done prior to hanging.

Workmanship

One mistake people make is to assume that the house is level and then pitch the gutter off of this. Homes are rarely if ever perfectly level, hence water can remain standing in the gutter if not pitched properly.

Do-It-Yourself

This could be a job for the adventurous do-it-yourselfer.

Costs per running foot

Treated fir, 4-foot by 5-inch:
    Materials: $10.00
    Labor: $ 2.36
    Total: $12.36
Copper, 5-inch half-round:
    Materials: $7.25
    Labor: $1.89
    Total: $9.14
Aluminum, white enamel, seamless:
    Materials: $1.76
    Labor: $3.97
    Total: $5.73
Vinyl, 5-inch, colored or white:
    Materials: $1.42
    Labor: $1.29
    Total: $2.71
Steel, 6 inch:
    Materials: $2.00
    Labor: $1.47
    Total: $3.47

Driveways

IMPROVEMENT: CONCRETE DRIVEWAY

Products/Materials

Concrete is the main material used. Contractors routinely have it delivered by truck.

How the Job Is Done

First the driveway is staked off with boards and string, then 6 or 7 inches of soil are removed and the area is leveled.

A base of sand or gravel is poured on top of this. Wire reinforcing mesh is placed, and the concrete is poured, leveled, and finished.

Workmanship

Many concrete drives fail because the job is done improperly. For best results have a 2-inch bed of sand laid, followed by ⅛-inch-diameter 6-inch square wire reinforcing mesh and then 4 inches of concrete. A good-quality job would involve three bags of sand or four bags of "concrete sand" (sand with rocks in it) for every bag of cement used. After the concrete is poured, the reinforcing wire should be lifted up 2 inches off the base so that it sits more or less in the middle of the concrete.

The driveway should be made in as straight a line as possible in relation to the street and slightly pitched for water runoff, or crowned—made higher in the middle than the edges. If water can puddle, the driveway will eventually deteriorate.

Asphalt expansion strips—4-inch-wide strips of asphalt-impregnated material—should be installed every 20 feet or so. When the ground bulks up from frost and heaves, the driveway sections will have some give and it won't crack. There should also be a strip between the end of the driveway and the garage-floor slab.

Possible Rip-offs

Sometimes a contractor will try to pour less concrete or a weaker mix. Write the mix formula into your contract. It will give a thief pause. And check the delivery invoice the concrete truck driver has to ensure that it reflects what you contracted for.

Cost

Cost per square foot for a 4-inch-thick driveway with a 4-inch sand base and wire reinforcing:

Materials: $1.67
Labor: $1.37
Total: $3.04

IMPROVEMENT: ASPHALT DRIVEWAY

Products/Materials

The main material used in this job is a hot-mix blend of asphalt, tar, and sand. Quality asphalt is black or dark brown—no streaks of white or brown—and must be installed hot (the warm months are the best times).

Gravel and other fillers are used in preparing the base for the asphalt if one is required.

How the Job Is Done

First the ground is prepared. If the soil is good (it drains well), then all that is necessary is to tamp it down and install a minimum of 4 inches of well-compacted asphalt. If the soil is clay, which doesn't drain well, then the contractor will dig this out and lay a bed of well-compacted gravel of 4 to 7 inches and then 4 inches of asphalt over that. After a year or so a sealer will be applied.

Workmanship

Complaints about asphalt driveways rank high in consumer protection departments around the country. In a number of states it is the most complained-about job.

The chief complaint has to do with cracking, but there are also complaints about water puddling in the driveway, the asphalt not getting hard, and damage to the surrounding property.

The main reason asphalt cracks is that the soil has not been prepared for it properly. Water under the asphalt can cause problems, and so can a base that moves—when it moves, the asphalt cracks.

Cracking can also be caused by too thin a layer of asphalt. Contractors may install a heavy base of gravel, then only 2 inches of asphalt. It's far better to have 4 inches of asphalt.

Puddling is caused by poor crowning of the material. It must be higher in the middle than on the sides and be sloped to the curb so that water can run down it.

Possible Rip-offs

Trying to do a quick and dirty job on soil preparation is one way contractors will try to rip people off. Pouring only an inch or two of material instead of 4 inches is another way. You also want the material to be the proper mix. The best insurance for this is to get an honest contractor. Contact the Asphalt Institute and they will give you the name of asphalt producers in your area; the producers know who uses the best mixes. For more information contact: Asphalt Institute, Research Park Drive, P.O. Box 14052, Lexington, Ky 40512-4052.

Cost

250 square feet or more:

New driveway (4-inch base of sand or stone, plus 4 inches of asphalt): $416.00 basic price, plus $1.96 per square foot.

Asphalt redo (2 inches of asphalt over a solid base): $264.00 basic price, plus $1.20 per square foot.

Patios and Walkways

IMPROVEMENT: BRICK-ON-SAND PATIO AND WALKWAYS

Products/Materials

The standard size of brick is 8 inches long, 4 inches wide, and 2¼ inches thick. Most brick is red, but it can also be obtained in other colors—black, white, and tan, for example—and in many different shades. It also comes glazed (shiny) and unglazed. Additionally there are bricks for special uses, such as those designed strictly for paving.

Brick is durable, but the most durable of all is "well-burned," which is a deep red color as opposed to brick that is pinkish; the latter is known as green brick because it's not as readily available.

Many people like used brick, and this could actually cost more than new material.

When buying brick, the mason should buy it from one yard all at once. Brick color tends to vary from batch to batch—it is a man-made product—and you want the color from brick to brick to be as close as possible.

How the Job Is Done

The first step in doing the job is to excavate it to a depth of 7 or 8 inches and remove the topsoil. Next some sort of edging, such as brick mortared together, and then some sort of material for drainage, such as gravel or stone, is laid. Then a layer of felt paper is laid, or else polyethylene sheeting, on top of this to prevent vegetation from growing through and penetrating the surface (weeds can grow through sand and stones). And then a 1- to 2-inch layer of sand is laid and tamped thoroughly to make the base flat and firm for the brick.

As the bricks are installed, they are tamped firmly into place and are cut to fit against the edging as needed. Even spacing of bricks is maintained throughout.

Finally sand is sprinkled in the joints and the area sprayed with water.

The same procedure may be used for brick walkways.

For an even more solid installation, mortar can be mixed with sand; the brick will then be one mass that can't move.

Workmanship

The key consideration in a brick or sand patio or walkway is proper excavation and preparation of the soil. All the topsoil must be removed, and the ground must be leveled and tamped.

Do-It-Yourself

Laying a brick-on-sand patio is well within the province of the do-it-yourselfer.

Cost

$10.00 per square foot.

IMPROVEMENT: FLAGSTONE-ON-SAND PATIO AND WALKWAYS

Products/Materials

Flagstone is a natural stone material ranging from ½ to 2 inches thick and that comes in various shapes, from free-form to rectangles, and in various lovely colors (soft yellows, browns, greens, grays, and reds). It is much more expensive than brick—four or five times the cost—but installation is no more problematic.

How the Job Is Done

The job is done the same way as with brick. Prepare the base carefully, then lay each stone in place, tamping it carefully and well.

Workmanship

As with brick, the key is proper preparation of the ground.

Cost

¾ to 1-inch thick: $11.25 per square foot.

Decks

In the last 15 years or so, decks have become very popular, perhaps because they maximize the living area—although outdoors—that people have.

In their earliest forms, decks tended to be simple rectangles, no more than floors, but today they are truly designed, with multiple angles, flooring laid in many different patterns such as herringbone, diagonal, parquet, and with plantings . . . shrubs, trees, groundcover as elements of design. Indeed, many decks are built around trees.

A popular feature today is a hot tub on the deck. These are made in various sizes and can accommodate a number of people simultaneously.

Depending on house design, decks may be built on the ground, or be raised, even multilevel.

Design is critical and it is suggested that one plan carefully here. Look at how other decks have been built for houses that are the same or similar to your own. There is also much literature available on the subject in terms of design, and of course, there are books, magazines and videos mentioned in chapter 2.

You should also consult with your local building code department to see what is required by the code. Commonly, for example, the balustrades, or vertical fence rails, must be certain distances apart on a raised deck so that no one can fall through them.

One of the relatively newer deck materials is **pressure-treated lumber**, which means that it is regular lumber such as pine that is treated with chemicals which help it resist rot and insects. The problem with such wood is that the chemicals injected into the wood are poisonous, and they must be handled with care and treated with respect. Once it cures, however, there is no longer any problem with it. Controversy currently surrounds the use of pressure-treated lumber. We suggest that you discuss the use of pressure-treated lumber with your contractor and your local health department.

IMPROVEMENT: RAISED DECK

Products/Materials

Deck lumber is commonly cedar, redwood, or pressure treated (CCA) and it's availability will depend on where you live. For example, in the west, redwood would be more readily available—because that's the home of redwood trees—than in the east. In fact, redwood is invariably used in the west.

All three kinds of materials can work well. **Redwood** is probably the most expensive of the three, followed by **cedar**, and then **pressure treated**. All can take the weather without finishing but will last up to 20% longer when finished.

As you might guess, all three materials come in various grades, which differ in price and appearance.

How the Job Is Done

Essentially this is a deck set on a supporting structure of some sort and stairs.

One way to save money on it is to use pressure-treated

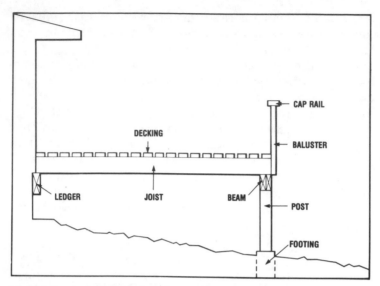

84. Details of a raised-level deck.

lumber for the supporting structure and cedar or redwood, which is prettier, for the decking material.

The removal of some of the siding from the house where the joists are located is necessary. Then a ledger board—a hefty 2 by 10 or the like—is bolted or screwed to the house sheathing. This serves as one component in supporting the joists on which the decking, or floorboards, will be secured.

Piers or posts, which are perhaps 4 by 4's or larger, are set on concrete-filled footings which are basically holes, dug deeper than the frost line to guard against frost heaving. The hole depth would depend on the area you live in. For example, in Minneapolis they have to go down around 3½ feet. It is less in the northeast, and probably negligible or nonexistent in some southern states. Posts used must be pressure treated to resist decay.

These posts are located to form intermediate supports for the deck. There is also usually a large beam placed on the perimeter of the deck parallel to the ledger board.

With the posts and beam in place, joists are nailed into

position, and then decking nailed to this, allowing certain space between boards for drainage.

Steps are also built and a railing added.

Cost

Decking and support structure, $700.00 plus $5.75/square foot if done with pressure treated lumber; $9.50 if done with construction-grade redwood. Deck rails: With pressure treated: $8.20/linear foot. With construction grade redwood: $11.17/linear foot.

Stairs (48″ wide) with two 2 by 6's per tread: $38.50 for pressure treated per step; $64.50 for construction grade redwood.

IMPROVEMENT: MODULAR GROUND-LEVEL DECK

Products/Materials

This deck is built with pressure-treated lumber modules which may be placed directly on the ground. Each module may be built to whatever size you wish—4 by 4, 4 by 6, 4 by 8—and then laid together on the ground to form the deck.

How the Job Is Done

The ground is prepared first. If it is level a 6-inch trench is dug around what will be the perimeter of the deck, then filled with gravel. This helps water runoff.

If the ground is uneven then the whole area is excavated and filled with 3 inches of gravel followed by 3 inches of sand and leveled.

Modules are built next, as shown in the sketches, and then simply laid in place.

85. Modular deck. (Courtesy of Western Wood Products Association)

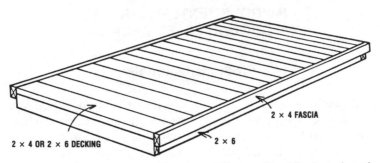

86. One of the deck modules. (Courtesy of Western Wood Products Association)

Do-It-Yourself

This project is well within the capabilities of the beginning do-it-yourselfer.

Cost

See above.

Porch

IMPROVEMENT: PORCH

Products/Materials

There are a variety of ways to construct a porch, and you can use a number of different materials. One of the least expensive is **pressure-treated wood**. Here pressure-treated pine, **CDX plywood, galvanized nails**, and **asphalt shingles** are the main materials used. See p. 317 for more on pressure-treated wood.

How the Job Is Done

Like many extensions, the porch is first laid out with stakes and string. To facilitate this process, batter boards are constructed consisting of long 2 by 4s driven into the ground with 1 by 6s nailed horizontally to them. These are used as reference points to determine where the **foundation** should be placed.

Next the **excavation** is done. In the case pictured here

87. Before the porch was added. (Photo courtesy of Western Wood Products Association)

88. Porch framing in place. It's built just like a house, only smaller. (Courtesy of Western Wood Products Association)

89. Another view of framing. (Courtesy of Western Wood Products Association)

90. The completed porch. (Courtesy of Western Wood Products Association)

the ground sloped (3 feet in an 8-foot area), and the area had to be cleared of shrubs and greenery.

Next **concrete footings** are installed, just as for a house, in a step fashion and to accommodate the slope of the land. Block is installed on top of that, with openings left in the block for covering with lattice.

Then the porch is constructed, again like a house. First 2-by-6 pressure-treated sill boards are attached to the tops of the foundation. Next perimeter joists are secured to the sills and the house opened up to accommodate a ledger, to which the ends of the joists are secured.

Next the 2-by-10 pressure-treated pine joists are nailed in place. Roof framing supports are erected next, followed by roof framing, just as when building a house or adding a room. (The roof slope is calculated to match the slope of the house roof.)

CDX ¾-inch sheathing is applied to the roof framing; ½-inch exterior plywood was used to box in the triangular ends of the roof, and rake boards added on the side and fascia in the front. Here asphalt roof shingles are used over a base of felt.

Following this, the flooring is installed, in this case 1-by-6 pressure-treated pine; these are secured to the joists with hot-dipped galvanized nails.

With the flooring in place, electrical fixtures are added between ceiling joists. In the present example 3½-inch tongue-and-groove pine boards are nailed to the joists forming the ceiling, and the porch is finished with an alkyd exterior paint.

Do-It-Yourself

Not for the beginner.

Cost

As built here, $1,400.00 basic price, plus $14.50 per square foot.

Termite Control

IMPROVEMENT: TERMITE CONTROL

Products/Materials

Ninety-five percent of all the termites in America are characterized as being the subterranean type, meaning that they live in nests deep in damp soil and arise periodically for food—that is, wood.

They leave signs such as mud tubes up the sides of **foundation walls**. Also, wood that has been attacked may be softened and thus easily penetrated by a sharp object.

The other kind of termites, seen mostly in the south and in California, are the flying type.

The top city in the country for termites, according to the Orkin Pest Control Company, is Miami.

How the Job Is Done

Ridding a house of termites is a job for a pro. Essentially he must inject chemicals into the ground between the house and the nests, building a chemical shield against them. This might well entail drilling through walks and other masonry around the house, an extensive and expensive process.

On new construction, say an addition, it is important to have the contractor install a termite shield, a piece of bent-over metal or other material that will keep the termites from gaining entry.

Since drywood termites fly and don't depend on nests, it is more difficult to rid a house of them. Sometimes it can be done by poisoning their nest, but sometimes the whole house has to be sealed up and fumigated.

Possible Rip-offs

Occasionally scamsters go door-to-door selling termite inspections, and you can believe they'll find termites—those they brought in with them.

If you suspect termites, ask neighbors if they've had the problem and for the name of someone they've used. Or contact a company that has been around for several years.

Cost

$400 to $1,400, depending on the extent of the job.

Waterproofing

IMPROVEMENT: WATERPROOF BASEMENT

Products/Materials

A variety of products and materials are used to handle moisture in the basement, depending on severity. Details are listed below.

How the Job Is Done

This will depend on what the problem is. If the walls are just damp, which comes from condensation (warm air condensing on a cold surface), the problem may be solved by reducing the amount of water vapor in the home by making sure driers are vented to the outside, cold-water pipes are covered with insulation, and other general efforts (such as, perhaps, reducing showers) are made. If the problem persists, a dehumidifier may be a wise buy.

Water may also come through hairline cracks or porous masonry foundation walls, or may seep through masonry.

Commonly such water comes from **gutters** not transporting water away properly. Water saturates the ground next to the foundation and seeps in. Solution: repairing leaky or wrongly pitched gutters.

Another cause could be that the ground is not pitched to carry water away from the house but instead is routing it toward the foundation. Regrading or filling in the depressed area with gravel usually solves the problem.

In some cases a small flow of water may be stopped by applying hydraulic (quick-drying) cement ⅛-inch thick to the leaking area, or ⅜-inch thick mortar.

In the vast majority of cases where porous masonry is the problem, application of a waterproofing paint, such as UGL Drylock, will cure the problem. It is made of rubber and cement and locks into masonry pores. But to be effective—and keep a virtual lake out—it can be used only on raw masonry.

In other cases relieving the pressure of earth or water against the foundation wall may be required. This would be done by digging up the earth around the foundation, buttressing the wall, installing drain tile, or other methods.

In still other cases a high water table may be the problem; handling this—but not curing it—has to be done with a sump pump. Here a hole is dug in the basement floor, and the pump is installed; when the hole or sump fills with water, it is pumped out.

Possible Rip-offs

This is a prime rip-off area. Be sure to get a number of diagnoses and estimates. If the cause is not obvious, this would be a good spot to hire an **ASHI** (American Society of Home Inspectors) inspector.

Do-It-Yourself

Applying waterproofing paint to masonry is an easy do-it-yourself job. So may be repairing or resetting gutters, as well as repairing active leaks with hydraulic cement or mortar cement. Jobs that require repairing the wall from below grade or installing drain tile is a job for a professional.

Costs

To apply waterproof paint, per 125 square feet: $35.

APPENDIX A:
Sample Contract

Following is a sample contract that does a good job of spelling out the agreement between a contractor and homeowner. While the contract was prepared for a new home, it is, as Reynolds Graves (attorney and partner in the Oakdale, Long Island, firm of Graves, Gold and Darbee, who provided it) says, "interchangeable with contracts for major renovations and extensions of homes."

The contract was drawn several years ago, and while it does a generally good job, based on my research—and Graves agrees—it could go even farther in the amount of detail it provides on products and materials. Also, I would not agree with the idea of giving any money up front, because of the lien law. Graves points out, however, that in New York State—where this contract was drawn—the law is "permeated with good faith. If the homeowner has acted out of good faith in paying for the job, there is no way," says Graves, "that he is going to lose anything under the lien law." (Still, a lawyer might be needed to fight the lien.)

The document below, incidentally, is just one of a number of others, such as permits and drawings, that would become part of the contract.

Also, it identifies neither the company, the homeowner, nor the address where the home was built.

It should be emphasized that this contract would be for a major job. For many jobs just making sure that the agreement with the contractor includes the points suggested in the contract chapter would be enough.

GENERAL CONDITIONS

ARTICLE I—DEFINITIONS

Wherever used in these General Conditions, or in the contract documents annexed hereto and made a part hereof, the following terms shall have the meanings indicated hereunder and said meanings shall be applicable to both the singular and plural thereof:

1. *Agreement*—the written Agreement between Owner and Contractor covering the work to be performed, including these General Conditions, the plans, specifications, blueprints and other Contract Documents attached to these General Conditions and made a part hereof.

2. *Application for Payment*—form to be used by Contractor in requesting progress payments, including the schedule of values required by Paragraph 1 of Article III and the Affidavit of Contractor that progress payments theretofore received from Owner on account of the work performed have been applied by Contractor to discharge in full all of Contractor's obligations incurred in connection with the work covered by all prior applications for payment.

3. *Change Order*—a written order to Contractor, signed by the Owner, authorizing an addition, deletion or revision in the work, or an adjustment in the Contract Price or the Contract Time issued after the execution of the Agreement.

4. *Contract Documents*—the Agreement, including these General Conditions, any bid submitted by Contractor, the specifications, drawings and modifications thereto.

5. *Contract Price*—the total of all monies payable to Contractor under the Contract Documents.

6. *Contract Time*—the number of calendar days stated in the Agreement for the completion of work.

7. *Contractor*—the person, firm or corporation with whom Owner has contracted for the performance of this Agreement.

8. *Drawings*—the drawings that show the character and scope of the work to be performed which have been prepared or approved by _____ and which are referred to in the Contract Documents.

9. *Field Order*—a written order issued by Owner or Owner's agent, such as an architect or engineer, that clarifies or interprets the Contract Documents in accordance with Paragraph 1 of Article II of these General Conditions, or which orders minor changes in the work in accordance with Paragraph 1 of Article IV of these General Conditions.

10. *Modification*—As used herein, "Modification" shall be defined as any of the following:

a. a written amendment of the Contract Documents signed by both parties; or

b. a Change Order; or

c. a written clarification or interpretation issued by Owner or Owner's agent (architect or engineer) in accordance with Paragraph 1 of Article IV; or

d. a written order for a minor change or alteration in work issued by _____ (architect or engineer) pursuant to Paragraph 1 of the Article IV.

A modification may only be issued after execution of this Agreement.

11. *Owner*—a public body or authority, corporation, association, partnership or individual for whom the work is to be performed.

12. *Project*—the entire construction to be performed as provided in the Contract Documents.

13. *Shop Drawings*—all drawings, diagrams, illustrations, brochures, schedules and any other data prepared by Contractor, a subcontractor, manufacturer, supplier, or distributor which illustrate the equipment or material to be used, or any portion of the work to be performed.

14. *Subcontractor*—an individual, firm or corporation having a direct contract with the Contractor or with any other subcontractor for the performance of a part of the work at the Project.

15. *Substantial Completion*—a date when the construction of the Project or a specified part thereof is sufficiently completed, in accordance with the Contract Documents, so that the Project

or specified part thereof can be utilized for the purposes for which it was intended; or the date when final payment is due in accordance with Paragraph 1 of Article IX.

16. *Work*—any and all obligations, duties and responsibilities necessary to successfully complete the Project undertaken by Contractor under the Contract Documents, including the furnishing of labor, materials, equipment and other incidentals.

ARTICLE II—DESCRIPTION OF WORK

1. Contractor shall perform the following described work, in accordance with the Contract Documents, at the following location: 1 Newhome Place, Greenlawn, New York; vacant land, 80 × 100 lot said premises appearing on the Suffolk County Tax Map at District _____Section _____ Block _____Lot _____, and being more particularly described on Schedule A annexed hereto.

Description of Work: Construct a one-family dwelling in accordance with plans and specifications prepared by Gerald Allenby, on vacant land of Owners located on Newhome Place, Greenlawn, New York. Said Model being Scottsdale III (revised Scottsdale I) with 1½-car garage and 12 × 14 den behind garage.

ARTICLE III—CONTRACT PRICE

1. Owner agrees to pay the Contractor, for the work herein described, the total sum of ONE HUNDRED SIX THOUSAND SEVEN HUNDRED THIRTY-SIX ($106,736.00) DOLLARS. This price includes the cost of two (2) storm doors. However, this price does not include New York State Energy Conservation update as of April 1, 1987, which requires insulation factor R-19 in exterior walls and basement floor. The Village of Patchogue will determine method of construction technique required for New York State Code. The price will not exceed additional cost of Two Thousand ($2,000.00) Dollars to comply with the foregoing. Payment of this amount shall be subject to additions or deductions in accordance with the provisions of these General Conditions and the Contract Documents. Payment on the total Contract Price is to be made in installments as follows:

a. Upon the signing of this Contract, receipt of $ 10,673.00
    which is acknowledged
b. Upon completion of the foundation walls $ 16,010.50

c.	Upon completion of the framing and sheathing	$ 28,683.50
d.	Upon installation of the rough plumbing and electric work and installment of insulation	$ 16,010.50
e.	Upon completion of Sheetrock, taping, spackling and painting	$ 16,010.50
f.	Upon final installation of plumbing, electric, flooring, trim and cabinets	$ 16,010.50
g.	Upon the issuance of a Certificate of Occupancy	$ 5,337.50
	Total Payments	**$108,736.00**

2. *Applications for Payment*—at least two (2) days before each progress payment falls due, Contractor will submit to Owner an application for payment duly executed by Contractor and covering the work completed as of the date of application. Such application shall include a statement, in affidavit form, establishing Owner's title to the material and equipment described in said application for payment, including the rights to any insurance or insurance proceeds covering same. Said statement shall further warrant and guarantee that title to all work, materials and equipment covered by the application has passed to Owner, free and clear of all liens, claims, security interests and encumbrances, excepting Contractor's Mechanic's Lien, which shall be released to the extent that payment is received. Upon verification of the statements contained in said application, Owner shall make progress payments to Contractor in accordance with the schedules set forth in paragraph 1 above.

3. *Progress payments may be withheld if:*
a. Work is found defective and not remedied;
b. Contractor does not make prompt and proper payments to Subcontractors;
c. Contractor does not make prompt and proper payments for labor, materials or equipment furnished to Contractor;
d. Claims or liens are filed on the Project.

4. Prior to withholding any progress payment under this paragraph, Owner shall give Contractor written notice of said defect and fourteen (14) days opportunity to cure same.

ARTICLE IV—CHANGES IN THE WORK

1. Without invalidating this Agreement, Owner may order additions, deletions or revisions in the work; however, such ad-

ditions, deletions or revisions shall *only* be authorized by a Change Order. Upon receipt of a Change Order, Contractor shall promptly deliver to Owner by personal delivery, at the address set forth herein, a statement setting forth the total additional charge generated by said Change Order. Unless Owner shall revoke said Change Order by written notice of same within forty-eight (48) hours after receipt of Contractor's statement of additional charge, Owner shall be deemed to have accepted same and shall make full payment for the cost of said Change Order within two (2) days after receipt of an Application for Payment of same, with certification as described in Article III, paragraph 2 hereof.

2. Any additional work performed by Contractor without a Change Order authorization, shall not entitle Contractor to any increase in the Contract Price, unless same shall have been caused by a casualty covered by Owner's insurance or Owner's breach of this Agreement.

ARTICLE V—RESPONSIBILITIES OF OWNER; WARRANTIES OF OWNER

1. Owner covenants and represents that it is the Owner in fee simple absolute of the premises described herein, upon which Contractor's work is to be performed. Owner further warrants and represents that there are no liens, easements, covenants or restrictions, nor any other encumbrance affecting Owner's ability to secure the construction loan referenced herein, or which would be violated by the work described herein.

2. Owner shall furnish all necessary surveys and subsurface tests.

3. If required to gain access to the subject premises, Owner will provide Contractor with easements, rights-of-way or licenses authorizing Contractor to make use of adjoining lands and traverse same while performing its obligations hereunder.

4. Owner will furnish all data required of him under the Contract Documents and make all payments due Contractor promptly after receipt of an Application for Payment and certificates ancillary thereto.

ARTICLE VI—CONTRACTOR'S RESPONSIBILITIES

1. Contractor will supervise and direct the work efficiently and with its best skill and attention. Contractor will be solely responsible for the means, methods, techniques, sequences and

procedures of construction. Contractor shall insure that all finished work complies with Contract Documents.

2. Contractor will furnish all materials, equipment, labor, transportation, construction equipment, machinery and tools necessary for execution, testing, commencement and completion of the work.

3. All materials and equipment will be new, unless otherwise provided in the Contract Documents. If required by Owner, Contractor will furnish satisfactory evidence as to the kind and quality of materials and equipment used. If indicated in the specifications, Contractor may make use of substitute materials or equipment; however, any substitute materials or equipment must be of similar and equal quality to that specified in the Contract Documents and must be capable of performing the same function as those materials or equipment specified.

4. All materials and equipment shall be applied, installed, connected, erected, used, cleaned and conditioned in accordance with the instructions of the applicable manufacturer, fabricator or processor, unless otherwise provided in the Contract Documents.

5. Contractor will give all notices and comply with all laws, ordinances, rules and regulations applicable to the work. If Contractor observes that the specifications, drawings or Contract Documents are at variance therewith, it will give Owner prompt written notice thereof and any necessary changes shall be made by an appropriate Change Order.

6. Contractor will purchase and maintain such insurance as will protect it from claims under Worker's Compensation Laws and Disability Benefit Laws. Contractor shall purchase and maintain comprehensive general liability insurance with limits of not less than $300,000. In addition, Contractor shall not contract with, hire or allow any Subcontractor to perform any work about the demised premises until and unless Contractor shall have received Certificates of Insurance certifying that said Subcontractor has obtained all required Workmen's Compensation Insurance, Employee Disability Insurance and other similar employee benefit insurance. In addition, Contractor shall employ no Subcontractor to perform work at the subject premises without receiving Certificates of Insurance indicating that said Subcontractor has obtained comprehensive general liability covering said Subcontractor in the work to be performed with limits of liability of not less than $300,000.

ARTICLE VII—INSURANCE COVERING THE WORK

1. Owner shall purchase and maintain insurance upon the work to be performed hereunder for the full insurable value thereof. This insurance shall include the interests of the Owner, Contractor, Subcontractors and any Sub-subcontractors in the work and shall insure against the perils of fire, extended coverage, vandalism and malicious mischief.

2. Any insured loss under the Owner's property insurance is to be adjusted with Owner and made payable to Owner as trustee for the insureds, as their interests may appear, subject to the requirements of any applicable mortgage clause. Owner will file a copy of all policies with Contractor prior to Contractor's installation of foundation footings. If Owner shall fail to obtain said insurance or file same with Contractor, Contractor may then purchase such insurance and, by appropriate Change Order, the cost thereof shall be charged to Owner. If Contractor is damaged by the failure of Owner to purchase or maintain such insurance and to so notify Contractor, Owner shall bear the reasonable costs properly attributable thereto.

3. Owner, Contractor, Subcontractor and all Sub-subcontractors waive all rights as against each other for damages caused by fire or other perils to the extent covered by insurance provided under this Article, except such rights as each may have to the proceeds of such insurance held by the Owner as trustee.

4. Owner, as trustee for Contractor and all other insureds under the policy referenced in this Article, shall have the power to adjust and settle any loss or claim with the insurer. Nothing contained herein shall be construed as relieving Owner from his obligation as trustee and fiduciary to settle said claim in good faith to protect the interests of all insureds under the policy referenced herein.

ARTICLE VIII—CONTRACT TIME

1. The work shall be completed within six (6) calendar months after obtaining all Building Permits.

ARTICLE IX—FINAL PAYMENT

1. Owner shall make final payment to Contractor within five (5) days after a Certificate of Occupancy is obtained for the work described herein except for punch-list items. At the time of final payment, Contractor shall deliver to Owner a complete release

of all liens arising out of the Contract herein, or receipts covering, in full, all labor, materials and equipment for which a lien could be filed. All claims generated under this Agreement shall be merged and shall not survive final payment, except any claims generated by the following:

a. Work which does not comply with the Contract Documents; or

b. Outstanding claims or liens generated by the work; or

c. Failure of Contractor to comply with any special guarantees required by the Contract Documents.

2. Contractor, by accepting final payment, waives all claims except those which it has previously made in writing and those which remain unsettled at the time of acceptance.

3. In addition to the documents referenced above, at closing Contractor shall deliver to Owner a Certificate of Occupancy covering all work performed under this Agreement, a Fire Underwriter's Certificate covering all electrical work performed and a Contractor's Guarantee which shall survive final payment and continue for a period of one (1) year from the date the Certificate of Occupancy was obtained.

4. Contractor's liability under the foregoing shall be limited to remedying the defect and none other.

ARTICLE X—MISCELLANEOUS

1. It is expressly agreed by and between the parties hereto that Owner shall not be entitled to use or occupy the work referenced herein, nor any part of the subject premises, prior to the final payment. In the event Owner shall use or occupy any part of the subject premises, Contractor shall be specifically authorized to maintain summary eviction proceedings to evict Owner from said premises.

2. Upon substantial completion of the work described herein, a final acceptance shall be scheduled and a punch list prepared listing all defects or variations which must be completed by Contractor prior to final payment. All work called for in said punch list shall be completed by Contractor within thirty (30) days after preparation of the said punch list.

3. Neither Owner nor Contractor may assign their rights under this Agreement without the other's prior written consent.

4. It is expressly understood and agreed that all prior representations, stipulations, agreements, promises, memoranda and understandings between the parties are merged in this Agreement and that this Agreement states the entire agree-

ment between the parties. This Agreement is binding upon the heirs, executors, administrators and successors of the respective parties.

SPECIFICATIONS

1. Permits: Contractor shall obtain the Building Permits from the Village of Greenlawn authorizing the construction of a one-family dwelling. Any variance, special exception, or other special permit required for insufficient road frontage is not included in Contractor's obligations under this provision.

2. Survey: Owner shall provide general overall survey including stake-out, set foundation, and final survey.

3. Tree Removal: Contractor will only remove trees that obstruct construction of the dwelling and all existing stumps.

4. Excavation: Contractor will clear site, excavate for foundation, backfill, and perform final grading of property. Nothing in this paragraph shall be construed so as to require Contractor to perform any extraordinary excavation in the event Contractor encounters any abnormal subsurface conditions such as the presence of abnormal debris, abnormal rock foundation, etc. Any extraordinary excavation required as a result of the discovery of any such abnormal subsurface condition shall be authorized only upon the issuance of an appropriate Change Order, which said Change Order shall encompass Contractor's increased costs as a result thereof. In addition Contractor shall remove all debris.

5. Foundation: Contractor will install foundation as per plans and specifications, with 8-foot-high walls, 3,000 psi concrete, and damp-proofing on exterior foundation walls only.

6. Utilities: All utilities to the subject premises, including electric, gas, water, telephone, cable TV, and any other utility of whatsoever nature, whether furnished by public or private entity, shall be supplied by Owner. Contractor shall be under no obligation to hook up any part of the subject premises to any such utility, nor shall Contractor be under any obligation to install any mains, hookups, or other devices necessary for such hookup. Any delay caused Contractor by lack of utilities at the subject premises shall entitle Contractor to an extension of the Construction Period provided for in the General Conditions annexed hereto. Owner agrees to execute and deliver to Contractor any Change Order requested as a result of lack of availability of utilities.

7. Cesspools: Contractor shall install "high line" cesspool system with tank and 900-gallon pool. In the event Board of Health approval is withheld because of an alleged insufficiency in such system, Contractor will install a different system only upon the issuance of an appropriate Change Order.

8. Framing: All framing shall be done in accordance with modified plans. All framing shall be 2 × 4 Douglas fir Construction grade. All plywood decking shall be ¾-inch tongue and groove. All sheathing shall be ½-inch plywood. All windows shall be Terratone Andersen windows with screens, and all doors shall be Benchmark Steel.

9. Siding: Contractor will install 1-by-6 tongue-and-groove Common cedar (knotty) and Tyvek vapor barrier.

10. Roofing: Contractor will install No. 235 asphalt roof shingle over 15-lb. felt with continuous ridge venting and continuous soffit vent. In addition Contractor will install brown seamless leaders and gutters.

11. Electric. All electric work shall be as per plan, Contractor agreeing to install 150-amp service, two (2) sets of spotlights, deluxe Builder's-grade features, provisions for four (4) ceiling fans, seven (7) hi-hats, receptacles for washer/dryer/dishwasher/range/range hood included, and decorative switches. In addition Contractor will install service for the dishwasher, range, and washer/dryer hookup. Contractor will install two (2) exterior outlets, the cost of which will not exceed Seventy-Five ($75.00) Dollars. Owner will supply the following major fixtures: kitchen, bath strips, dining room, front door, or any other decorative fixture. Contractor shall be under obligation to install major lighting fixtures. The parties specifically agree that "major" lighting fixtures include kitchen lighting fixtures, breakfast-nook lighting fixtures, dining room lighting fixtures, bathroom lighting fixtures, and exterior front-door and rear lighting fixtures. Basement and garage to include one (1) extra outlet each, not to exceed $80.00.

12. Plumbing: All plumbing work shall be done as per plans, with Contractor installing an oil hot-water-retention head boiler 275-gallon oil tank in basement, a 4-foot shower modular, 5-foot tub modular, 2-zone heating, American Standard toilet bowl, and standard sinks. In addition Owner shall receive a $200 allowance for the selection of faucet fixtures, including the kitchen faucet. Contractor will consult with the plumber regarding the selection of bathroom facilities and fixtures, taking into consideration any medical problems Owner may have.

13. Insulation: Contractor shall install R-19 insulation in all

walls and floors, R-19 insulation in ceilings, R-30 for cathedral ceilings, and 3½-inch insulation in basement ceilings.

14. Sheetrock: Contractor shall install as per plans, ½-inch Sheetrock throughout the interior of the premises, excepting bathrooms and garage. Contractor shall install ½-inch "green" Sheetrock in all bathrooms and ⅝-inch Sheetrock throughout the garage.

15. Taping and Spackling: Contractor shall provide three coats of taping and spackling throughout the interior of the entire house. Contractor shall provide two coats of taping and spackling throughout the garage and all closets.

16. Interior Painting and Staining: Contractor shall provide one coat of Benjamin Moore primer and one coat of Benjamin Moore finish paint throughout entire house and garage. In addition Contractor shall provide Cabots stain for trim. Polyurethane finish is not included. Notwithstanding the foregoing, nothing included herein shall be construed as to require Contractor to provide any stain or varnish of any type, said staining or varnishing being authorized only upon the issuance of an appropriate Change Order. *Exterior Stain:* Benjamin Moore exterior stain one (1) coat.

17. Trim: Contractor shall provide 2½-inch pine clamshell moldings with flush luan doors.

18. Stairs: Contractor shall install basic pine stairs, which stairs shall be sufficient to accept carpeting.

19. Dining Room Floor: Contractor shall install No. 2 red oak flooring in dining room only. Contractor shall install, at no extra charge, red-oak runway from front door to dining area.

20. Wall-to-Wall Carpeting: Contractor will install wall-to-wall carpeting in the bedrooms, den, and living room. However, nothing contained herein shall be construed so as to require Contractor to expend more money than the allowance granted Owner herein. For the purposes of this provision, Owner shall be granted a $3,000 allowance toward the purchase of wall-to-wall carpeting, which allowance shall include installation costs. Any expenditure over said allowance shall be authorized only by the issuance of an appropriate Change Order.

21. Ceramic Tile: Contractor shall install ceramic tile in the two bathrooms. However, Owner's ceramic-tile allowance shall extend only to the following particulars: $3.59 per square foot for materials only. Any cost over the foregoing shall be authorized only by the issuance of an appropriate Change Order.

22. Linoleum: Contractor shall install linoleum in the kitchen.

Owner shall receive an allowance of $1,000 toward the cost thereof, including installation. Any cost over said amount shall be authorized only by the issuance of an appropriate Change Order.

23. Vanities: Contractor shall install two (2) vanities, one in each of the bathrooms. Owner shall be given an allowance of $500 toward the selection of said vanities. The $500 allowance shall cover the cost of purchasing the vanities. Any cost over and above said $500 shall be authorized only by the issuance of an appropriate Change Order.

24. Kitchen Cabinets: Contractor shall install mica style cabinets with oak trim in the kitchen area. Owner shall receive an allowance of $2,500 for materials only toward said kitchen cabinets. Any cost over and above said allowance shall be authorized only by the issuance of an appropriate Change Order.

25. Driveway: Contractor shall install one (1) 30-foot-long, 10-foot-wide one-car asphalt driveway. Upon Owner's request and with the properly signed Change Order, Contractor shall install a 1½-car asphalt driveway or a 2-car asphalt driveway, at the extra cost of $210.00 or $500.00, respectively. Any cost over and above said allowance shall be authorized only by the issuance of an appropriate Change Order.

26. Fireplace: Not included.

27. Garage Door: Contractor shall give Owner a $300.00 allowance toward the purchase of a garage door. Any cost over and above said allowance shall be authorized only by the issuance of an appropriate Change Order.

28. Materials: Contractor shall utilize the following materials in constructing the project referenced herein:

—Framing: Contractor shall use 2 × 4 Douglas fir for all exterior framing; or 2 × 4 plus insulating sheathing;

—All decking shall be ¾-inch tongue-and-groove plywood;

—All sheathing shall be ½-inch plywood;

—All windows installed on the project shall be Andersen casement;

—Exterior door shall be Benchmark steel insulated;

—Exterior siding shall be 1 inch × 6 inch tongue-and-groove No. 2 cedar.

29. Leaders and Gutters: All leaders and gutters shall be Tyvek Vapor Barrier, seamless, and sufficient to service the entire structure.

30. Landscaping: Contractor shall rake, seed, and plant six (6) bushes. Contractors will not use rye seed.

31. Architect: Contractor shall provide Owner with plan alterations and working sets to construct model-type Scottsdale III (Revised Scottsdale I) with a 1½-car garage with a 12-by-14 den. Owner shall be responsible for any architectural services beyond Contractor's providing for plan alterations and working sets and/or reverse plans at customer's option.

32. Road Improvements: Contractor shall be responsible for roadside curb that presently exists. Owner acknowledges and agrees that Contractor shall have no responsibility for road improvements, including sidewalks, drains, repairing or replacing of current curbs and sidewalks, or any other roadside improvement.

33. Appliances: Contractor shall install kitchen appliances. Owner shall receive a $2,000 allowance for materials only. Any cost over and above said allowance shall be authorized only by the issuance of an appropriate Change Order.

34. Miscellaneous: Owner acknowledges and agrees that Contractor shall have no responsibility for providing medicine cabinets, mirrors, shower doors, or any bathroom accessories. In addition Contractor shall have no responsibility to remove existing fencing at the subject premises. Contractor shall install a stainless-steel double sink in the kitchen.

35. Oil Tank: Contractor shall provide a 275-gallon fiberglass oil tank and install same.

36. N.Y.S. Energy Code as of April 1, 1987 (see attached).

37. Interior architectural plans to be corrected on den with windows and upstairs room sizes, bedrooms, closet and bathroom. No extra charge.

APPENDIX B:
Glossary

Backfill: The gravel or earth replaced in the space around a building wall after foundations are in place.

Baseboard: Boards along the floor against walls and partitions to hide gaps.

Bearing Wall: A wall that supports a floor or roof of a building.

Bridging: Small wood or metal support pieces placed diagonally between floor joists.

Building Paper: Heavy paper used in walls or roofs to damp-proof. Also called 15-pound felt.

Collar Beam: A horizontal beam fastened above the lower ends of rafters to add rigidity.

Crawl Space: A shallow, unfinished space beneath the first floor of a house that has no basement, used for visual inspection and access to pipes and ducts. Also a shallow space in the attic, immediately under the roof.

Cripples: Cut-off framing members above and below windows.

Door Buck: The rough frame of a door.

Eaves: The extension of a roof beyond the house walls.

Fascia: A flat horizontal member of a cornice placed in a vertical position.

Flashing: Noncorrosive (aluminum or copper) metal used around angles or junctions in roofs or exterior walls to prevent leaks.

Floor Joists: Framing pieces that rest on outer foundation walls and interior beams or girders.

Footing: Concrete base on which the house foundation sits.

Foundation: Masonry lower parts of walls on which the structure is built. Foundation walls are mainly below ground level.

Framing: The rough lumber of a house—joists, studs, rafters, and beams. In sum, the shell.

Furring: Thin wood or metal applied to a wall to level it for various purposes.

Gable: The triangular part of the wall under the inverted V of the roof line.

Gambrel Roof: A roof with two pitches, designed to provide more space on upper floors. The roof is steeper on its lower slope and flatter toward the ridge.

Girder: A main member in a framed floor supporting the joists that carry the flooring boards. It carries the weight of a floor or partition.

Headers: Double-wood pieces supporting joists in a floor or double-wood members placed over windows and doors to transfer the roof and floor weight to the studs.

Hip Roof: A roof that slants upward on three or four sides.

Jamb: An upright surface that lines an opening for a door or window.

Lally Column: A big steel pipe sometimes filled with concrete, used to support girders or other floor beams.

Lath: One of a number of thin, narrow strips of wood nailed to rafters, ceiling joists, wall studs, and so on to make a base or key for slates, tiles, or plastering.

Lintel: The top piece over a door or window that supports walls above the opening.

Load-Bearing Wall: A strong wall capable of supporting weight. These run perpendicular to the joists.

Louver: An opening with horizontal slats to permit passage of air, but excluding rain, sunlight, and view.

Masonry: Walls built by a mason, using brick, stone, tile, or similar materials.

Molding: Wood strips used to hide gaps at wall junctures and for decoration.

Mullion: Slender framing that divides the "lights," or panes of windows.

Oriented-Strand Board (OSB): Made into panel form from wood flakes 1 to 3 inches long that have been bonded together under pressure. It is normally available 4 feet wide and in lengths of 8, 10, and 12 feet and in six or seven thicknesses ranging from ⅜ to ¾ inch. Cheaper and stronger than plywood, it can be used for wall sheathing, subflooring, and sometimes roof decking; but where high humidity or moisture intrusion are possible, plywood is better.

Particleboard: Made of wood scraps that have been ground up and glued together in panel form. Heavy and tough to cut, but cheap, it is not suitable for exterior use or where it will contact water. Commonly used as a base material for kitchen countertops, where it is covered by plastic laminate.

Partition Wall: A wall that divides space but does not support the structure of the house.

Plasterboard: Gypsum board, used instead of plaster. Also known by the brand name Sheetrock.

Plates: Wood members placed on wall surfaces as fastening devices. The bottom member of the wall is the sole plate and the top member is the rafter plate.

Plywood: One of the main building materials. It is made of panels glued together in criss-cross fashion called plies, or is "lumber core"—two panels of wood that sandwich a series of boards. It comes in a variety of thicknesses, commonly from ⅜- up to ¾-inch, and usually in 4-by-8-foot panels, and is available in both exterior and interior forms, depending on whether outdoor or indoor glue has been used to adhere the plies.

Plywood grade is characterized by letter designations indicating the clarity of the veneer panels. A is the best, followed by B, C, and D, which has the most knots and mars.

Glue type is sometimes indicated. For example, CDX, a common plywood used for sheathing, means that one side is grade C, the other grade D, while the X signifies exterior glue.

Pressure-Treated Lumber: Ordinary wood, such as pine, that has had chemicals injected into the wood fibers at high pressure to yield a product that is resistant to decay and insects.

Rafter: One of a series of structural roof members spanning from an exterior wall to a center ridge beam or ridge board.

Ridge: A thick longitudinal plank to which the ridge rafters of a roof are attached.

Riser: The upright piece of a stair step, from tread to tread.

Roof Sheathing: Sheets, usually of plywood, which are nailed to the edges of trusses or rafters to tie the roof together and support the roofing material. Also called a deck.

Sash: The movable part of a window—the frame in which panes of glass are set.

Septic Tank: A sewage-settling tank in which part of the sewage is converted into gas and sludge before the remaining waste is discharged by gravity into a leaching bed underground.

Sheathing: The first covering of boards or panel material on the outside wall or roof prior to installing the finished siding or roof covering.

Shell: House framing. It is the essential support structure for all other materials and products.

Shim: A thin, tapered piece of wood used for leveling or tightening a stair or other building element.

Sill Plate: The lowest member of the house framing resting on top of the foundation wall. Also called the mud sill.

Skirtings: Narrow boards around the margin of a floor; baseboards.

Slab: Concrete floor placed directly on the earth or on a gravel base and usually about 4 inches thick.

Sleeper: Strip of wood laid over a concrete floor to which the finished wood floor is nailed or glued.

Soffit: The visible underside of structural members such as staircases, cornices, beams, a roof overhang, or an eave.

Stringer: A long, horizontal member that connects uprights in a frame or supports a floor or the like. One of the enclosed sides of a stair supporting the treads or the risers.

Studs: In wall framing, the 2-by-4-inch vertical members to which horizontal pieces are nailed. Studs are spaced either 16 inches or 24 inches apart.

Subfloor: Usually, plywood sheets that are nailed directly to the floor joists and that receive the finished flooring.

Toenailing: A method of nailing where the end of one wood member is placed against the side of another wood member and nails are driven at an angle near the bottom of the first member into the second.

Tongue and Groove: A carpentry joint in which the jutting edge of one board fits into the grooved end of a similar board.

Tread: The horizontal part of a stair step; the part stepped on.

Underlayment: A layer of plywood or other wood material sometimes used over subflooring and directly under the finish flooring.

Valley: The depression at the meeting point of two roof slopes.

Waferboard: Like oriented-strand board, waferboard is bound with glue under high pressure. It is available in roughly the same thicknesses, lengths, and widths, but is cheaper. However, it tends to swell if moisture contacts it, though it can be used for wall sheathing and roof decking in selected circumstances.

Wall Sheathing: Sheets of plywood, or other material nailed to the outside of studs as a base for exterior siding.

INDEX

Page numbers in bold indicate illustrations.

Acoustical ceilings
  cost, 270
  do-it-yourself, 269
  how job is done, 269
  products/materials, 268, **269**
  workmanship, 269
Air Conditioning
  who installs, 18
Aluminum siding
  cost, 299
  how job is done, 299
  products/materials, 298–99
American Institute of Architects, 31
American Society of Home Inspectors, 26
American Subcontractors Association, 11
Architects
  fees, 30
  necessity of, 26–27
  and plans, 29–30, 31
Asphalt-driveway scam, 7
Asphalt driveways, 119
  being there to oversee, 118–19
  cost, 312
  how job is done, 311
  possible rip-offs, 7, 311–12
  products/materials, 310–11
  workmanship, 311
Asphalt Institute, 312
Asphalt shingle roofing
  cost, 282
  how job is done, 279–81,
    279, 281
  possible rip-offs, 282
  products/materials, 277–79
  workmanship, 281
ASTM (American Society of
  Testing and Materials), 278

Attic conversion, **153**
  cost, 127, 151
  do-it-yourself, 151
  how job is done, 147–48, **150**
  products/materials, 146–47
  sealing a joint, **150**
  subflooring, 146–47
  workmanship, 150
Awning windows
  cost, 227
  products/materials, 227

Baessler, Bill, 5, 99
Balloon payments, 35
Bartlett, Harold, 7
Basement finishing, 151–54
  cost, 154
  do-it-yourself, 154
  how job is done, 152, **152**
  products/materials, 151
  workmanship, 153–54
Basement waterproofing
  cost, 329
  do-it-yourself, 328–29
  how job is done, 327–28
  possible rip-offs, 328
  products/materials, 327
Bath (addition)
  cost, 125
  designers, 30
  designers, when required, 31
  plans and, 30
Bath (remodeling)
  cost, 125
  designers, 30
  designers, when required, 31
  exhaust fans, 188–89
  fixtures, 175
  lavatories, 175, 180–82
  lavatory faucets, 185–86

Bath (remodeling) (*cont.*)
  plans and, 30
  showers, 187–88
  toilets, 175, 182–85
  tub faucets, 186
  tubs, 175, 176–79
  See also Faucets; Lavatories;
    Toilets; Tubs
Bay or bow windows, **229**
  cost, 229
  products/materials, 228–29
Better Business Bureaus, 43–44
  directory of, 76–85
Bids, 86–94
  middle as best, 92–93
  multiple, 15
  over the phone, 86
  presentation, 87
  records, keeping, 88–89, 90–91
  small versus large compa-
    nies, 88
  written, 92
Blanket (batts) insulation, **255**
  cost, 255
  do-it-yourself, 255
  how job is done, 254
  possible rip-offs, 255
  products/materials, 254
  workmanship, 255
Blown-in insulation
  cost, 259
  how job is done, 258
  possible rip-offs, 258–59
  products/materials, 257–58,
    258
Board siding
  cost, 303
  how job is done, 302, **302**
  products/materials, 301–2
Bonding, 46
Brick-on-sand patios & walkways
  cost, 314
  do-it-yourself, 314
  how job is done, 314
  products/materials, 313
  workmanship, 314
Brown, Byron, 12
Builders/designers, 31
  fees, 30
  and plans, 30–31

Built-ins
  who installs, 19

Cabinet refinishing
  cost, 173
  how job is done, 172–73
  products/materials, 172
  workmanship, 173
Cabinet remodeling
  basic types, **166**
  cost, 170
  do-it-yourself, 169
  how job is done, 169
  mortise-and-tenon joint, **167**
  products/materials, 165–68
  who installs, 19
  workmanship, 169
Carpeting
  cost, 197
  how job is done, 196
  possible rip-offs, 197
  products/materials, 195–96
Casement windows
  cost, 224
  possible rip-offs, 224
  products/materials, 223
  workmanship, 224
Cedar shakes roofing
  cost, 289
  how job is done, **288**, 289
  products/materials, 288
Cedar shingle roofing
  cost, 287
  how job is done, 287
  products/materials, 287
Cedar shingle/shake siding
  cost, 304
  how job is done, 303, **304**
  products/materials, 303
Ceiling light, installing fixture
  cost, 234
  how job is done, 234
  products/materials, 233–34
Ceilings (acoustical tile)
  cost, 270
  do-it-yourself, 269
  how job is done, 269
  products/materials, 268, **269**
  workmanship, 269
Ceilings (sheetrock)

cost, 238
do-it-yourself, 238
how job is done, 237–38
products/materials, 236–37
workmanship, 238
Ceilings (suspended)
cost, 271
how job is done, 270–71, **271**
products/materials, 270
Ceramic tile, 249
cost, 252
how job is done, 251
products/materials, 250–51
workmanship, 252
Changing Times magazine, 3
Circular staircases
cost, 262
do-it-yourself, 262
how job is done, 261
products/materials, 261
Clay tile roofing
cost, 286
how job is done, 285
products/materials, 283–85
workmanship, 285, **285**
Concrete driveways, 118
being there to oversee, 118–19
cost, 310
how job is done, 309
possible rip-offs, 310
products/materials, 309
workmanship, 309–10
Concrete tile roofing
cost, 286
how job is done, 286
products/materials, 286
workmanship, 286
Conser, Tom, 22
Consumer affairs investigator, 4
Consumer protection offices,
45–47
directory of, 49–75
Contractor-arranged loans, 38
Contractors
as businessmen, 10–11
checking out, 15, 95–97
as craftsmen, 9–10
rip-off artists, 6–8, 122
Contractors (checking out), 15,
95–97

credit, 96
visiting place of business, 96–97
Contractors (finding), 39–85
Better Business Bureaus,
43–44, 76–85
bonding, 46
by elimination, 39–40, 43–45
conflict of interest, 41–42
consumer affairs depart-
ments, 45–47, 49–75
contacting, 47–48
patience, 48
refund plans, 46–47
sources to avoid, 42–43
using friends & family, 39
Contractors (how to hire)
being on sight, 118–20
bids, 86–94
contractor, checking out, 95–97
contractor, finding a, 39–85
educating yourself, 22–28
needing a plan, 29–31
payment schedule, 98–103
reducing risks, 3–21
where to get money, 32–38
written contracts, 104–17
Contracts, 15, 104–17
clauses to include, 108–11
lien laws. *See under* Lien Laws
necessity of, 104–5
sample, 106–7, 331–44
specifications test, 113–17
states requiring, 105
Cost of jobs, 121–131
Countertops (plastic-laminate)
cost, 172
do-it-yourself, how job is
done, 171
possible rip-offs, 172
products/materials, 170–71
who installs, 19
workmanship, 171

Decks, 316–17
cost, 129
Decks (modular ground-level),
320 cost, 320
do-it-yourself, 320
how job is done, 319

Decks (modular ground-level)
    (*cont.*)
  products/materials, 319
  who installs, 19
Decks (raised)
  cost, 319
  details, **318**
  how job is done, 317–19
  products/materials, 317
  who installs, 19
Designers (kitchen & bath), 30
  fees, 30
  when required, 31
Dirt, 21
Disruption, **20**, 21
Do-it-yourself, 122, 131
  acoustical tile ceilings, 269
  attic conversion, 151
  basement finishing, 154
  basement waterproofing,
    328–329
  cabinet remodeling, 169
  decks, 320
  fireplaces (freestanding), 273
  gutters, 308
  painting (exterior), 247
  patios & walkways, 314
  porch, 324
  sheetrock walls/ceilings, 238
  tub improvement, 179
  wallpaper, 241
  windows (double-hung), 222
Do-it-yourself (doors)
  fiberglass entry, 214
  wood, 210
Do-it-yourself (electrical im-
    provement)
  ground fault circuit inter-
    rupter, installing, 233
  receptacle, installing, 232
  replacing switch, 231
  replacing switch with dim-
    mer, 231
Do-it-yourself (insulation)
  batts/blanket, 255
  loose-fill, 257
  rigid on basement wall, 256
Do-it-yourself (staircases)
  circular, 262
  simple wood steps, 263

Doors
  framing, 135, **136**
  who installs, 18
Doors (fiberglass entry)
  cost, 214
  do-it-yourself, 214
  products/materials, 214
Doors (garage)
  cost, 201
  how job is done, 201
  products/materials, 198–201,
    199, 200
  who installs, 18
Doors (patio)
  cost, 205
  how job is done, 204–5
  products/materials, 201–4,
    202, 204
Doors (steel entry)
  cost, 213
  how job is done, 213
  possible rip-offs, 213
  products/materials, 211–13,
    211, 212
Doors (wood exterior/interior)
  cost, 210
  do-it-yourself, 210
  how job is done, 209–10
  products/materials, 206–9, **208**
  workmanship, 210
Dormers (improvement), 154–57
  cost, 156, 157
  framing, **156**
  gable dormers, 154–56, **155**
  how job is done, 155, 157
  products/materials, 154–55,
    156–57
  shed dormers, **155**, 156–57
Double-hung windows
  cost, 223
  do-it-yourself, 222
  double insulated window
    glazing, **221**
  how job is done, 221
  possible rip-offs, 222–23
  products/materials, 215–18
  products/materials (pure
    vinyl), 217–18, **218**
  products/materials (solid-
    aluminum), 220–21

products/materials (solid
wood), 218–20, **219**
products/materials (wood
clad with vinyl), 220
styles, 216
workmanship, 222
Downspouts
who installs, 18
Drainage
who installs, 17
Driveways (asphalt), 119
being there to oversee, 118–19
cost, 312
how job is done, 311
possible rip-offs, 7, 311–12
products/materials, 310–11
workmanship, 311
Driveways (concrete), 118
being there to oversee, 118–19
cost, 310
how job is done, 309
possible rip-offs, 310
products/materials, 309
workmanship, 309–10
Drywall
who installs, 19

Educating yourself, 15, 22–28
products/materials, knowledge of, 22–23
plans, necessity of, 27–28
sources, using reliable, 15
sources of information, 25–27
warranties & guarantees,
23–25
Electrical improvement
how system works, 144–45
who installs, 17
Electrical improvement (installing ceiling light fixture)
cost, 234
how job is done, 234
products/materials, 233–34
Electrical improvement (installing ground fault circuit interrupter)
cost, 233
do-it-yourself, 233
how job is done, 233

products/materials, 232–33
Electrical improvement (installing receptacle)
cost, 232
do-it-yourself, 232
products/materials, 232
Electrical improvement (replacing switch)
cost, 231
do-it-yourself, 231
how job is done, 231
products/materials, 230–31
Electrical improvement (replacing switch with dimmer)
cost, 232
do-it-yourself, 231
products/materials, 231
Electrical improvement (upgrading service to 150 amps)
cost, 235
how job is done, 234–35
products/materials, 234–35
Engelhardt, Tom F., 6–7
Excavation
who's responsible, 17
Exhaust fans, 188–89
cost, 189
how job is done, 189
products/materials, 188–89
workmanship, 189

Family member as contractor, 39
Family-room
cost of addition, 126
Faucets (lavatory), 175
cost, 186
how job is done, 185
products/materials, 185
Faucets (tub), 175
cost, 186
how job is done, 186
products/materials, 186
See also Lavatories; Toilets;
Tubs
Fiberglass entry doors
cost, 214
do-it-yourself, 214
products/materials, 214
Fiberglass shingle roofing
cost, 282

Fiberglass shingle roofing
(*cont.*)
how job is done, 279–81,
279, 281
possible rip-offs, 282
products/materials, 277–79
workmanship, 281
Financing, 32–38
balloon payments, 35
contractor-arranged loans, 38
401 (k), 37
home equity line, 34–35
home equity loans, 33–34
home-improvement loans, 36
HUD, 37
life insurance, 37
refinance mortgage, 35–36
shopping around, 32–33
unsecured personal loans,
36–37
Fireplace
who installs, 19
Fireplaces (brick)
cost, 276
how job is done, **275**, 276
products/materials, 275–76
Fireplaces (built-in)
cost, 274
how job is done, 274
products/materials, 274
Fireplaces (freestanding)
cost, 273–74
do-it-yourself, 273
how job is done, 273
possible rip-offs, products/
materials, 272–73
workmanship, 273
Fixed windows
cost, 225–26
products/materials, 224–25,
225
Fixtures, 175
See also Lavatories; Toilets;
Tubs
Flagstone-on-sand patios &
walkways
cost, 315
do-it-yourself, 315
how job is done, 315
products/materials, 315

Flooring
who installs, 19
See also Subflooring
Flooring (carpeting)
cost, 197
how job is done, 196
possible rip-offs, 197
products/materials, 195–96
Flooring (hardwood)
cost, 195
how job is done, 195
installation, **193, 194**
products/materials, 193–94
Flooring (resilient tile/sheet)
cost, 192
do-it-yourself, 192
how job is done, 191–92
installing, **193**
products/materials, 190–91
workmanship, 192
Footings, 132–33, **133**
Formal plans. *See under* plans
Foundation
who installs, 17
Foundations, 132–33, **133**
401 (k), 37
Framing
a house, 133–35, **137**
stairs, **137**
who's responsible, 17
window and door framing,
135, **136**
Friends as contractor, 39

Garage doors
cost, 201
how job is done, 201
products/materials, 198–201,
199, 200
who installs, 18
Garages (attached), improving,
161–63
cost, 163
how job is done, 162
products/materials, 161–62
workmanship, 163
Garages (detached), improving,
163–64
cost, 164
how job is done, 163

products/materials, 163
workmanship, 164
Garthe, Bill, 9, 13, 99
General contractors, functions of, 16
Glazing, double insulated window, **221**
Gorman, Fred, 87, 98–99
Grant, Peter, 4
Grant, Susan, 7, 9, 39–40
Graves, Reynolds, 32, 99
Green, Mark, 13
Ground fault circuit interrupter (installing)
cost, 233
do-it-yourself, 233
how job is done, 233
products/materials, 232–33
Gutters
cost, 308
do-it-yourself, 308
how job is done, 307–8
products/materials, 306–7
types, **307**
who installs, 18
workmanship, 308

Hardboard siding
cost, 305
how job is done, 305
products/materials, 305
workmanship, 305
Hardwood flooring
cost, 195
how job is done, 195
installation, **193, 194**
products/materials, 193–94
Heating
who installs, 18
Home equity line, 34–35
Home equity loans, 33–34
Home office
cost of addition, 127
Home Show (ABC TV), 7–8
Home Time (TV program), 25–26
Home-improvement loans, 36
Hopper windows
how job is done, 228
products/materials, 228
Horror stories, 3–5

House (building), 132–40
footings, 132–33, **133**
foundation, 132–33, **133**
framing, 133–35, **137**
insulation, 138
joists, 133–34, **134**
rafters, 135, **136**
sheathing, 135, 138
stair framing, **137**
stud walls, 134–35
trim, 138
window and door framing, 135, **136**
See also Electrical; Plumbing
HUD (Federal Housing Administration), 37

Improvements
cost, 13, 122. *See also under* Cost
do-it-yourself, 122. *See also under* do-it-yourself
how the job is done, 122. *See also under specific job*
possible rip-offs, 122. *See also under* Rip-offs
products/materials, 121. *See also under specific job*
satisfaction with, 5
workmanship, 122. *See also under specific job*
Increasing space
attic conversion, 146–51
basement finishing, 151–54
dormer improvement, 154–57
garages, 161–64
room additions, 157–59
upper-story additions, 159–61
Informing yourself. *See* Educating yourself
Insulation, 253–54
being there to oversee, 119
installing, 138
R-value, 253–54, **255**
who installs, 18
Insulation (batts/blanket), **255**
cost, 255
do-it-yourself, 255
how job is done, 254
possible rip-offs, 255

Insulation (batts/blanket)
(*cont.*)
  products/materials, 254
  workmanship, 255
Insulation (blown-in)
  cost, 259
  how job is done, 258
  possible rip-offs, 258–59
  products/materials, 257–58,
  258
Insulation (loose-fill)
  cost, 257
  do-it-yourself, 257
  how job is done, 257
  products/materials, 257
Insulation (rigid on basement
  wall)
  cost, 256
  do-it-yourself, 256
  how job is done, 256
  products/materials, 256

Jalousie windows
  products/materials, 227
Job sight (being there), 14–15,
  118–20
  asphalt driveway, 119
  concrete driveway, 118
  paint job, 119
  roof job, 119
  wall insulation, 119
  windows, 119
Johnson, Sue, 104–5
Joists
  installing, 133–34, **134**
  wood to use, 140
Jones, Francis, 30

Kitchen remodeling
  cost (major), 124
  cost (minor), 124
  designers, 30
  plans and, 30
  possible rip-offs, 170
  when required, 31
Kitchen remodeling (cabinet
  refinishing)
  cost, 173
  how job is done, 172–73
  products/materials, 172

  workmanship, 173
Kitchen remodeling (cabinets)
  basic types, **166**
  cost, 170
  do-it-yourself, 169
  how job is done, 169
  mortise-and-tenon joint, **167**
  products/materials, 165–68
  workmanship, 169
Kitchen remodeling (plastic-
  laminate countertop)
  cost, 172
  do-it-yourself, how job is
  done, 171
  possible rip-offs, 172
  products/materials, 170–71
  who installs, 19
  workmanship, 171
Kitchen remodeling (refrigerator refinishing), 173–74
  cost, 174
  how job is done, 173
  products/materials, 173
  workmanship, 174
Kraeger, Ken, 10

Lagowski, Barbara, 23, 25, 88, 92
Landscaping
  who's responsible, 19
Lavatories (improvement), 175,
  180–82
  cost, 182
  how job is done, 182
  products/materials, 180–82,
  181
  See also Faucets; Toilets;
  Tubs
Lien laws, 11–12, 15, 100
  and written contracts, 111–12
Life insurance, borrowing on, 37
Lindstadt, Ed, 278
Loose-fill insulation
  cost, 257
  do-it-yourself, 257
  how job is done, 257
  products/materials, 257
Lumaghi, Peter, 4

Mahoney, Matt, 32
Master suite

cost of remodeling, 126
Materials, knowledge of, 22–23
Miller, Dan, 30
Modular ground-level decks, **320**
  cost, 320
  do-it-yourself, 320
  how job is done, 319
  products/materials, 319
  who installs, 19
Molding
  who installs, 19
Money magazine, 13
Mortise-and-tenon joint, **167**
Mosaic tiles, 250
  See also Ceramic tile

National Kitchen and Bath
  Association, 27

Painting (exterior)
  being there to oversee, 119
  cost, 247–48
  do-it-yourself, 247
  possible rip-offs, 247
  products/materials, 246–47
  who's responsible for, 19
  workmanship, 247
Painting (interior)
  being there to oversee, 119
  cost, 246
  how job is done, 245
  possible rip-offs, 245
  products/materials, 244–45
  who's responsible for, 19
Paneling, **243**
  cost, 243
  how job is done, 242
  products/materials, 242
  who installs, 19
Patio doors
  cost, 205
  how job is done, 204–5
  products/materials, 201–4, **202, 204**
Patio tiles, 251
  See also Ceramic tile
Patios (brick-on-sand)
  cost, 314
  do-it-yourself, 314

how job is done, 314
  products/materials, 313
  workmanship, 314
Patios (flagstone-on-sand)
  cost, 315
  do-it-yourself, 315
  how job is done, 315
  products/materials, 315
Pavers (tiles), 250
  See also Ceramic tile
Payment schedule, 98–103
  as incentive, 101–3
  lien laws, 11–12, 15, 100
  special orders, 100–101
Plank flooring, installation of, **193**
  See also Flooring (hardwood)
Plans, 15, 29–31
  architects, 26–27, 29–30, 31
  builder/designers, 30–31
  designers (kitchen & bath), 30
  fees, 30
  necessity of, 27–28
Plastic-laminate countertops, 172
Plates, wood to use, 140
Plumbing
  how system works, 141–43
  typical system, **142**
  who installs, 18
Plywood, 140
Plywood siding
  cost, 301
  how job is done, 301
  products/materials, 300–301
Porch, **322, 323**
  cost, 324
  do-it-yourself, 324
  how job is done, 321–24
  products/materials, 321
Prefab fold-up staircases
  cost, 261
  how job is done, 261
  products/materials, 260–61
Pregrouted tiles, 251
  See also Ceramic tile
Product, knowledge of, 22–23

Quarry tiles, 250
  See also Ceramic tile

Rafters
  installing, 135, **136**
  wood to use, 140
Raised decks
  cost, 319
  details, **318**
  how job is done, 317–19
  products/materials, 317
  who installs, 19
Receptacles(electrical),installing
  cost, 232
  do-it-yourself, 232
  products/materials, 232
Records
  keeping, 88–89
  sample, 90–91
Refrigerator refinishing, 173–74
  cost, 174
  how job is done, 173
  products/materials, 173
  workmanship, 174
Refund plans, 46–47
Resilient tile flooring
  cost, 192
  do-it-yourself, 192
  how job is done, 191–92
  products/materials, 190–91
  workmanship, 192
Rigid insulation (on basement
    wall)
  cost, 256
  do-it-yourself, 256
  how job is done, 256
  products/materials, 256
Rip-offs, 6–8, 122
  basement waterproofing, 328
  asphalt-driveway scam, 7
  asphalt/fiberglass shingle
    roofing, 282
  cabinets, 170
  doors (steel entry), 213
  flooring (carpeting), 197
  plastic-laminate countertops,
    172
  siding (vinyl), 298
  termite control, 326
  tub improvement, 179
  upper-story additions, 161
Rip-offs (driveways)
  asphalt, 7, 311–12

  concrete, 310
Rip-offs (insulation)
  batts/blanket, 255
  loose-fill, 258–59
Rip-offs (painting)
  interior, 246
Rip-offs (windows)
  casement, 224
  double-hung, 222–23
Risks, reducing, 3–21
  asphalt-driveway scam, 7
  dirt, disruption & thievery, 21
  getting involved, 14–15
  horror stories, 3–5
  lien laws, 11–12, 15
  poor businessmen, 10–11
  poor craftsmen, 9–10
  rip-off artists, 6–8, 122
  "spiking," 8, **9**
  a strategy, 13–14
  who does what, 17–19
  who's who, 16–17
Roll roofing
  cost, 283
  how job is done, 283, **284**
  products/materials, 283
Roofing
  being there to oversee, 119
  who installs, 18
Roofing (asphalt or fiberglass
    shingle)
  cost, 282
  how job is done, 279–81,
    279, 281
  possible rip-offs, 282
  products/materials, 277–79
  workmanship, 281
Roofing (cedar shakes)
  cost, 289
  how job is done, **288**, 289
  products/materials, 288
Roofing (cedar shingles)
  cost, 287
  how job is done, 287
  products/materials, 287
Roofing (clay tile)
  cost, 286
  how job is done, 285
  products/materials, 283–85
  workmanship, 285, **285**

Roofing (concrete tile)
    cost, 286
    how job is done, 286
    products/materials, 286
    workmanship, 286
Roofing (roll)
    cost, 283
    how job is done, 283, **284**
    products/materials, 283
Roofing (slate)
    cost, 290
    how job is done, 289
    products/materials, 289
    workmanship, 290
Room additions, 157–61
    cost, 159
    how job is done, 158–59
    products/materials, 157–58
    workmanship, 159
Rooney, Bill, 10, 16
R-value (insulation), 253–54,
    255

Sculptured tiles, 251
    See also Ceramic tile
Sheathing
    installing, 135, 138
    who's responsible, 17
Sheet flooring
    cost, 192
    do-it-yourself, 192
    how job is done, 191–92
    products/materials, 190–91
    who installs, 19
    workmanship, 192
Sheetrock (walls and ceilings)
    cost, 238
    do-it-yourself, 238
    how job is done, 237–38
    products/materials, 236–37
    workmanship, 238
Shingle roofing (asphalt)
    cost, 282
    how job is done, 279–81,
        279, 281
    possible rip-offs, 282
    products/materials, 277–79
    workmanship, 281
Shingle roofing (cedar)
    cost, 287

    how job is done, 287
    products/materials, 287
Shingle roofing (fiberglass)
    cost, 282
    how job is done, 279–81,
        279, 281
    possible rip-offs, 282
    products/materials, 277–79
    workmanship, 281
Shirley, David, 11–12, **12**
Showers (improvement)
    cost, 188
    products/materials, 187, **187**
Siding, 291–93
Siding (aluminum)
    cost, 299
    how job is done, 299
    products/materials, 298–99
Siding (board)
    cost, 303
    how job is done, 302, **302**
    products/materials, 301–2
Siding (cedar shakes or shingles)
    cost, 304
    how job is done, 303, **304**
    products/materials, 303
Siding (hardboard)
    cost, 305
    how job is done, 305
    products/materials, 305
    workmanship, 305
Siding (plywood)
    cost, 301
    how job is done, 301
    products/materials, 300–301
Siding (steel)
    cost, 300
    how job is done, 300
    products/materials, 299
Siding (vinyl), **297**
    cost, 298
    how job is done, 296, **297**
    possible rip-offs, 298
    products/materials, 293–96
    types, **294**
    workmanship, 296
Slate roofing
    cost, 290
    how job is done, 289
    products/materials, 289

Slate roofing (*cont.*)
  workmanship, 290
Siding
  cost of replacement, 128
  who installs, 18
Sills, wood to use, 140
Skiles, Theron, *xvii*
Skylights
  cost, 267
  glass, **265**
  how job is done, 265, **266, 267**
  products/materials, 264–65
  who installs, 18
  workmanship, 267
Sliding windows
  cost, 226
  how job is done, 226
  products/materials, 226
Sources
  to avoid, 42–43
  Better Business Bureaus,
    43–44, 76–85
  consumer protection offices,
    45–47, 49–75
  of information, 25–27
  using reliable, 15
Space (Increasing)
  attic conversion, 146–51
  basement finishing, 151–54
  dormer improvement, 154–57
  garages, 161–64
  room additions, 157–59
  upper-story additions, 159–61
Specialty contractors, functions
  of, 17
"Spiking," 8, **9**
Staircases (circular)
  cost, 262
  do-it-yourself, 262
  how job is done, 261
  products/materials, 261
Staircases (custom wood steps)
  cost, 263
  products/materials, 263
Staircases (simple wood steps)
  cost, 263
  do-it-yourself, 263
  how job is done, 262
  products/materials, 262
  workmanship, 262–63

Staircases (prefab fold-up)
  cost, 261
  how job is done, 261
  products/materials, 260–61
Stairs, framing, **137**
Standard tiles, 251
  See also Ceramic tile
Steel entry doors
  cost, 213
  how job is done, 213
  possible rip-offs, 213
  products/materials, 211–13,
    211, 212
Steel siding
  cost, 300
  how job is done, 300
  products/materials, 299
Stembridge, Jim, 14
Stoeppelwerth, Walt, 5, 10, 93
Strip flooring, installation of,
  193, 194
  See also Flooring (hardwood)
Stud walls, installing, 134–35
Studs, wood to use, 140
Subcontractors
  functions of, 16
  how good, 94
Subflooring (attic conversion),
  146–47
Suspended ceilings
  cost, 271
  how job is done, 270–71, **271**
  products/materials, 270
Switches (electrical), replacing
  cost, 231
  do-it-yourself, 231
  how job is done, 231
  products/materials, 230–31
Switches (electrical), replacing
  with dimmer
  cost, 232
  do-it-yourself, 231
  products/materials, 231

Termite control
  cost, 326
  how job is done, 325–26
  possible rip-offs, 326
  products/materials, 325
Thievery, 21

This Old House (TV program), 25
Tile (ceramic), 249
  cost, 252
  how job is done, 251
  products/materials, 250–51
  workmanship, 252
Toilets (improvement), 175,
  182–85
  cost, 184–85
  how job is done, 184
  products/materials, 182–84,
   183
  See also Faucets; Lavatories;
   Tubs
Top-hinged windows
  how job is done, 228
  products/materials, 228
Trim, installing, 138
Tubs (improvement), 175, **176**
  cost, 179
  do-it-yourself, 179
  how job is done, 177–78
  possible rip-offs, 179
  products/materials, 176–77
  whirlpools, **178**
  workmanship, 178
  See also Faucets; Lavatories;
   Toilets
Two-story addition, cost of, 123

Upper-story additions, 159–61
  cost, 161
  how job is done, 160–61
  possible rip-offs, 161
  products/materials, 159–60
  workmanship, 161

Vinyl siding, **297**
  cost, 298
  how job is done, 296, **297**
  possible rip-offs, 298
  products/materials, 293–96
  types, **294**
  workmanship, 296

Walkways (brick-on-sand)
  cost, 314
  do-it-yourself, 314
  how job is done, 314
  products/materials, 313

  workmanship, 314
Walkways (flagstone-on-sand)
  cost, 315
  do-it-yourself, 315
  how job is done, 315
  products/materials, 315
Wallcovering
  who installs, 19
Wallpaper
  cost, 241
  do-it-yourself, 241
  how job is done, 241
  patterns, **240**
  products/materials, 239–41
  who installs, 19
Walls (paneling), **243**
  cost, 243
  how job is done, 242
  products/materials, 242
Walls (sheetrock)
  cost, 238
  do-it-yourself, 238
  how job is done, 237–38
  products/materials, 236–37
  workmanship, 238
Walls (wallpaper)
  cost, 241
  do-it-yourself, 241
  how job is done, 241
  patterns, **240**
  products/materials, 239–41
Waterproofing (basement)
  cost, 329
  do-it-yourself, 328–29
  how job is done, 327–28
  possible rip-offs, 328
  products/materials, 327
Webster, William, 7
Whirlpools, **178**
Who does what, 17–19
  cabinets/built-ins/counter-
   tops, 19
  decks/landscaping, 19
  doors, 18
  drainage, 17
  drywall, 19
  electrical, 17
  excavation, 17
  fireplace, 19
  flooring, 19

Who does what (*cont.*)
  foundation, 17
  framing, 17
  garage doors, 18
  gutters/downspouts, 18
  heating/air conditioning, 18
  insulation, 18
  interior & exterior painting,
    19
  molding, 19
  paneling/wallcovering, 19
  plumbing, 18
  roofing, 18
  sheathing, 17
  siding, 18
  windows/skylights, 18
Who's who, 16–17
  general contractors, 16
  specialty contractors, 17
  subcontractors, 16
Williamson gang, 7
Windows
  being there to oversee, 119
  cost of replacement, 128
  framing, 135, **136**
  who installs, 18
Windows (awning)
  cost, 227
  products/materials, 227
Windows (bay or bow), **229**
  cost, 229
  products/materials, 228–29
Windows (casement)
  cost, 224
  possible rip-offs, 224
  products/materials, 223
  workmanship, 224
Windows (double-hung)
  cost, 223
  do-it-yourself, 222
  double insulated window
    glazing, **221**
  how job is done, 221
  possible rip-offs, 222–23
  products/materials, 215–18
  products/materials (pure
    vinyl), 217–18, **218**

products/materials (solid-
    aluminum), 220–21
products/materials (solid
    wood), 218–20, **219**
products/materials (wood
    clad with vinyl), 220
styles, 216
workmanship, 222
Windows (fixed)
  cost, 225–26
  products/materials, 224–25,
    225
Windows (hopper)
  how job is done, 228
  products/materials, 228
Windows (jalousie)
  products/materials, 227
Windows (sliding)
  cost, 226
  how job is done, 226
  products/materials, 226
Windows (top-hinged)
  how job is done, 228
  products/materials, 228
Wood (exterior/interior) doors
  cost, 210
  do-it-yourself, 210
  how job is done, 209–10
  products/materials, 206–9,
    208
  workmanship, 210
Wood steps (custom)
  cost, 263
  products/materials, 263
Wood steps (simple)
  cost, 263
  do-it-yourself, 263
  how job is done, 262
  products/materials, 262
  workmanship, 262–63
Written contracts, 15, 104–17
  clauses to include, 108–11
  lien laws. *See under* Lien Laws
  necessity of, 104–5
  sample, 106–7
  specifications test, 113–17
  states requiring, 105